WHEN
GOD
GOES TO
STARBUCKS

Other books by Paul Copan

Creation Out of Nothing: A Biblical, Philosophical, and Scientific Exploration (coauthored with William Lane Craig)

"How Do You Know You're Not Wrong?" Responding to Objections That Leave Christians Speechless

"That's Just Your Interpretation": Responding to Skeptics Who Challenge Your Faith

"True for You, but Not for Me": Deflating the Slogans That Leave Christians Speechless

Will the Real Jesus Please Stand Up? A Debate between William Lane Craig and John Dominic Crossan (editor)

WHEN GOD GOES TO STARBUCKS

A Guide to Everyday Apologetics

PAUL COPAN

BakerBooks

a division of Baker Publishing Group
Grand Rapids, Michigan

Published by Baker Books
a division of Baker Publishing Group
P.O. Box 6287, Grand Rapids, MI 49516-6287
www.bakerbooks.com

Printed in the United States of America

Library of Congress Cataloging-in-Publication Data
Copan, Paul.
    When God goes to Starbucks : a guide to everyday apologetics / Paul Copan.
        p.   cm.
    Includes bibliographical references.
    ISBN 978-0-8010-6743-3 (pbk.)
    1. Apologetics. I. Title.
BT1103.C65 2008
239—dc22   2008012697

To my precious daughter Johanna,
who enjoys Starbucks and loves conversations about God
and whose life shows forth the sweetness of Christ.

Contents

Introduction 9

Part I: Slogans Related to Truth and Reality

1. Why Not Just Look Out for Yourself? 15
2. Do What You Want—Just as Long as You Don't Hurt Anyone 22
3. Is It Okay to Lie to Nazis? 28

Part II: Slogans Related to Worldviews

4. Why Is God So Arrogant and Egotistical? 41
5. Miracles Are Unscientific 53
6. Only Gullible People Believe in Miracles 61
7. Don't People from All Religions Experience God? 67
8. Does the Bible Condemn Loving, Committed Homosexual Relationships? 77
9. Aren't People Born Gay? 94
10. What's Wrong with Gay Marriage? 108

Part III: Slogans Related to Christianity

11. How Can the Psalmists Say Such Vindictive, Hateful Things? 121
12. Aren't the Bible's "Holy Wars" Just Like Islamic Jihad? Part One 136

Contents

13. Aren't the Bible's "Holy Wars" Just Like Islamic Jihad?
    Part Two   144
14. Aren't the Bible's "Holy Wars" Just Like Islamic Jihad?
    Part Three   149
15. Was Jesus Mistaken about an Early Second Coming?
    Part One   162
16. Was Jesus Mistaken about an Early Second Coming?
    Part Two   174
17. Why Are Christians So Divided? Why So Many
    Denominations?   191

Notes   203

Introduction

Cafés are a natural place to engage in conversations about God. Many of us don't just swing by for a quick caffeine fix and then dash out. We like to sit down, relax, and read a book or engage in conversation with a friend over a cup of coffee with espresso brownies or cranberry-orange muffins.

I've enjoyed many hearty discussions at coffee shops—exchanging stories, problems, and questions with friends, students, and strangers. A coffee shop is a superb place to talk about what's important— what makes for a good life, why we should be moral, what is really real. I have not only discussed such coffee-shop topics on location, but I've also tried to write on these often-challenging topics in an accessible manner. You may want to check out my earlier popular-level coffee-shop books—*"True for You, but Not for Me," "That's Just Your Interpretation," "How Do You Know You're Not Wrong?"* and *Loving Wisdom: Christian Philosophy of Religion.*[1] As the subtitle— *A Guide to Everyday Apologetics*—suggests, this book attempts to guide readers, Christian or not, into practical answers to tough questions and hard-to-handle slogans.

As with my aforementioned books, this book follows a threefold structure. First, in our café chats, we may have to *begin with issues of truth and reality*—the fundamentals of any philosophy of life. Many people will deny that there's such a thing as truth at all. But despite their most valiant attempts to deny the stability of truth and reality, they can't do so. They keep bumping up against the inescapable. For when they deny objective truth, they are actually affirming the existence of truth ("It's true that there is no truth"). In claiming that they can make up their own reality, they are affirming something they take to be universally real ("The reality is that all people make up their own reality"). But truth and reality aren't in the eye of the beholder.

Second, given the bedrock nature of reality and truth, we need to *ask which worldview or philosophy of life is the true one.* That is, which one best matches up with the way things really are? I have repeatedly argued that the existence of a good personal God who created the world and made humans with value and dignity ("theism") does a better job of explaining the features of this universe and of human experience than alternative nontheistic worldviews—whether the view is naturalism ("nature is all there is") or nontheistic religions like Buddhism, Shintoism, Confucianism, and the like. For those who are serious-minded seekers (rather than halfhearted dabblers), there are abundant indicators of God's existence; indeed, they are quite difficult to explain if there is no God. Consider the profuse beauty of the world and the elegance of certain scientific laws, the dignity and rights of human beings, the universe's beginning and astonishing bio-friendliness, and human awareness of a transcendent presence—to name a few.

Third, if a personal God makes better sense of the world and also better helps interpret human experience, we have to *ask if this God has actually done something to help us* out of our misery, suffering, and alienation from him, from one another, from our world, and from our own selves. This brings us to the question of *Christian apologetics*—reasons to believe that God's revelation in Christ is more intellectually satisfying than the other theistic alternatives of Judaism and Islam. Topics such as the deity and resurrection of Jesus, the doctrine of the Trinity, or the reliability of Scripture fit in here. Why should I be a Christian rather than a Muslim? Why take a trinitarian view of God rather than a unitarian one?

In claiming that the Christian faith provides a more robust explanation than its theistic competitors, I am not saying that we can remove all mysteries and questions. God's greatness is truly unsearchable, and the mystery of the incarnation is profound. At times we may have only partial answers and see things only dimly (1 Cor. 13:12); at other times we may simply have to confess, "I don't know." And when we're talking with people in pain or when people just want to tell their stories, we should be quick to listen and slow to speak (James 1:19); we shouldn't jump in with answers when we haven't truly understood the questions.

Finally, discussing such questions in the context of a gracious, respectful relationship (1 Peter 3:15) goes a long way to setting the context for robust, in-depth conversations. Moreover, Christians should engage their non-Christian friends *prayerfully*, in dependence on God's Spirit to awaken, convict, and provoke.[2] While people can resist God's gracious initiative (e.g., Isa. 5:4; Luke 7:30; Acts 7:51; Rev. 2:21), they can't wake up to their need without it.

Part I

SLOGANS RELATED TO TRUTH AND REALITY

Why Not Just Look Out for Yourself?

The human basis for morality is *self-interest* or *egoism* (from the Latin *ego*, "I"), according to Russian-born philosopher Ayn Rand, who popularized the idea of *egoism*.[1] This viewpoint has its own version of the Golden Rule: we should "do unto others" who will eventually/hopefully do the same to us. If I scratch someone's back, eventually someone will scratch mine. In fact, each person has a moral *duty* to pursue her own self-interest exclusively. According to the egoist, *I* am the one who best knows what I need—much better than any other person. So self-interest comes before the interests of others. This is what the good life is all about—pursuing what I want.

This view fits quite nicely with today's relativistic "true for you, but not for me" mentality. Relativists aren't interested in finding truth but in preserving their own autonomy. This isn't a logical argument against relativism, of course. I'm just trying to point out that the *true*(!) basis for relativism is ultimately rooted in its motivation rather than in any good reasons or persuasive arguments.

If self-interest is the basis for decision making and setting our priorities, we run into a host of problems.

First, this view often fails to distinguish between self-interest and selfishness. In the Disney movie *Ice Age*, Sid the Sloth—a really nice guy—is being discussed by two female sloths. Says one, "He's not much to look at, but it's so hard to find a family man these days." The other replies, "Tell me about it. All the sensitive ones get eaten."[2] The implication is this: if you want to survive, look out for yourself, not others. Rand's discussion of this subject seems to suggest that self-sacrifice and self-preservation are opposed to each other. If I am deeply concerned about others, then I am less likely to preserve my own life.

Such thinking is confused. Taking care of oneself isn't the same as selfishness. The Scriptures themselves assume that we already love ourselves; so we're commanded, "Love your neighbor as [you already love] yourself" (Mark 12:31). A normal self-love means that we will, for example, feed and take care of our bodies. As Paul writes, "No one ever hated his own flesh, but nourishes and cherishes it" (Eph. 5:29). Self-love isn't a *goal* to pursue (Paul warns Timothy to avoid those who are "lovers of self" in 2 Tim. 3:2, 5), but rather a *fact* to be acknowledged.[3] The fact that we love ourselves is to guide us in our love for others: given our knowledge of how we want to be treated, this should serve as a model for how we treat others (Matt. 7:12).

Second, this view commits the "naturalistic fallacy," illegitimately moving from "is" to "ought." We all recognize that we can easily cater to our self-centered tendencies and our wants. Too often we are inclined to look out for our own well-being and disregard the welfare of others (Phil. 2:3–4). The problem with Rand's view is that it makes an illegitimate jump from the way we *are* to the way we *ought to be* (known as the "naturalistic fallacy"). However, such a conclusion—moving from the *descriptive* to the *prescriptive*—doesn't follow. Why accept Rand's view? Why not affirm that we should resist our self-centeredness rather than give in to it? There is nothing logically compelling about making Rand's recommended move.

Third, when we speak about how we "ought" to live, we are speaking of universally applicable ideals—but this flies in the face of egoism. It's ironic that an egoist would announce far and wide that selfishness (or self-interest) is a virtue to be pursued. If we're talking about ethics, then we're talking about universal relevance—a stance all should embrace. But this works at cross-purposes for the egoist. Presumably, Ed the Egoist wants others to embrace this view as intellectually superior and to act on it, but this would mean that Ed is recommending that others cater to *themselves* rather than to Ed! As egoism becomes universalized and practiced, it actually undermines itself. It tells others to live for themselves rather than to live for *me*! This suggests that egoism is a deficient view. Why would egoists want their views universalized? Instead, they should keep quiet about them!

Fourth, we can never trust an ethical egoist. The ethical egoist can't be trusted when offering moral advice to others, because it will ultimately be to his own advantage—not another's—to follow it. After all, the egoist is always me-deep in conversation! Advocates of egoism only create a climate of suspicion around themselves. This, of course, renders egoism suspect; it turns out to be a very counterintuitive notion.

Fifth, the egoist's desire to get what he "wants" turns out to be an empty or trivial concept—or worse. The egoist says that what he "wants" is the primary drive to all that he (or anyone else) does. People usually don't betray their friends—even if doing so under severe pressure or possibly torture would give them considerable relief. They *want* to be loyal. If some cave in to pressure, it's because they *want* relief more strongly than loyalty.

The problem here is fourfold:

- *The term* want *becomes unhelpful.* When anyone acts, the egoist tells us that this action was in response to the strongest desire someone had—when one *really* wanted. The term *want* then comes to mean whatever supports egoism. No matter what potential counterexample one gives, the egoist appeals to some stronger "want" lurking in the background. This, however, leads to another problem.
- *What I decide to do is nothing I have control over, because all my choices and actions are necessarily determined by my strongest desire.* But why should I assume this? In fact, wouldn't one's holding a belief in egoism be determined by his own deepest desires rather than freely or rationally choosing it? This kind of an approach simply assumes that egoism is right rather than offering any good arguments for it.[4]
- *People may "want" all kinds of things that are self-destructive.* Alcoholics *want* more alcohol; drug addicts *want* to continue

their habit; pedophiles *want* to engage in illicit sex. But surely simply "wanting" something is not justification for egoism.

• *What if people "want" to live lives of self-sacrifice and devotion to others?* Persons like Mother Teresa and William Wilberforce are examples of people wanting to help others. Why should the egoist dispute such other-centered dedication as wrongheaded? The egoist's view seems arbitrary this way: Why should I opt for my own good as opposed to society's good? It seems that the egoist can give no real reasons for why his view is to be preferred.

Sixth, even if egoists lay claim to self-interest rather than selfishness, we're left with the problem of arbitrariness—why only this virtue and no others? Some philosophers make the distinction between being selfish and being an egoist. To be selfish means we show no concern for others. An egoist, on the other hand, may show concern for others, but this is driven by *her own* feelings of pity, not the condition of the poor or unfortunate. For example, the seventeenth-century British philosopher Thomas Hobbes claimed that he gave to beggars because of *his own* sense of pity. He didn't want to walk away feeling guilty.[5]

Even so, it seems that self-interest is only part of the moral picture. Why think that this alone would be the only moral virtue? While a person may legitimately consider his own concerns as an object to pursue (within limits), this need not be the only one.

So we can see that the egoist is on to something—even if he is misguided. Indeed, our lives are often helped by boundaries we create for ourselves—to get the necessary rest, for instance; in doing so, however, we'll be better able to serve other people. If we're cranky without our sleep, we should make sleep a priority. It benefits us as well as those around us. There is more to the moral world than our own self-interest.

Seventh, the pursuit of power or self-interest isn't an end in itself; it is a means to something else. But how is that goal to be determined? Perhaps the best example of egoism in the field of philosophy is Friedrich Nietzsche's emphasis on "the will to power." He despised Christianity, which, he claimed, sprang from a doormat theology. For Nietzsche, the pursuit of power mattered. We're left wondering, however, why this is the supreme value. And isn't pursuing power a means to something else rather than an end in itself? "Power" is just an arbitrary value.

Eighth, even if I may end up getting some benefit from a charitable act (e.g., someone recognizes my service), it doesn't follow that this was my motive for acting charitably. The egoist says that we all inescapably act from self-centered motives—even apparently self-sacrificing persons like Mother Teresa, who, according to this line of thinking, was seeking a reward in the afterlife and avoiding punishment.

However, when human creatures show love for God and others, this doesn't mean such actions are motivated by nothing more than punishment-avoidance and reward-mindedness. The sheer enjoyment of God's presence—the greatest good of humans—and his approval of us are reward enough. C. S. Lewis offers a delightful picture:

> Money is not the natural reward of love; that is why we call a man mercenary if he marries a woman for the sake of her money. But marriage is the proper reward for a real lover, and he is not mercenary for desiring it. . . . Those who have attained everlasting life in the vision of God know very well that it is no mere bribe, but the very consummation of their earthly discipleship.[6]

Ninth, there will inevitably be a conflict of interests (or egos). What happens if my interests clash with another's? How do we adjudicate between conflicting personal agendas? What happens when an ethical egoist becomes a powerful dictator? At this point, the egoist doesn't want to have his viewpoint embraced by another (despotic) egoist.

Tenth, any "obligation" to self-interest is merely a matter of convenience for the egoist. Since the egoist's moral rules are really ones of convenience or expediency, the "duty" to self-interest will only exist as long as it is convenient. When it isn't convenient (e.g., when an egoistic dictator is pursuing his own self-interest), the oppressed egoist can't appeal to higher moral principles without inconsistency.

There are some fairly hefty problems with the mind-set of "looking out for number one." The other-centered life that the other-centered triune God calls us to is not only far more attractive, but to live this way is in keeping with how God designed us. God has made us to relate to him and to one another—to love God and to love our neighbor as ourselves (Mark 12:28-33; Luke 9:57-62). Ultimately, we flourish when living by "the Jesus Creed."[7] God's commands have our best interests in mind—they are "for your good" (Deut. 10:13; cf. 8:16; 30:9). We harm ourselves when we try to "create our own reality." This egoistic pursuit actually flies in the face of reality.

Summary

- Some egoists distinguish between self-*centeredness* (which they reject) and self-*interest* (which may involve others).
- Egoism wrongly moves from "is" (that we tend to be self-concerned) to "ought" (that we ought to live this way). This is called the "naturalistic fallacy."
- Why would we ever trust the advice of an egoist since we know that it is always directed toward his own interests?
- When we speak about how we "ought" to live, we are referring to universally applicable ideals. But this is opposed to the self-interested goal of the egoist.
- The egoist's desire to get what he "wants" is empty and trivial.
- Why pursue self-interest as opposed to being other-centered in our orientation? Why prefer self over others? Why stop with the self? Why this virtue and no others?
- To pursue self-interest or power can't be an ultimate goal, but is rather a means to something else. How then do we determine what that goal is?
- What happens when two or more personal agendas or egos conflict with one another (e.g., in a dictator)?
- The egoist's "duty" to self is merely a matter of convenience, not principle.
- Even if I may end up receiving some benefit from a charitable act (e.g., someone recognizes my service), this doesn't mean that this was my motive (or primary motive) for acting charitably.
- How do we handle any conflict of interest or egos?

Further Reading

Frankena, William K. *Ethics.* 2nd ed. Englewood Cliffs, NJ: Prentice-Hall, 1973. Chapter 2.

Graham, Gordon. *Eight Theories of Ethics.* London: Routledge, 2004. Chapter 3.

Lewis, C. S. "The Weight of Glory." In *The Weight of Glory and Other Addresses.* New York: Macmillan, 1965.

McKnight, Scot. *The Jesus Creed: Loving God, Loving Others.* Brewster, MA: Paraclete Press, 2004.

2

Do What You Want—
Just as Long as You
Don't Hurt Anyone

Jack Kevorkian, known as "Dr. Death" and author of *Prescription Medicide: The Goodness of Planned Death,* has been responsible for euthanizing or assisting in the suicides of more than a hundred people. The standard Hippocratic Oath invoked by doctors across the ages includes the promise: "I will neither give a deadly drug to anybody if asked for it, nor will I make the suggestion to this effect. . . . In purity and holiness I will guard my life and my art." That is, the doctor must be committed not to killing even when the patient asks him to.

In July 1996 at the National Press Club, Kevorkian was asked about his philosophical beliefs. He replied, "Yeah, it's quite simple: Absolute personal autonomy. I'm an absolute autonomist. Do and say whatever you want to do and say at any time you want to do or say it, as long as you do not harm or threaten anybody else's person or property." This statement was greeted by hearty applause.[1]

This statement of personal autonomy is quite commonly heard in our society that stresses "rugged individualism." What are we to make of this philosophy of the "absolute autonomist"? And what about that qualifier, "just as long as you don't hurt anyone"?

First, it's an irony in our society that people will deny moral standards or assert absolute autonomy but then slip other (universal) standards in the back door when no one seems to be looking. We commonly hear people make sweeping relativistic claims, but then they'll tack on an absolute, inviolable standard at the end:

- "People can do what they want—*just as long as they don't hurt anyone.*"
- "You can do whatever you want—*as long as it's between two consenting adults.*"
- "You can do whatever you want—*as long as it's in the privacy of your own home.*"
- "People can believe and do whatever they want; *they should just be tolerant of others' views.*"
- "You can do what you want; *just don't violate another person's rights.*"

In essence, they're saying, "You don't have any limits whatsoever—well, except for this or that." Let the autonomist fish or cut bait: why can't people just do what they want—*period*? Why should they have *any* regard for others at all? Why should privacy be respected? Why not be intolerant? The "absolute autonomy" of someone like Kevorkian is seriously compromised by the qualification "as long as you do not harm or threaten anybody else's person or property." Ironically, Kevorkian has fatally harmed other persons!

Second, upon scrutiny, such slogans end up self-destructing. In a purely autonomous world, why insist on standards at all? Why be concerned about others at all? Let's revisit these slogans for a moment:

- "People can do what they want—*just as long as they don't hurt anyone.*" But what's wrong with hurting another person if you can get away with it? Why think that humans have value in themselves—especially if we've naturalistically evolved from valueless processes? And aren't there certain things that are wrong and harmful even if private (e.g., pornography)?

- "You can do whatever you want—*as long as it's between two consenting adults.*" What if the two consenting adults engage in sadomasochistic acts? Aren't such actions deviant? And why limit the discussion to adults? What's ultimately wrong with lowering the age of sexual consent, as the North American Man/Boy Love Association desires?

- "You can do whatever you want—*as long as it's in the privacy of your own home.*" Again, why should absolute autonomists insist on privacy as opposed to doing whatever one wants in *public*—including shouting, "Fire!" in a crowded theater or "Bomb!" on a transatlantic flight? And is child abuse or wifebeating okay since it's done in the "privacy" of one's home?

- "People can believe and do whatever they want; *they should just be tolerant of others' views.*" If the relativist believes that her views are true for her but not necessarily for others, then why should she insist on laying this standard of tolerance on everyone—relativist or not? Where does *that* standard come from? What if a person doesn't want to be "tolerant" (whatever that means)?

- "You can do what you want; *just don't violate another person's rights.*" Why respect anyone's rights? Where do rights even come from in a godless world? How can the relativist believe we can do what we want but, out of the other side of her mouth, insist that others' rights ought to be respected? Isn't it ironic (and contradictory) that our society both freely accepts the "true for you but not for me" relativism as well as insists on watching out for people's "inviolable rights"? If relativism is justified, humans don't have rights that ought to be respected. If humans have genuine rights, then relativism is false.

Third, one can do a number of things without "hurting" others, but they would still be wrong and should still be avoided. We're familiar with "date rape" drugs (GHB, rohypnol, and ketamine) and what they are intended for. Let's apply this slogan of "doing what you want without hurting others": Let's say that a young man wants to "do what he wants" to an unsuspecting woman at a party. He places such a drug in her drink . . . and you can guess the rest. Suppose he takes certain "precautions" so that there are no "consequences" to his violating her. He does all of this "without hurting" her—or even without her knowing what has taken place. Hasn't the young man then been able to do what he wants without harming the woman?

We still recognize that this act is intolerable. While the man may not have technically "hurt" the woman physically or even psychologically, he took terrible advantage of her by raping her while she was under the influence of the drug. We know that certain things are wrong even if they don't injure another. Another example might be mocking mental hospital patients whose minds are no longer connected to reality, leaving them incapable of making sense of the hateful things being said of them. Such actions don't "hurt" the patients—these acts actually damage the soul of the mocker—but engaging in them is still wrong.

Furthermore, what if a teenager wants to commit suicide, exercising his own autonomy? We wouldn't say that this is a good or noble thing, would we? If autonomy is what ultimately matters and one determines that life isn't worth living, then why not let the teenager commit suicide? Isn't that his "right"? Philosopher John Stuart Mill noted a similar problem—having the "right" to enslave oneself: "The principle of freedom cannot require that [one] should be free not to be free. It is not freedom, to be allowed to alienate his freedom."[2] That is, my placing absolute power in the hands of a slaveholder undermines my human dignity. This isn't true freedom. Such questions of suicide or self-slavery expose the inadequacy of this autonomous philosophy of life.

Fourth, while human freedom and choices are important, they must be considered in the context of broader issues, such as community, life's being a gift, and the existence of moral standards. Ironically, Kevorkian's philosophy of "absolute autonomy" is undermined by his qualifier ("as long as you do not harm or threaten anybody else's person"). Despite his individualism, he's assuming (a) that we are part of a larger community, and (b) that we should take commitments to this community seriously. "Absolute (personal) autonomy" assumes I don't need to regard others and I don't have moral duties to others; a better term to use would be "personal responsibility," which suggests that human choices are meaningful in the context of a broader community of loyalties and moral commitments.

Another reason to reject absolute autonomy is that our lives are a gift from God; they are not a right. It's one thing to let a dying person die when the "great organs" (brain, lungs, and heart) are starting to shut down, since death must come to us all. It's another thing to intentionally take an innocent person's life—even when she may want to die. We ought always to *care*, even if we can't *cure*.[3]

Fifth, freedom is not an end in itself, and it can often be coercive. Despite our positive associations with the word *freedom*, freedom is a relative term. We're not "free" to rape, murder, or steal. We must first know what the freedom is for.

Furthermore, freedom may actually serve as justification for coercion, as Stanley Hauerwas has written. Think of "women's freedom" or "reproductive rights": unborn children are coerced to comply with a woman's "ethic of convenience"; mentally handicapped children can be coerced into an institution by their "independent-minded" parents: "For when freedom and its enhancement becomes an end in itself, we lose any account of human life that gives content and direction to freedom."[4]

A final thought: Absolute autonomists tend not to be interested in philosophical or logical consistency. They are committed to their own personal programs. Given their personal motivations, they won't likely be persuaded by arguments. (While poor motivations don't disprove their position, they should still be taken seriously.) They'll be drawn to beautiful lives that are well lived and loving relationships that, by God's grace, can break into their self-enclosed worlds.

Summary

- Ironically, many who deny moral standards (e.g., relativists) or who assert absolute freedom will slip absolute standards in the back door: "You can do whatever you want—just don't hurt anyone, just be tolerant, just do it with consenting adults," and the like.

- These sorts of slogans end up in a mire of contradictions. If we can be "absolute autonomists," why insist on these standards of tolerance or not hurting others?
- Moral standards and concern for others are hard to square with this pure autonomy. We can do a lot of things without "hurting others" (e.g., using a date rape drug, mocking the mentally impaired), but we know instinctively that such acts are wrong.
- Human freedom and choice are important, but they must be placed in the context of community, life's being a gift, and the existence of moral standards.
- Freedom isn't absolute, and it can itself be coercive and intolerant (e.g., abortion, institutionalizing the mentally handicapped when they could be kept at home).

Further Reading

Beckwith, Francis J., and Gregory Koukl. *Relativism: Feet Firmly Planted in Mid-air*. Grand Rapids: Baker, 1998.

Copan, Paul. *"That's Just Your Interpretation."* Grand Rapids: Baker, 2001. Part 1.

———. *"True for You, but Not for Me."* Minneapolis: Bethany, 1998.

3

Is It Okay to Lie to Nazis?

My great-aunt, "Tante" Lilly Schweitzer Franzkeit, lived with her relatives in a German-speaking area of Kaunas, Lithuania, called Schanzen. She had served as a young nurse on the Russian front during World War I; she lived through the turmoil of the Russian Revolution of 1917; and then she witnessed the invasion of the Soviets who occupied this Baltic state in June 1940—in accordance with Hitler's secret treaty with Stalin of August 1939. She had been helping Ukrainians and others who were fleeing from the ruthless Communists cross the border. Refugees would cross the Lithuanian-German border at Kybarten near Königsberg (Prussia), hoping to make it to a less-threatening Germany.

Someone reported Tante Lilly to the authorities, who put her in prison. Before her arrest, she was able to give her purse with important papers—including a list of refugees she was helping—to a doctor. Also in the purse was a gold medal bearing Czar Nicholas's image that she had received for serving on the Russian front—not exactly something to show Soviet soldiers! This purse was delivered to her sisters, Lorchen and Vody, just before the NKVD (later known as the KGB) arrived to search the house. Vody, sick in bed, hid the purse under her blanket, and the medal was put under a saucer. Thankfully, the soldiers left, finding nothing, and Tante Lilly was released from prison a half year later.

Were my great-aunts obligated to turn over papers to inquiring authorities, meaning the death or imprisonment of innocents? Or consider this: Do you tell an abusive husband who shows up at your door that you are harboring his (battered) wife? Do you tell a questioning burglar where you keep your stash of money? The eighteenth-century philosopher Immanuel Kant (who happened to be from Königsberg) was utterly committed to "absolutes" (the "categorical imperative"). In fact, he determined that, rather than ever deceive, he would be obligated to be "truthful" about his friend's whereabouts to an ax murderer seeking to kill him! If a murder were to take place, Kant argued, he wouldn't share any responsibility for it, because he had told the truth. The blame would rest entirely on the ax murderer![1]

Such a position is truly counterintuitive, despite Kant's valiant attempt at consistency. I'll argue that deception is morally permissible—a point reinforced by Scripture—under certain specific conditions.

First, we must differentiate between "lying" and "deceiving." Lying involves breaking trust with another when we have a duty to tell the truth: "Do not withhold good from those to whom it is due, when it is in your power to do it" (Prov. 3:27). *Deception,* on the other hand, need not involve breaking trust, because some people (e.g., criminals) forfeit their right to the truth by violating the rights of others. So while lying is clearly deceptive, not all deception is lying. We'll explore this below.

Second, when discussing truth-telling and deception, we must first consider the matter of personal character. We shouldn't look to those who are regularly rationalizing, telling lies (white or black), or acting unscrupulously at work to learn when deception is morally permissible. Rather, those who are steadfast, faithful, and true to their word are in the best position to judge this. For example, consider Sophie Scholl, a committed Christian who was a university student and an active participant in The White Rose—a German resistance movement during World War II.[2] She and her friends devoted their lives to exposing the Nazis' propaganda and lies by quietly publicizing the truth to their fellow Germans. When she, along with her brother, was caught on February 18, 1943, and interrogated, she sought to deceive her interrogators to protect her innocent comrades. But when she was found out, she refused to say anything that might endanger her friends. Indeed, her life had been characterized by virtuous character and commitment. So the deception used by such persons can't be misinterpreted as self-serving. It is precisely the person of truthful and faithful character who is in touch with reality and is best able to discern when deception is permissible.

Third, while certain acts are always wrong, we must also consider motives, the context, and the consequences of other actions in assessing their rightness or wrongness. Skeptic Michael Shermer criticizes biblical ethics for its alleged preoccupation with "absolutes"—for disallowing any ethical tensions or exceptions.[3] I've met people who have concluded that since ethical tensions exist (telling the truth to Nazis versus protecting innocent Jewish lives), this means moral standards don't really exist.

Such conclusions aren't accurate, however. In fact, the very tension that exists between truth-telling and preserving innocent life assumes that we take seriously two or more important moral obligations. Furthermore, these tensions may not be of equal value and may call for properly ordering/prioritizing them according to God's kingdom purposes. That is, we have to consider a moral hierarchy or ordering of our moral priorities when various moral considerations converge. Biblical ethics is more subtle and nuanced than many imagine.

Now some people might protest, "This is situation ethics—a denial of moral absolutes!" Joseph Fletcher's book *Situation Ethics*[4] argues for the justification of questionable (indeed, immoral) practices under the vague cloak of "love." He raises the question of "sacrificial adultery": Mrs. Bergmeier, a Berlinese woman picked up by the Soviets during World War II, was placed in a prison camp in the Ukraine. She heard that her husband and three children were seeking her and desperately needing her. She knew that she could only get out of prison alive and return home if she would be found "with child." So out of "love" for her family, she had sex with a prison guard, conceived, and, according to plan, was sent back home. Her family "welcomed her with open arms, even when she told them how she managed [to get out]." And when the child was born, "[the parents] loved him more than all the rest."

This adultery-justifying scenario, however, is hardly what we are talking about when we refer to a nuanced ethical stance. Rather, we should consider various factors:

- As we saw above, moral choices are not made in a vacuum; (a) *character* is an important backdrop for ethical decision making.
- However, as with Mrs. Bergmeier, (b) certain *acts*—such as rape, adultery, or torturing babies for fun—are always wrong and never justified.
- Besides this, (c) *motives* are an important factor for judging moral actions. For example, Jack and Jill visit their "Gramgram" in a nursing home. Jill visits because she wants to inherit a portion of her grandmother's fortune. Jack, though, doesn't care about money; he visits because he loves Gramgram. Even though their outward actions may be identical, Jill's actions are wrong because of her warped, mercenary motives.
- Furthermore, (d) *circumstances* or *contexts* are also relevant for determining the rightness of an action. Take the act of killing. In one context (protecting one's family when a burglar intrudes), killing (in self-defense) would be morally justified. In another context (strangers in a crowded street or supermarket), killing would be cold-blooded murder. While all murder is killing, not all killing is murder.
- Finally, we must consider the *consequences* of our actions. We don't always speak what comes to mind, because it may bring harm to others. When we confront a person with a serious problem, we try to keep it proportional to those directly affected rather than disseminating the news widely and causing great harm.

These considerations are relevant when it comes to truth-telling and deception. We must not only consider an act itself, but the character, motive, and context (or relationships) involved. In defending deception in certain circumstances, I'm not advocating lying when you've gotten yourself into deep trouble! For example, the adulterer who thinks he is preserving his marriage by not telling his wife of his betrayal is misguided. As Lewis Smedes points out, "[This] would turn adultery itself into its own justification for lying. Since adultery always threatens to destroy a marriage, lying about it is almost always required to save the marriage. So the offense itself guarantees the 'right to lie.' The irony is too great."[5]

When Christians speak of "absolutes," they can often give the wrong impression about Scripture's moral framework. They lead others to believe that circumstances have no bearing on moral considerations, that no weighing is necessary, that no tensions exist, and that the moral course is always easy. This isn't true, and Christians should be prepared for a nuanced discussion of such issues.[6]

Fourth, we human beings find ourselves flourishing in the context of trusting covenantal relationships, to which we are obligated, but truthfulness and trust are not expressed in identical ways. Parents and children, husbands and wives, employers and employees, professors and students, state and citizens—these relationships require trust and truthfulness in different ways. Governments should be truthful to their citizens, though this doesn't mean giving away delicate state secrets (even to the media), which would jeopardize national security. Auto manufacturers are obligated to make safe cars for consumers and to disclose and correct any deficiencies, but truthfulness doesn't demand that these companies reveal their long-range engineering and production plans to their competitors. Doctors ought to explain clearly and carefully the nature of their patients' condition to them—but not post their medical charts on the Internet!

In other words, trusting covenant relationships require different levels of disclosure, and full disclosure is not always a requirement. A truthful person need not always tell the whole truth, and it isn't right for just anyone to demand the whole truth from just anyone else. For example, parents rightly seek to protect their children from consuming worry, insecurity, and fear; parents don't need to tell their young children that they are having financial challenges, that they may be out of a job, or that there are a certain number of known child molesters living in the county! Think of the notable Norman Rockwell painting *Freedom from Fear* (1943): a mother is tucking her children into bed while the father stands alongside holding a newspaper whose headlines mention the Nazi bombing of London and the horrors of World War II.[7] Parents shouldn't burden their children of a tender age with workplace problems, financial or insurance challenges, or personal issues that adults should be grappling with. Given the circumstances, a parent does not owe her children "the truth," which can overwhelm them and which they can't understand.

Furthermore, what can be spoken in certain contexts (e.g., family relationships) should not be brought up in public. The German theologian Dietrich Bonhoeffer, who himself engaged in deception to protect innocent persons from being destroyed by the Nazis, wrote wisely about considering such contexts.[8] He gives the example of a child who may be embarrassed or ashamed of issues at home, such as a father's alcoholism. A prying teacher asks him in front of the class if his father often comes home drunk. The child doesn't know how to handle this conflict and so, doing the best he can, denies it. The teacher, however, is in the wrong, and the child has an obligation to keep certain things within the family: "The family has its own secret and must preserve it." Even though the child denies the situation, Bonhoeffer says, he bears more truth than if he had betrayed his father's weakness.

Because we live in a fallen, sinful world, some secrecy and hiding are necessary. (God gave Adam and Eve clothing to wear!) To humiliate ("You're ugly") or to betray someone is not justified in the name of "speaking one's mind" or "being honest." This is actually a *distortion* of reality, which often requires silence or concealment in certain relationships in order to build others up or simply to protect the innocent and vulnerable. Telling the truth takes place in real situations; different situations, different times, and different relationships demand different things of us: "All speech is subject to certain conditions. . . . it has its place, its time and its task, and consequently also its limits."[9] Lying is more than an intentional discrepancy between thought and speech: "The lie is the denial, the negation and the conscious and deliberate destruction of the reality which is created by God and which consists in God, no matter whether this purpose is achieved by speech or by silence."[10]

A government should allow freedom for elections, presses, and houses of worship while trying to protect the innocent and stop criminals. When a government is evil or corrupt, however, Christians "have no covenant . . . to tell them such truth as will help them do their evil."[11]

Fifth, the Scriptures actually give insight into when deception is permissible and when it is not—in three general areas. Let's look more closely at them:

1. *Criminal activity/oppression.* The Hebrew midwives Shiphrah and Puah in Egypt (Exod. 1:15–21) engaged in deception. Because they "feared God," they resisted Pharaoh, who wanted to put innocent Hebrew male babies to death. These women "did not do as the king of Egypt had commanded them, but let the boys live" (v. 17). When confronted by Pharaoh, they used deception: "Because the Hebrew women are not as the Egyptian women; for they are vigorous and give birth before the midwife can get to them." The divine response? "God was good to the midwives"; and "because the midwives feared God, He established households for them" (vv. 20, 21). Note the close connection between fearing God, resisting Pharaoh (including using deception), and receiving God's approval.

The same is true of Rahab of Jericho (Joshua 2). She is commended elsewhere (Heb. 11:31; James 2:25) as one who displayed "faith" in God by hiding two Hebrew spies, deceiving the authorities, and sending the spies off in a different direction. According to James 2, she is praised in part for her deception: "she received the messengers and sent them out by another way."

In our day we don't seem to think that there is a moral problem with leaving on our house lights when going on vacation or going out at night. Why do we seek to give the *impression* that someone is home when no one *really* is home? We're preemptively attempting to deceive would-be thieves. Police use deceptive tactics when conducting sting operations to catch drug lords, break up prostitution rings, or trap money launderers. Certainly such deception is justified, and we implicitly assume the legitimacy of deception in such instances.

Deception in such cases becomes even clearer when God gets involved directly. In 1 Samuel 16:1–5, God told Samuel to anoint a king, and Samuel replied that if King Saul heard of it, he would kill Samuel. God gave this advice to him: "Take a heifer with you and say, 'I have come to sacrifice to the LORD'" (v. 2). Because of Saul's jealousy and evil intent, God urged Samuel to deceive anyone who asked. Because of Saul's irrational ruthlessness that threatened to violate others' rights, he had forfeited a right to full or even partial disclosure of what Samuel was doing.[12]

2. *Warfare.* The very principles of warfare in the Old Testament presuppose deception, and God is often involved in helping Israel. For example, Joshua is *told by God* to set an "ambush" (Josh. 8:2). In one instance, *God himself* sets an ambush (2 Chron. 20:22). Even though God is "true" (Rom. 3:4) and "cannot lie" (Titus 1:2), he still deceives the enemies of Israel in warfare.

Jael deceived the Canaanite commander Sisera and ended up killing him in his sleep using a tent peg (Judg. 4:17–21). Elsewhere, we see Elisha deceiving the Syrian army, which resulted in their capture—and a peaceable resolution to war with Israel (2 Kings 6:18–23).

3. *Light, inconsequential social/conventional arrangements.* Sporting events and board games often require deception (e.g., pitchers throwing curveballs, quarterbacks faking a running play in order to pass the ball, a chess player attempting to put his opponent in check), but this is an agreed-upon convention that is built into these activities.

Jokes presuppose some kind of deception; punch lines often come as a surprise. Harmless practical jokes and surprise parties can be great fun—even if they involve deception. Social conventions also often allow for mild deception, and this is not taken as lying—withholding the truth from whom it is due. In some Oriental cultures, it is understood that a guest says "no" several times to the offer of a second helping before finally accepting. In our culture, when we are asked, "How are you?" it is not immoral to say, "Okay" or "Doing all right" when we are feeling less than okay. Unless the asker is a close friend, he likely isn't looking for any deep self-disclosure. After the walk to Emmaus, Jesus himself "acted as though He would go farther" (Luke 24:28), but the two disciples urged him to stay. Jesus wasn't really "pretending" but was simply exhibiting modesty: he wouldn't force his presence on them but gave them an opportunity to freely invite him in.[13]

We live in an age of falsehood. Flattery, mere idle chatter, always saying what one thinks, and even certain silences (which ought to be articulated) could be categorized as "lies." They fail to match up to the reality that God has created.

There are times, however, when a person may in good conscience deceive—in cases of (a) ruthless political oppression and criminal activity, (b) (just) warfare, and (c) certain conventional social situations. Deception in the cases of (a) and (b) should still have the overarching goal of restoring or creating an environment that is conducive to truth-telling. As Glen Stassen and David Gushee write, "Those . . . who are threatened and oppressed may be permitted in times of moral emergency to suspend truth-telling temporarily in some contexts in order to honor central covenant obligations—and to work clandestinely, if necessary, for a just and peaceful public square in which truth may be freely spoken once again."[14]

Summary

- It may be helpful to distinguish between "lying" and "deceiving" (as with "murder" and "killing"): while all lying is deceiving, not all deceiving is lying.
- Personal character helps set an important context for deception.
- Certain acts (like adultery, rape, torturing for fun) are always wrong, but we should also consider the motives, context, and consequences of an act to discern whether it is right or wrong.
- Humans flourish in trusting covenantal relationships, but we express truthfulness and trust in various ways.
- The Bible mentions three areas where deception is permissible: criminal activity and ruthless oppression, warfare, and light social deception.

Further Reading

Bonhoeffer, Dietrich. *Ethics*. Trans. Neville Horton Smith. New York: Macmillan, 1965. Part 5, "What Is Meant by 'Telling the Truth'?"

McQuilkin, J. Robertson. *Introduction to Biblical Ethics*. Wheaton: Tyndale, 1990.

Smedes, Lewis. *Mere Morality: What God Expects from Ordinary People.* Grand Rapids: Eerdmans, 1983. Chapter 8.

Stassen, Glen H., and David P. Gushee. *Kingdom Ethics: Following Jesus in Contemporary Context.* Downers Grove, IL: InterVarsity, 2003. Chapter 18, "Truth-telling."

Part II

SLOGANS RELATED TO WORLDVIEWS

4

Why Is God So Arrogant and Egotistical?

In an open forum, a woman from the local humanist society raised her hand to ask me, "Why does God tell us to worship, praise, and glorify Him? It sounds so vain and conceited. Why is it wrong for *us*—but not *God*—to be proud?"

To many, God seems to be arrogant. Atheist philosopher Bede Rundle makes a similar point:

> If you are going to make your god in the image of man, you might at least filter out some of the less desirable human traits. God should be above any sort of attention-seeking behaviour, for instance, and an insistence on being told how unsurpassably wonderful one is does not rate highly. As Hume, in the guise of Philo, observed: "It is an absurdity to believe that the Deity has human passions, and one of the lowest of human passions, a restless appetite for applause." True, this objection assumes that God commands us to worship him in order to gratify some self-regarding desire on his part, when it could be that the point of singing God's praises was protective—to propitiate a God who could be angry or jealous, for instance—but this hardly shows God in a better light.[1]

Theologians and philosophers have traditionally talked about God's loving himself, contemplating himself, enjoying himself. We read in Scripture that God wants to "make a name for Himself" (2 Sam. 7:23; cf. Neh. 9:23). He delivers his people from Egypt "for the sake of His name" (Ps. 106:7; cf. Isa. 63:12; Jer. 32:20; Dan. 9:15). On the surface, it may appear as though God has an unhealthy preoccupation with himself. Isn't this the height of vanity and arrogance? Surely God can't be humble![2]

There are some important perspectives to keep in mind as we try to think about God's demand to worship. In fact, we can make the case that God's very nature and his interaction with humans express gracious humility and astonishing condescension.

First, we should get clear on definitions of "pride" (an inflated view of self) and "humility" (an appropriate acknowledgment and realistic self-assessment). Clarifying and defining our terms is often the first step in attempting to settle disagreements, and this case is no exception. To those asserting that God is vain and proud, we should ask, "How do you define *pride*?" We all know that pride is a kind of false advertising campaign. We promote an image of ourselves because we suspect that others won't accept who we really are.[3] Pride is actually a lie about a person's identity or achievements. To be proud is to live in a world propped up with falsehoods about oneself, taking credit where credit isn't due.[4]

Now, we're not talking about being gratified or "taking pride in" one's work (as Paul did as an apostle, 2 Cor. 10:17) or "being proud of" a person's progress in faith (2 Cor. 7:14; 9:3–4) and in the proper use of God-given abilities. In all of this, we recognize the grace of God that makes these things possible. Of course, to "boast in the Lord" (2 Cor. 10:17) and in the cross of Christ (Gal. 6:14) puts into proper perspective our deep dependence on God. The pull-yourself-up-by-your-own-bootstraps type of self-reliance is an expression of pride—a failure or refusal to acknowledge our proper place before God. Grace is given to the humble, not the proud.

Humility, on the other hand, involves having a realistic assessment of oneself. This includes recognizing not only weaknesses but also strengths. Obviously, it's delusional to claim you've invented aluminum foil or Post-it notes when you really haven't. But it's also delusional to say you "really can't play piano all that well" when you're an award-winning pianist who regularly performs with the

Cleveland Orchestra or the London Philharmonic! This would be a *false* humility that's equally out of touch with reality—not to mention (possibly) being a backdoor attempt to get others' attention! A truly humble person won't deny his abilities, but he will at the same time acknowledge that his gifts come from God and that he can't take credit for them. So *to be humble is to know our place before God*.[5]

Upon closer examination, we can see that God can't be called proud by this definition. Rather, he has a *realistic* view of himself, not a false or exaggerated one. His view of himself isn't distorted or exaggerated—after all, he *is* God! We can't ascribe too much greatness to God, because he's the greatest conceivable being! God doesn't take more credit than he deserves. For example, he doesn't lay claim to choices that morally responsible humans must make; nor does he make himself out to be the author of evil in the name of "sovereignty" (which some Christians tend to do when they praise God for evil things). No, God doesn't "think more highly of himself than he ought to think" (Rom. 12:3). Rather, he thinks accurately about himself.

Second, Jesus' call for his followers to be humble isn't inconsistent with other concerns to allow our deeds of love to be noted by others. When we are tempted to show off our "religion," we should engage in the discipline of secrecy. When we are tempted to stifle our witness, we should "let our light shine." Atheist philosopher Michael Martin claims that Jesus' exhortations to humility, if applied as he commanded, can be self-contradictory and problematic. He claims that the warning about giving alms and praying—and we could add fasting—for the public to see (Matt. 6:1–18) shouldn't be absolute prohibitions: "Sometimes public displays of ostensibly altruistic [i.e., apparently selfless] actions—ones that could have been done privately—may be done for completely altruistic motives. Jesus may have wrongly supposed otherwise."[6]

Martin is right about the importance of motives; he's wrong to suggest that Jesus may not have been sophisticated enough to consider different situations. In this same context of Matthew 6, Jesus assumes that his disciples will engage in corporate—not merely private—prayer ("Our Father"), implying that they won't all squeeze into a prayer "closet"[7] to do so! And just earlier in the Sermon on the Mount, Jesus tells his disciples (who are "the light of the world") to "let your light so shine"—like a city on a hill—before people that "they may see your good works, and glorify your Father who is in heaven" (Matt. 5:13–16).

At the tomb of Lazarus, Jesus (who often tries to avoid crowds and spends time in solitary prayer) prays in public to make a deliberate point to those around him: "Father, I thank You that You have heard Me. I knew that You always hear me; but because of the people standing around I said it, so that they may believe that You sent Me" (John 11:41–42). Later on Paul says that Christians, in their behavior and loving demeanor, should "adorn the doctrine of God our Savior" (Titus 2:9–10; cf. 1 Tim. 4:15; John 13:35).

In all of this, Jesus and the rest of the New Testament offer a twofold exhortation against pride: *show when tempted to hide* (e.g., Matt. 5:13–16) and *hide when tempted to show* (Matt. 6:1).[8] We may at times want to stifle or resist doing the right thing in front of others—a manifestation of pride. That's the time to demonstrate our commitment to Christ—an act of humility (e.g., instead of arguing about who's the greatest, we should serve one another). But at other times, we may feel like advertising our religious commitment—an expression of pride. However, out of humility, we should keep this secret. Rather than being preoccupied with our own image in front of others, we should "place our public relations department entirely in the hands of God."[9]

Third, God's making us in his image isn't a mark of divine pride. It's a gift he bestows on us and one to receive gratefully. To be made in God's image and to receive his salvation are expressions of God's kindness, not of divine arrogance. When God created human beings, he uniquely equipped them to rule the world with him (a kingly role) and to walk with and worship him (a priestly role). Being made in God's image as priest-kings brings with it the ability to relate to God, to think rationally, to make moral decisions, to express creativity, and to share in God's rule over creation. But some have claimed that God's making us in his image is arrogant—like a vain toy maker creating dolls that look just like him.

We can look at the matter from another angle, though. By making us in his image, God is "spreading the wealth." Historian Arthur Lovejoy (1873–1962) tracked the concept of "the great chain of being"—that God's rich goodness overflows to his creation, which lives, moves, and has its being in him.[10] Though God created freely and without constraint, God is bursting with joy and love to share his goodness with his creatures. God allows us humans, his image-bearers, to share—in a limited way—in who he is. God enables us to participate in the life of the divine community, the Trinity—a life that fills him with great joy and pleasure (2 Peter 1:4). This image is a gift to be received. God bestows on us a great compliment by endowing us with a privileged position and with important capacities—ones that reflect God's own wonderful nature. By God's image and Spirit, we are equipped to carry out our kingly and priestly duties on this earth (Rev. 5:10). That we can so fully participate in God's remarkable purposes involves "things into which angels long to look" (1 Peter 1:12).

Fourth, worshiping God doesn't diminish our humanity, but rather fulfills it. To worship God is to realize our very purpose (a relationship with God), and such worship reflects our place in the universe (we are creatures and God is Creator). The Old Testament repeatedly declares how God desires his name to be known among the nations ("that they may know that I am the LORD"). This "knowing" can be either in blessing/deliverance or in judgment (e.g., Ezek. 25:7, 11, 17). At the temple dedication, Solomon prays that "all the peoples of the earth may know" God's name and "fear" him as Israel does (2 Chron. 6:33).

Worship—which comes from the Old English word *worth-ship*—is an appropriate recognition of who the triune God is and of our relationship to him. Worship is simply self-forgetfulness as we remember and acknowledge God.[11]

So when God calls for our worship, this isn't a manifestation of pride. The knowledge and worship of God is the highest good possible. Not only this, worship expresses an awareness of God's—and thus our—proper place in the order of things, and it also transforms us into what we were designed to be. To be connected with God in worship not only humbles us. It's a lofty, lifelong endeavor that expands our minds, enriches our souls, makes us wise, and enables us to have a proper self-understanding. Knowing God is the highest human pursuit possible. The loving and creating triune God is worthy of our allegiance, love, and attention.[12]

God's call for our worship, then, is not because he thinks more highly of himself than he ought or because he has false beliefs about himself. God's desire to be known by us stems from his being deeply in touch with reality. He calls us to acknowledge what he has known all along—in order that we might be transformed. Biblical scholar Richard Bauckham writes: "For a human being to seek such universal and eternal fame [as God does] would be to aspire to divinity, but God must desire to be known to be God. The good of God's human creatures requires that he be known to them as God. There is no vanity, only revelation of truth, in God's demonstrating his deity to the nations."[13]

Fifth, God's jealousy is aroused when human beings turn creatures or false ideas into God-substitutes. Just as a woman will not share her husband with another, so God is jealous to protect the love relationship for which all human beings were designed. We often think of jealousy in negative terms: it smacks of insecurity when someone feels threatened by another; it promotes resentment; and it can create all kinds of unpredictable reactions. So when people read that God is a "jealous God" who won't share his glory with another (Exod. 20:5), they promptly apply to God this negative view of jealousy!

There's an appropriate kind of jealousy, though. Just imagine a wife who's unconcerned when another woman flirts with her husband. If she wasn't jealous or committed to protecting that sacred marital relationship, we would rightly see her lack of concern as warped and morally deficient.

Similarly, we should think of God's jealousy as noble and virtuous—a jealousy not springing from an inferiority complex that makes prideful, selfish demands. Rather, divine jealousy springs from a human denial that God is God, that a relationship with him isn't really needed for ultimate human flourishing. Indeed, divine *jealousy* in Scripture is used in the context of idolatry and false worship.[14] To choose this-worldly pursuits over a relationship with God is spiritual adultery (James 4:4; cf. 2 Cor. 11:2), which makes God legitimately jealous.

God is the all-good Creator and Life-giver, who wills the flourishing of his creation. When a person acts in life-denying ways (e.g., engaging in adultery, pornography, or promise breaking—or simply suppressing the truth about God), God's jealousy surfaces so that the person might abandon her death-seeking goals and return to an abundant life. Divine jealousy should be seen as God's willing the best for his creatures.[15]

Sixth, when the Scriptures enjoin us to praise God, God is not the one commanding praise. Rather, the call to praise comes from creatures spontaneously calling upon one another to recognize God's greatness, goodness, and worth-ship. Naturally flowing praise simply completes and expresses the creature's enjoyment of God. Some people, however, suggest that the idea of praise in Scripture is nothing more than God's fishing for compliments and flattery. Nonsense! God is self-sufficient and content in and of himself. He doesn't need frail humans for some sort of ego boost (Ps. 50:11: "If I were hungry I would not tell you, for the world is Mine, and all it contains"). God freely created us to share in the joys of his triune life. He hardly needs our praise, which would be pathetic, as Bede Rundle's earlier caricature indicates.

The critic might ask, "Then why does God command us to praise him?" Ah, this is the seriously misunderstood part. Contrary to popular criticism, praise isn't commanded by God. It's called for by creatures caught up with God's greatness, power, goodness, and love. Praise is the climax of realizing God's excellencies, and creatures fittingly erupt in praise, spontaneously beckoning the rest of us to do the same.[16]

C. S. Lewis had his own misconceptions about this notion of praise and wrote of the lesson he learned:

> But the most obvious fact about praise—whether of God or anything—strangely escaped me. I thought of it in terms of compliment, approval, or the giving of honor. I had never noticed that all enjoyment spontaneously overflows into praise. . . . The world rings with praise—lovers praising their mistresses, readers their favorite poet, walkers praising the countryside, players praising their game. . . . I think we delight to praise what we enjoy because the praise not merely expresses but completes the enjoyment; it is appointed consummation.[17]

Lewis came to see that praise stems from doing what one couldn't help doing—giving utterance to what we regard as supremely valuable: "It is good to sing praises to our God." Why? "For it is pleasant and praise is becoming" (Ps. 147:1). We can also add that although praise is often spontaneous and springing from an overflowing heart of joy, there are times when praise is an expression of deliberate trust in God's goodness and sovereignty in the face of hardship and loss (Job 1:21: "The LORD gave and the LORD has taken away. Blessed be the name of the LORD").

Seventh, God's humility is expressed in offering praise to human beings for their trust and obedience. Not only do we praise God, but the humble God is also willing to "praise" human beings who have trusted in his grace: their "praise" isn't from human beings, "but from God" (Rom. 2:29). The other-centered God delights in praising humans who seek to please him.

Another related point: when we creatures show love for God, we aren't doing so because of a crass desire for rewards or the avoidance of punishment. The sheer enjoyment of God's presence—the greatest good of humans—and his approval of us are reward enough. This quotation by Lewis is worth citing again: "Money is not the natural reward of love; that is why we call a man mercenary if he marries a woman for the sake of her money. But marriage is the proper reward for a real lover, and he is not mercenary for desiring it. . . . Those who have attained everlasting life in the vision of God know very well that it is no mere bribe, but the very consummation of their earthly discipleship."[18]

Eighth, the triune God is humble in himself, and he continually manifests his humility in his interactions with human beings. Jesus of Nazareth turns out to be a remarkable example of the humility of God, who comes to serve us. God is inherently loving and self-giving within the relationships of the divine family, the Trinity. This divine inter- (and inner-) connection of mutuality, openness, and reciprocity has no individualistic competition among the family members, but only joy, self-giving love, and transparency. Rather than being some isolated self or solitary ego, God is supremely relational in his self-giving, other-oriented nature.

Furthermore, God particularly manifested his humility in the incarnation and death of his Son. Jesus describes himself as "gentle and humble in heart"—this in the very same context as his declaration of (1) uniquely knowing, relating to, and revealing the Father and (2) being the one who gives the weary rest for their souls (Matt. 11:27–29)! Jesus' greatness and humility don't contradict each other; Jesus sees himself clearly and accurately.

Jesus not only declares his humility, but he models servant leadership for his disciples. He reminds them that the one who is greatest among his people is the one who serves: "I am among you as the one who serves" (Luke 22:27). This "Lord" and "Teacher" displays his self-humbling servanthood by taking the slave's role by washing his disciples' dirty feet (John 13:5–20). Truly, God in Christ didn't come to be waited on but to "serve" and "give His life a ransom for many" (Mark 10:45). Philippians 2 marvelously displays the depths to which God is willing to go for our salvation: God the Son humbles (empties) himself, becoming a slave who dies in great shame and humiliation (2:6–8).

This is just like the triune, self-giving God, who is humble by nature. Furthermore, God's interactions with human beings reflect continuous acts of humility. God doesn't only act humbly and condescendingly in the temporary earthly mission of Christ. God is *characteristically humble*. The "high and exalted God" dwells "with the contrite and lowly of spirit" (Isa. 57:15). Throughout his dealings with humans, God consistently displays a gracious self-humbling. In fact, God in Christ shares in and identifies with the joys and sorrows of Jesus' brothers and sisters—"the least of these" (Matt. 25:40, 45). When Saul persecutes Christ's body, Jesus confronts him: "Why are you persecuting *Me*?" (Acts 9:4, emphasis added). In the final state of the redeemed—after Christ returns and the new heavens and earth are established—he himself ("the master") will "gird himself" and "wait on" his own servants, his disciples (Luke 12:37).

Ninth, the ultimate picture of divine humility is evident in the humiliating and degrading death of Jesus of Nazareth on the cross, which is simultaneously God's greatest, most glorious achievement. I was once speaking with a Muslim friend, Abdul, who expressed his difficulties with the idea of God's becoming man and dying on the cross. "It's such a humiliation!" he exclaimed. From the Christian perspective, he spoke better than he knew! For the Muslim, God is so utterly transcendent and therefore doesn't stoop to the level of humans. How different is God who sits down at table with society's undesirables and outcasts!

Just after the September 11 terrorist attacks, I watched with interest *Larry King Weekend*. The panel—a couple of Christians, a Jewish rabbi, a Hindu, and a Muslim—discussed the topic "Where was God?" One of the Christians spoke of God's incarnation in Christ, who came to provide atonement for us. The Muslim (Dr. Maher Hathout) expressed his disagreement with the "the incarnation part," because "we don't believe in that. We believe that God is way beyond being imprisoned in space or in place. He is beyond perception, beyond concretization."[19]

In response to the question, "Where was God?" the Christian—not the Muslim—has the far more remarkable and richer contribution to make. The sovereign God stoops and condescends. The triune, self-giving God is Immanuel, "God with us" and God for us. Isaiah 57:15 proclaims that God is not only exalted, but that he also dwells with the contrite and lowly. The compatibility of greatness and humility is marvelously demonstrated in Jesus' own crucifixion—a display of God's humiliation that turns out to be his own mark of distinction and moment of glory!

On the one hand, the Romans intended for crucifixion to be a barbaric, humiliating, and painful death. Crucified victims (typically runaway slaves or criminals) were severely beaten, stripped naked, and placed at crossroads or on a high hill for all to see. And to make the humiliation complete, their bodies would be left on the crosses to be devoured by vultures.[20]

Of course, it appeared to the Jews that Jesus, by hanging on a tree/cross, was cursed by God (Gal. 3:13; cf. Deut. 21:23); so he couldn't be the Messiah. But Jesus, who was faithfully living out Israel's story as God had intended it, was actually enduring the curse of exile so that God's new community could receive blessing.

In the book of Isaiah, God's "servant" of Isaiah 52–53 suffers and faces humiliation ("despised and rejected"), but this same "servant" is also "lifted up" and "glorified" (Isa. 52:15; cf. 6:1; 57:13 with John 12:38–48). John's Gospel, referring back to these Isaianic passages, shows that Jesus' being "lifted up" on the cross (John 12:32; cf. 3:14–15; 8:28) is both *literal* (being physically raised up onto a cross) and *figurative* (exaltation/honor from God, including the drawing of the nations to salvation, 12:32). The moment of Christ's humiliating death is precisely when he is "glorified" (John 12:23–24; 13:31–32). God's great moment of glory is when he experiences the greatest humiliation and shame—when he takes the form of a slave and suffers death on a cross. Thus, Richard Bauckham writes, this Servant "in both his humiliation and exaltation, is therefore not merely a human figure distinguished from God, but, in both his humiliation and his exaltation, belongs to the identity of the unique God."[21]

This is how low God was willing to go for our salvation![22] This act of servitude was utterly unique in antiquity. No wonder the German

New Testament scholar Martin Hengel wrote, "The discrepancy between the shameful death of a Jewish state criminal and the confession that depicts this executed man as the preexistent divine figure who becomes man and humbles himself to a slave's death is, as far as I can see, without analogy in the ancient world."[23]

Once a Muslim expressed to me his disbelief and even scorn at the idea of Christians wearing crosses: "How can Christians wear with pride the instrument of torture and humiliation? If your brother were killed in an electric chair, would you wear an electric chair around your neck?" I replied that it depends: "If my brother happened to be Jesus and his death in an electric chair brought about my salvation and was the means by which evil was defeated and creation renewed, then he would have transformed a symbol of shame and punishment into something glorious." Indeed, Paul boasts in the cross, which humbles the pride of human self-reliance (Gal. 6:14). Because of this magnificent salvation, we can follow the humble Christ, "bearing His reproach" (Heb. 13:13).

The evidence of God's self-revelation reveals a God very different from the one described by Bede Rundle and other critics. The late theologian Colin Gunton remarked that "it is as truly godlike to be humble as it is to be exalted."[24] Indeed, God's other-centered character and activity in history reveal that he is indeed humble—inescapably so.

Summary

- We should get clear on our terms first. *Humility* involves an appropriate acknowledgment and realistic assessment of oneself. *Pride* is an inflated view of oneself or one's accomplishments. So then, "pride" or "vanity" doesn't accurately describe God, who has a realistic—rather than an unrealistic or distorted—view of himself.

- Humility isn't in conflict with allowing deeds of love to be seen by others. We are to "hide when tempted to show" and "show when tempted to hide."

- God makes humans in his image, not as a mark of divine pride, but as a gift he bestows on us, which equips us to become part of his family.

- To worship God fulfills our humanity rather than diminishes it. We are made to know and love God. To worship God reflects our place in the universe—God is Creator, and we are his creatures.
- Divine jealousy is appropriate when people turn creatures or creaturely ideas into God substitutes. Just as a right-thinking woman won't share her husband with another woman, so God is jealously protective of the loving relationship for which all human beings were designed.
- God's jealousy springs from a denial that God is God and a belief that one need not be rightly related to God as the ultimate good.
- The Scripture's call to praise God comes from creatures, not God himself; creatures spontaneously exhort one another to praise God, who is good and worthy of worship ("worth-ship"). Such praise simply completes and expresses creaturely enjoyment of God.
- God himself exhibits humility by giving praise to humans who trust in God and obey him.
- By his very nature, God is humble. He regularly displays humility in his interactions with human beings—especially in Jesus of Nazareth, who comes to serve humans.
- God's greatest achievement is his amazing act of humility—Jesus' self-humiliating and degrading death on the cross to rescue us from our exile and alienation from God.

Further Reading

Bauckham, Richard. *God Crucified: Monotheism and Christology in the New Testament.* Grand Rapids: Eerdmans, 1998.

Copan, Paul. "Divine Narcissism? A Further Defense of Divine Humility." *Philosophia Christi* 8 (January 2006).

Lewis, C. S. "The Weight of Glory." In *The Weight of Glory and Other Addresses.* New York: Macmillan, 1965.

Taliaferro, Charles. "Is God Vain?" In *Philosophy and Faith: A Philosophy of Religion Reader.* Ed. David Shatz. New York: McGraw-Hill, 2002.

5

Miracles Are Unscientific

President Thomas Jefferson, a Deist who believed Jesus to be merely a powerful moral teacher of reason, cut up and pasted together portions of the four Gospels that reinforced his belief in a naturalized, nonmiraculous, nonauthoritative Jesus. The result was the severely edited *Life and Morals of Jesus of Nazareth Extracted Textually from the Gospels*—or, *The Jefferson Bible*. He believed he could easily extract the "lustre" of the real Jesus "from the dross of his biographers, and as separate from that as the diamond from the dung hill." Jefferson believed Jesus was "a man, of illegitimate birth, of a benevolent heart, [and an] enthusiastic mind, who set out without pretensions of divinity, ended in believing them, and was punished capitally for sedition by being gibbeted [i.e., crucified] according to Roman law."[1] Jefferson edited Luke 2:40, "And [Jesus] grew, and waxed strong in spirit, filled with wisdom," omitting "and the grace of God was upon him." This "Bible" ends with a quite unresurrected Jesus: "There they laid Jesus, and rolled a great stone to the door of the sepulchre, and departed."

Deism's chief motivation for rejecting miracles—along with special revelation—was that they suggested an inept Creator: He didn't get everything right at the outset; so he needed to tinker with the world, adjusting it as necessary. The biblical picture of miracles, though, shows them to be an indication of a ruling God's care for and involvement in the world. Indeed, many in modern times have witnessed specific indicators of direct divine action and answers to prayer.[2]

The Christian faith stands or falls on God's miraculous activity, particularly in Jesus' resurrection (1 Corinthians 15). Scripture readily acknowledges the possibility of miracles in nonbiblical religious settings. Some may be demonically inspired,[3] but we shouldn't rule out God's gracious, miraculous actions in pagan settings—say, the response of the "unknown God" to prayers so that a destructive plague in Athens might be stayed. However, we'll note below that, unlike many divinely wrought miracles in Scripture, miracle claims in other religions are *incidental*—not foundational—to the pagan religion's existence.

I am assuming here that there are good reasons for thinking that (a) *a good, powerful, wise, personal God exists.* He's not some generic deity, but a covenant-making, initiative-taking God who responds to (b) *the human situation of sin, misery, alienation, suffering, and evil.* Philosophical discussions of God's existence and nature typically fail to ask, "If God exists, has he done anything to address this profound problem?" Unlike other religions, the Christian story emphatically answers, Yes! God's *existence* and his *concern* for humanity go hand in hand; he gets his feet dirty and hands bloody in Jesus, bringing creation and redemption together. His ministry and the salvation event signaled a new exodus and a new creation. His miraculous resurrection from the dead in particular guarantees hope and restoration, and this cornerstone event is accompanied by many publicly accessible reasons—historical, theological, and philosophical.[4]

Divine miracles don't *guarantee* belief, though: "If they do not listen to Moses and the Prophets, they will not be persuaded even if someone rises from the dead" (Luke 16:31). Miracles can be rationalized away (see, e.g., John 12:29) or even suppressed by people who don't want to believe anyway—such as Jesus' enemies seeking to kill miraculous evidence—the resuscitated Lazarus (John 12:1, 10)! Miracles don't compel belief, but for those willing to receive them, they do serve as sufficient indications of God's activity and revelation. John calls them *signs* that point beyond themselves to Jesus' *sign*ificance:

Jesus miraculously feeds bread to a crowd of more than five thousand and then declares, "I am the bread of life" (John 6); he says, "I am the light of the world," illustrating it by healing a man born blind (John 8–9); he affirms, "I am the resurrection and the life" and shows it by raising Lazarus (John 11). No wonder Jesus says, "Believe Me that I am in the Father and the Father is in Me; otherwise believe because of the works themselves" (John 14:11). His miracles, revealing the in-breaking reality of God's reign, are available for public scrutiny.

First, we should be clear on what miracles are. Definitions may include terms like "suspension of," "exception to," or "nonrepeatable counterinstance to" nature's order and laws. Simply put, they're *direct acts of a personal God that can't be predicted or explained by merely natural causes*; they wouldn't take place if left up to nature. Naturally, dead people don't live again; Jesus' bodily resurrection—impossible according to natural processes—is possible because God exists. God's involvement in the world, however, may be tied to apparently natural events but reveal their supernatural quality by their remarkable timing—say, an earthquake causing Jericho to fall at the precisely predicted moment. These are part of God's "extraordinary providence"—in distinction from his "ordinary providence" of sending sunshine and rain and fruitful seasons (Matt. 5:45; Acts 14:17). True-blue miracles, in contrast to these two workings of divine providence, simply cannot be accounted for—they can't happen—by any natural processes.

Second, "natural law" or "natural order" describes *how the world generally operates, but it doesn't* control *what happens in it.* Now, Hume called miracles "violations" of natural laws; since natural laws can't be violated, he reasoned, miracles can't happen! This argumentation is known as question begging (assuming what one wants to prove).

Consider this irony. Hume notably posed the "problem of induction": despite the past's unvaried, repeated sequence of sunrise and sunset, that's no guarantee the sun will rise tomorrow—although it's a prudent belief, Hume declares. Yet Hume's assumption of nature's fixed, unbreakable laws *disallows* miracles. But what if, as with the sunrise, these "laws" will be "violated" tomorrow?

If all knowledge comes through our senses, as Hume insists, then we'll draw conclusions about what has taken place in nature, not that things couldn't be otherwise. If science describes how the natural world operates, we shouldn't presume to know how things will look in advance of the evidence or experience. Science is *prescriptive*, not *descriptive*. Canceling a university class doesn't exactly "violate" the class schedule! In fact, the criterion that all things must conform to prior experience would make scientific progress impossible. And if the universe came into existence from nothing, that certainly couldn't be predicted by natural laws.

"Natural laws" could just be a *description* of nature's workings; they're a framework or pattern, but they do nothing and set nothing into motion. A "law of nature" simply describes what happens when no agent (divine, human, angelic) is acting on or "interfering" with the causal order.[5] In a sense, human activity in the world is a type of "miracle." So natural laws aren't "violated"; they're not even necessary.

Third, God's existence provides the necessary religious context or "background information" to affirm the possibility of miracles. Typically, people don't reject miracles like Jesus' resurrection because of lack of good evidence but rather due to philosophical assumptions that overwhelm the evidence (*"No matter what the evidence looks like, dead people don't come back to life—period!"*). One's openness to the supernatural makes a huge difference, and Scripture regularly illustrates that, despite signs and wonders, unbelief persists.

Radical theologian Rudolf Bultmann boldly claimed that since "the forces and the laws of nature have been discovered," we can't believe in good or evil spirits or miraculous cures from sickness and disease. "It is impossible to use electric light and the wireless and to avail ourselves of modern medical and surgical discoveries, and at the same time to believe in the New Testament world of spirits and miracles."[6] When people claim miracles just can't happen, they're implying that a Creator can't exist: if a God exists who can create a universe from nothing, then miracles are at least *possible*. A miracle-denying worldview simply won't be open to whatever evidence, because experience by itself is insufficient; any proposed evidence can always be explained away. As C. S. Lewis pointed out: "If anything extraordinary seems to have happened, we can always say that we have been the victims of an illusion. If we hold a philosophy which excludes the supernatural, this is what we always shall say."[7] If the context of God's existence and possible working in human history are granted, however, why think it impossible that God should raise the dead?

Too often philosophical considerations overwhelm the historical evidence, no matter how strong. Miracles are probable (or not) relative to the background information or context. Of course, miracles are "initially improbable" or "highly improbable" *if* God doesn't exist. Yes, naturalistically speaking, miracles defy all probability: dead people don't naturally come back to life. However, a miracle's probability greatly increases if "God's existence" is part of the relevant background information, making miracles a live option. We shouldn't decide in advance that miracles are impossible, particularly if the following are true: (a) God exists and creates and also has revealed himself in history; and, given this context, (b) there is good historical evidence to support such a miracle claim.

Against Hume, miracles aren't "violations" of nature; they become quite plausible given the triune God's saving intentions. So, given the appropriate, spiritually significant religious context, we shouldn't prefer naturalistic explanations—which may be inferior or even ridiculous—but rather supernaturalistic ones with far greater explanatory power. Hume got things terribly wrong. No wonder the prominent agnostic philosopher John Earman wrote *Hume's Abject Failure*[8] to make this very point.

So should we be "open" to reports of John Lennon or Elvis "sightings"? The background information is crucial: Does the Lennon scenario occur randomly, out of the blue? And how was he raised—by God? To what purpose? Why is Lennon so significant? By contrast, Jesus' resurrection involves a historical and theological context—including Jesus' own predictions—to make sense of that event. If God exists, miracles like the resurrection—and supernatural explanations—become a live option.

Fourth, the Christian faith's most theologically significant miracle is Jesus' resurrection—a historically well-supported event. Though history yields only probable—not absolute—knowledge, we don't have to be mired in historical skepticism. We can still have a good degree of confidence in our historical knowledge as we consider evidence for Jesus' resurrection. The following are the chief evidences surrounding this miracle:

1. Jesus' burial in Joseph of Arimathea's tomb
2. the discovery of Jesus' empty tomb
3. the postmortem appearances
4. the origin of the earliest disciples' belief in Jesus' resurrection

These are well-established historical facts accepted by the majority of critical scholars—including the most skeptical who reject Jesus' bodily resurrection.[9] For instance, some scholars may believe that these "appearances" were hallucinations or psychological/guilt projections, but they acknowledge that *something* triggered the disciples' belief in Jesus' postmortem appearances.

In themselves, these four lines of evidence aren't "miraculous facts" that are somehow beyond historical research; they're available to all historians. The point at issue is which interpretation or explanation— natural or supernatural—makes the best sense of these facts.

In addition to the ready explanation of God's raising Jesus from the dead, consider also the very low historical probability of available naturalistic explanations of the first Easter—the disciples stole the body; the women went to the wrong tomb; Jesus' followers suffered massive and widespread hallucinations; Jesus didn't really die but swooned, and the cool tomb revived him; the common, but virtually universally rejected view[10] that the resurrection is just another pagan or "mystery religion" legend. Their inadequacy reinforces the plausibility of the miraculous explanation.

While historical facts themselves are not miraculous, an explanation certainly may be; and if God exists, such an explanation is legitimate and theologically warranted. Historian N. T. Wright, quite judicious and not given to overstatement, concludes that the combined historical probability of *the empty tomb*—something his enemies assumed (Matt. 28:12–15)—and *the postmortem appearances* is "virtually certain," being on the level of Caesar Augustus's death in AD 14 or the fall of Jerusalem in AD 70.[11] To have one without the other wouldn't do: just an empty tomb would have been merely a puzzle or a tragedy, and Jesus' postmortem appearances alone could have been chalked up to hallucinations. But taken together, these two matters give the origin of the early church its powerful impetus. Jesus' resurrection isn't "beyond history."

The biblical testimony of (a) many, (b) independent, (c) credible and sincere eyewitnesses should be taken seriously. First Corinthians

15 reports that Jesus appeared to more than five hundred, to Peter, to the *unbelieving* James (Jesus' half brother), and though in visionary form, to the *hostile persecutor*, Paul. John 20 tells us that Jesus showed himself to the *skeptic* Thomas. Women were the first witnesses, whose testimony wouldn't have been taken seriously in first-century Palestine. The basic facts surrounding Jesus' resurrection are consistent in an array of sources—the Gospels, the early Christian sermons in Acts, Paul's epistles, and the very early Jerusalem tradition mentioned in 1 Corinthians 15, which dates to less than two years after Jesus' death.[12]

Furthermore, the Jews of Jesus' day (Second Temple Judaism) believed that "resurrection" entailed an empty tomb; a resurrection couldn't take place without a thoroughly dead body being made gloriously alive again. Naturalistic attempts to explain away the first Easter (hallucination theory, wrong-tomb theory, disciples-stole-the-body theory, swoon theory, and the like) are inadequate. The far more probable conclusion for Jesus' empty tomb and for postmortem appearances of an alive-and-well Jesus is that God raised Jesus from the dead.

Summary

- Deism—the belief that God "winds up" the universe and lets it proceed on its own without involvement through miracles or special revelation—assumes that God wouldn't need to tamper further with a well-ordered creation.
- Unlike a deistic deity, the biblical God actually shows concern for this world—rather than remaining aloof from it—by getting his hands and feet dirty to rescue humans from their miserable plight.
- Genuine miracles don't guarantee belief. From Israel in the wilderness to Jesus' own contemporaries, Scripture indicates that the most impressive miracles may be resisted.
- Miracles aren't "violations of natural law." They are *direct acts of a personal God that can't be predicted or explained by merely natural causes or processes.* Thoroughly dead people don't *naturally* come to life.

- Certain kinds of divine activity may involve God's "extraordinary providence" (as distinct from his "ordinary providence" in giving us rain, sunshine, and fruitful seasons)—apparently natural events that reveal God's agency through their remarkable timing (e.g., earthquake causing Jericho to fall at the precisely predicted moment). These are distinct from true-blue miracles.
- "Natural law" or "natural order" doesn't *control* what happens in the world; it simply *describes* how nature generally operates.
- God's existence and nature furnish the needed religious context or "background information" for the possibility of miracles. If nature is all there is, miracles are ruled out. But if God is part of the equation, the possibility of miracles is greatly increased.
- Apart from the issue of reliable eyewitnesses, JFK, John Lennon, or Elvis "sightings" have no theological significance or religious context to make sense of them.
- By contrast, the Christian faith's key miracle—Jesus' resurrection—is both historically supportable and has a well-formed religious context.
- The four facts of (1) Jesus' burial in Joseph of Arimathea's tomb, (2) the discovery of Jesus' empty tomb, (3) the postmortem appearances, and (4) the origin of the earliest disciples' belief in Jesus' resurrection are not "miraculous facts." These facts are available to all historians. However, there can be a supernaturalistic explanation to make sense of these facts; only a philosophical bias would rule this out.

Further Reading

Geivett, R. Douglas, and Gary Habermas. *In Defense of Miracles: A Comprehensive Case for God's Involvement in History*. Downers Grove, IL: InterVarsity, 1997.

Lewis, C. S. *Miracles*. New York: Macmillan, 1960.

Swinburne, Richard. *The Concept of Miracle*. New York: Macmillan, 1971.

Wright, N. T. *The Resurrection of the Son of God*. Minneapolis: Fortress, 2003.

6

Only Gullible People Believe in Miracles

The skeptic David Hume declared that those who believe in miracles are "ignorant and barbarous" peoples. They're apparently not so-phisticated, clear-thinking, and scrutinizing.

While we should certainly be careful about being gullible rather than believe just any sensational claim, Hume's claims go way too far. Besides the fact that modern science was established by Bible-centered thinkers, plenty of well-informed believers today hold to the possibility of the miraculous. Yet even in Jesus' day, his own disciples—especially Thomas—refused to believe initial reports that Jesus was raised. They hadn't expected an individual's resurrection before the final "day of the Lord." Or, Joseph, who knew where babies come from, didn't take the Virgin Mary's word for it, but an angelic messenger's instead. The believers gathered at Mary's house were skeptical about Rhoda's claim that Peter was out of prison and standing at the gate—even though they had been praying for him (Acts 12)! From Abraham to Zacharias, Scripture portrays plenty of miracle doubters in all their skeptical colors.

If we push Hume's logic, we can draw parallels between his view on miracles and on white racial supremacy. For Hume, "ignorant and barbarous" peoples (who believed miracle claims) were basically nonwhites—people he believed to be of "naturally inferior" intelligence. The implication? Despite having heard reports of exceptions, Hume's experience would have found the existence of an intelligent black person to be just as unreasonable as expecting a miracle. His "reasonable" presumption is always against intelligent nonwhites. The point here is simply this: if a person has made up his mind about what is uniform—whether white superiority or miracles—that person will always dismiss any counterexamples (of intelligent blacks or well-attested miracle claims) as going against probability.[1]

Let's look at some additional skeptical questions regarding miracles:

1. *Do extraordinary claims require extraordinary evidence?* Hume ("Of Miracles") claimed that no testimony is sufficient to establish a miracle unless that testimony's falsehood would be even more miraculous than the claim it's trying to establish: extraordinary claims demand extraordinary evidence. It initially sounds plausible: we shouldn't be gullible about all miracle claims we hear. However, it's simply false that Christians have an unusually heavy burden to bear. John Earman, an agnostic philosopher, calls it "nonsensical."[2] He's right: If God exists and we have an explanatory theological-religious context to make sense of a particular miracle, then we have the relevant background information to render miracles plausible. All we need to show for, say, the resurrection, is that, given this context, a supernatural explanation makes better sense of the historical facts than a naturalistic one.

2. *Must testimonies to miracles be evaluated in light of our own experience?* German theologian Ernst Troeltsch claimed that we should evaluate any testimony to miracles in light of our own experience; some *analogy* must exist between what we've experienced and the miracle claim itself. In response: (a) What if you witnessed an authentic miracle? Given Troeltsch's standard, *you'd have to reject it because you hadn't seen anything like it before.* You'd have to reject a whole string of miracles since you'd never have a starting point for declaring something miraculous. (b) What of unique miracles such as the incarnation or resurrection? No first miracle could occur, because nothing previous compares to it. (c) *All events are*

in some sense unique. No one sunrise is exactly like another, C. S. Lewis wrote—how much more miraculous events!

Philosopher John Locke once recounted the story of the king of Siam. This ruler thought it preposterous that in some parts of the world water could freeze so thickly that even elephants could walk on it. He'd had no previous experience with ice. Ultimately, Troeltsch's standard is simply arbitrary.

3. *Should we demand how miracles are performed before we believe them?* Atheist Bede Rundle says that virgin births and miraculous cures from diseases "are of no assistance at the point that concerns us; they do not advance our understanding of *how* things could come about in the way claimed. To claim that God said, 'Let there be light,' leaves us not one jot wiser as to how light came about."[3] Is this so? First, we *are* wiser in at least this sense—that creation can't be *naturalistically* explained. Also, when Rundle refers to "our understanding," he means "*naturalistic* understanding," which simply begs the question. Knowing *that* God created doesn't guarantee knowing *how* God did it. Why expect that we should? We're talking about miracles here, not combining vinegar and baking soda.

4. *What of miraculous claims in other religions—or even secular contexts?* Hume believed that miraculous claims in other religions would cancel each other out. However, whatever the source of miracle claims in other religions or "secular" claims that John Lennon or Elvis is alive, we should take them on a *case-by-case basis* rather than lumping them all together. It's unfair and misguided to say that conflicting miracle claims must cancel each other out. Anyone can make a claim; the question is, "What's the evidence for it?"

Consider the "miracle" of Osiris. His body is cut up into fourteen pieces that float down the Nile, and his wife-sister Isis gathers up thirteen of the pieces and eventually resuscitates him. Is this a "resurrection"? No, the myth's point is actually Osiris's death and Isis's mourning, not resuscitation. Additionally, such myths tend to be part of a cyclical view of history—with no datable event for this story—but this lack of historicity doesn't really matter anyway. None of these gods and goddesses is a historical person.[4]

Here are some further concerns: (1) *Miraculous claims in other religions tend to be incidental and not crucial to their validity.*

Muhammad's translation from Mecca to Jerusalem and back in one evening is hardly foundational to Islam—unlike the exodus, Jesus' exorcisms, and the resurrection. (2) Historian-philosopher Gary Habermas has investigated purported miracle claims from the ancient world, such as the resuscitation ("resurrection") or translation into heaven of great personages. He concludes that *the sources are generally late in their "recounting," they put forth questionable or contradictory accounts, and they are not open to any sort of verification.*[5] (3) *Nontheistic or pantheistic ("God is everything") worldviews have no conceptual room for miracles*; miracles associated with Buddha or Confucius just don't "fit" with their respective worldviews and thus don't offer any supporting evidence for Buddhism or Confucianism. (4) *Biblical miracles take place in a theologically plausible context that is historically/archaeologically supportable.* The places and historical events surrounding biblical miracles are quite unlike, say, the *Book of Mormon*'s claims of the Nephite civilization in North America and a massive battle in New York.[6] Not surprisingly, the Smithsonian Institution's 1996 statement rejects this book as "a scientific guide" and "has never used it in archaeological research."[7] Ironically, many skeptics tend to take more seriously the bizarre and ultimately insignificant miracle claims in other religions than they do the sane, sincere, reliable resurrection reports and other miracles of the New Testament.[8]

So, not all miracle claims are created equal. Conflicting miracle claims between religions don't imply that all claims are false or that one religion's claims can't be true. If the triune, self-revealing Creator exists, there's no reason he can't override the natural order he has put in place. He is *God*, after all.

Summary

- *Do gullible people believe in miracles?* (1) Scripture's miracles are often treated skeptically in their ancient text (e.g., Joseph knew where babies came from; Thomas and the other disciples were skeptical about Jesus' resurrection); (2) David Hume's parallel claims about "ignorant and barbarous" peoples believing in miracles and his not believing there could be any intelligent nonwhites reflect a question-begging posture: his mind was made up against either despite the evidence.

- *Do extraordinary claims demand extraordinary proof?* No (John Earman calls this requirement "nonsensical"): (1) If God's existence and an appropriate religious context make sense of a miracle, we have what we need to render it plausible. (2) We merely need to show that, say, God's raising Jesus from the dead makes better sense of the historical facts than any naturalistic theory.

- *Must testimonies to miracles be evaluated in light of our own experience?* The demand for some analogy (Ernst Troeltsch) is problematic: (1) This criterion suggests that you'd have to reject any authentic miracle you witnessed—or a whole string of them—just because you had never seen anything like it before! (2) There can be no "first miracle" for an incarnation or resurrection since nothing previous compares to it. (3) All events are in some sense unique.

- *Should we demand to know how miracles are performed before we believe them?* Why do we think we should know *how* God created ("Let there be light!") before believing *that* he did? We can at least say that creation can't be *naturalistically* explained.

- *What of miraculous claims in other religions—or even secular contexts?* Conflicting claims (e.g., "Jesus is alive" versus "Elvis is alive") don't cancel each other out; we take them on a case-by-case basis and consider the evidence for each (anyone can make a claim). (1) Religious resuscitation myths are short on evidence and tend to be part of a cyclical view of history (no datable events, etc.) (2) Miraculous claims in other religions tend to be incidental and not crucial to their validity. (3) Miracle claims from the ancient world (e.g., resuscitations or translations into heaven) come from sources that are generally late in their "recounting," are from questionable or contradictory accounts, and are not open to any sort of verification. (4) Nontheistic or pantheistic ("God is everything") worldviews don't have room for miracles. (5) Biblical miracles are both theologically plausible and historically and archaeologically supportable.

Further Reading

Copan, Paul, and Ronald K. Tacelli. *Jesus' Resurrection: Fact or Figment?* Downers Grove, IL: InterVarsity, 2000.

Geivett, R. Douglas, and Gary Habermas. *In Defense of Miracles: A Comprehensive Case for God's Involvement in History.* Downers Grove, IL: InterVarsity, 1997.

Habermas, Gary R., and Antony Flew. *Resurrected? An Atheist and Theist Dialogue.* Lanham, MD: Rowman & Littlefield, 2005.

Habermas, Gary R., and Michael R. Licona. *The Case for the Resurrection of Jesus.* Grand Rapids: Kregel, 2004.

Lewis, C. S. *Miracles.* New York: Macmillan, 1960.

7

Don't People from All Religions Experience God?

Many people throughout history and across cultures have claimed to have profound experiences of the transcendent.[1] In Athens, Paul noticed the "unknown God" altar—one of many dating back to the sixth-century BC, when the philosopher Epimenides helped deliver the plague-oppressed city, urging its citizens to sacrifice to the unknown God. Paul reminded the Athenians that "we live and move and exist" through this God and that "we . . . are His children" (Acts 17:28–29).[2]

Do people genuinely experience God—*even if not savingly*? Can non-Christians have a profound sense of God's presence, glory, and holiness? If heaven and earth are saturated with God's glory (Ps. 19:1–4; Isa. 6:3), it seems that people throughout the world would at least partly encounter the God who isn't far from each one of them—even if these encounters or experiences aren't necessarily salvific.

Across many cultures, people have had *mystical* encounters—a feeling of unity with God, an ecstasy or an overpowering awareness of his love. Others have had *numimous* experiences (Lat., *numem*

= "God," the "wholly other," a spiritual/transcendent presence or influence). Rudolf Otto's *The Idea of the Holy* considers the numinous the fundamental element cutting across religious traditions.[3] This is a sense of awe or dread—a *mysterium tremendum*—in the presence of a holy power. The subject feels unworthy—also astonished and awed—before this penetrating presence. Isaiah, for instance, felt unclean and unworthy before the thrice-holy God (Isa. 6:5); Peter told Jesus to depart, for "I am a sinful man" (Luke 5:8). Otto claims that encountering the transcendent also includes a certain fascination or irresistible attraction (*fascinans*). So these profound religious experiences are a dreadful and fascinating mystery (*mysterium tremendum et fascinans*).[4] Maybe Otto is onto something. Perhaps religious experience points us beyond—to a transcendent God.

Christians have come to know God through Christ and are made aware of God's loving presence and fatherly acceptance (Rom. 5:5; 8:15; Gal. 4:6). Such genuinely saving experiences are life-transforming and self-authenticating—not officially requiring evidence or argument (1 John 2:20, 27). Thoughtful Christians, though, must recognize the need to offer *public reasons* for belief to the questioning outsider. An argument from religious experience is only part of the broader explanatory case for our examinable faith. It can offer existential power—think of Paul's repeated testimony throughout the book of Acts—when added to the other reasons and arguments for believing in the biblical God. This God, concerned about our condition of alienation (from ourselves, others, and God) and our search for meaning and immortality, can be personally and directly known.

Several important, commonly asked questions about the merits of religious experience are worth discussing. Let's explore some of them.

First, why take religious experience seriously? A basic answer is that if something seems clearly present to me, if I'm profoundly aware of it, I shouldn't simply dismiss it as wholly false but should take it seriously and explore it further. We're back to the principle of credulity, a presumption of innocence: we typically assume that if something seems true, then we take it as true unless we have good reasons to question it. In Richard Swinburne's words, "How things seem to be is good grounds for a belief about how things are."[5] Plenty of honest, morally upright people have claimed some encounter with the divine. Even if they misinterpret their experience, should their testimony be casually dismissed? Maybe they're partly right, and perhaps there's something fundamental and basic to these experiences.

Second, what if people misinterpret religious experiences? What about non-Christians such as Mormons, who claim to have a true, deep experience of God—a "burning in the bosom"? The Mormon's faulty apprehension of God doesn't cancel out the genuineness and power of the Christian's experience—no more than a color-blind person's perception negates my seeing the color correctly.

People may and do "overreport"—that is, infer or extrapolate beyond—what their mystical or numinous experiences seem to allow. Meister Eckhart (1260–1328) interpreted his religious experience as him being indistinct from God—a problem indeed! *Union* with God is different from *identity* with God. Overreported interpretations don't necessarily undermine their veridicality (truthfulness). The mystic may be overemphasizing God's immanence while a person having a numinous experience might be glimpsing something of God's transcendent otherness—and both immanence and transcendence characterize the God of Scripture. Another point: why think overreporting must imply or favor the secularist's viewpoint? Indeed, despite conflicting interpretations, we actually have good reason to think something beyond nature exists.[6]

Delusional persons may claim to experience something "transcendent" or "divine," but they may be confused or be hallucinating or projecting something from their minds that isn't real. Despite this, creation is full of God's glory and is hardly a cold, hostile, and impersonal place. People may be appropriately awed and even overwhelmed by it. We would *expect* people around the world to sense God's presence and power. But because of their background or perspective, they may infer something less than personal from this experience: they may *select* or *focus on* certain apparently "impersonal" attributes of the "Ultimate Reality"—"otherness," infinity, greatness, power, sheer existence—and *filter out* any personal qualities such as love, grace, holiness, and goodness. Despite differing cultural or religious traditions in the world, real numinous or mystical experiences of God that share common features can occur—even if not savingly. Human religious experiences *reinforce* available public reasons for belief in God—for example, arguments from the universe's beginning or its design, or arguments for God's goodness as we discover human dignity and worth and moral obligations—even if such experiences turn out to be modest evidence for God's existence.

Third, how do we distinguish true religious experiences from false ones? The following points offer some guidance.[7]

- A genuine experience from God *won't serve as the basis for an immoral or self-destructive lifestyle*: Indian guru Bhagwan Shree Rajneesh claimed that permissive sexual encounters bring spiritual enlightenment. No, this wasn't from God, who by definition is good and worthy of worship.

- The *consequences of the experience are good for the person* in the long run. A true religious experience, even if initially troubling, ought not to lead to instability or mental disturbance, but to *greater wholeness*.

- The *consequences are good for others*. Does one's experience create a spirit of love and self-sacrifice—or self-absorption and aloofness?

- If "religious" experiences are *self-contradictory or self-refuting* (like a Buddhist's experiencing a nonself), then the religious object doesn't exist.

- If the Christian faith is true, then religious experiences, properly understood, will *match up with the Scriptures*.

The only true and triune God graciously allows believers to experience his loving presence in Christ in a saving way—a self-authenticating encounter. We don't need further evidence to persuade us of God's personal reality. Whether sudden or gradual, our transforming encounter with God is *properly basic*—what Calvin called the *sensus divinitatis* (the sense of the divine). This doesn't mean that basic beliefs are infallible; it's logically possible that I could be wrong. But a basic belief is proper if (a) *conditions or circumstances are right*, providing the context for belief that, say, God is near or has forgiven me or that I need his grace; that (b) *my faculties—rational, emotional, spiritual—are properly functioning in the way they've been designed*; and that (c) *these beliefs are successfully directed toward the truth.* While I may not be able to come up with arguments showing that other minds exist or that the earth is older than five minutes, these beliefs are still warranted in the absence of undermining arguments. The Christian's experience of God could be properly basic in this same way.

Let's get back to the Mormons' burning in the bosom. The Christian's simply asserting that "my experience is more legitimate than yours" won't get her very far. Here's where we must go beyond a properly basic, self-authenticating experience through Christ—or the occurrence of "mixed experiences of God" in non-Christian settings. We should winsomely, wisely present a *public case* for our faith; perhaps these reasons can create doubts, unsettling the Mormon's (or Muslim's or Hindu's) false convictions that give way to true ones. With grace and gentleness, we must appeal to reasons for the hope within us (1 Peter 3:15), which God's Spirit can graciously use.

Despite conflicting religious truth claims, a strong case can be made for the Christian faith—and the pervasive presence of God who isn't far from any one of us. We have solid reasons for believing in a personal, good, wise, and powerful God—namely, the beginning and fine-tuning of the universe, moral obligations/human rights, consciousness, rationality, beauty, and the further support of religious experience. The strong evidence for God's existence would undercut a large percentage of (nontheistic) belief systems, making the task far more manageable.

Fourth, those who try to reduce religious experience to the activity of the brain are misguided in their conclusions. In a small, dark hospital laboratory, Andrew Newberg and the late Eugene D'Aquili would receive signals from Robert, a Tibetan Buddhist, when his "meditative state" approached a "transcendent peak." (The same sort of experimentation was done with eight other Buddhist meditators as well as with several Franciscan nuns at prayer.) In light of distinct brain activity during these peak times, they concluded that "mystical experience is biologically, observably, and scientifically real."[8] They go on to ask: Are humans "biologically compelled to make myths"? Are mystics functioning properly, or are they deluded? Do religious experiences have a common biological basis? What their book tries to show is that the religious experiences of all kinds of religionists throughout the ages are "attributed to the brain's activity"; that is, there is a biological origin for specific religious beliefs.[9]

In response, one need not be surprised at such phenomena—particularly if we are made with the capacity to relate to God. If God's glory fills the universe and people can recognize its beauty and immensity, for instance, as a reflection of something transcendent, the brain activity described above isn't startling. If humans can physically respond to God's presence or even have some kind of powerful, life-transforming experience, we shouldn't be startled to see this register in the brain. But this brain activity doesn't mean God doesn't exist or that we don't have souls, as I have argued elsewhere.[10]

In fact, Justin Barrett—a well-respected cognitive science of religion (CSR) scholar, editor of the *Journal of Cognition and Culture*, and a Christian—has written *Why Would Anyone Believe in God?*[11] His research here and in other parts of the world (e.g., India) strongly suggests that through biological and environmental endowments, we are suited to believe in God/the divine; atheism is actually the aberration. Our "mental tools" encourage us to think about and be drawn toward belief in the divine, and our minds are structured to find such beliefs attractive. This is part of the *proper* function of human minds; it is not strange or weird. Barrett's research has led him to conclude that children are "intuitive theists"—that very early on they have an inclination to believe in a "nonhuman superbeing"—even prior to religious indoctrination. Belief in the existence of the divine is natural and normal—comparable to our belief in other minds. We find ourselves appropriately believing that other minds with intentions, desires, and the capacity for agency exist. That same kind of naturalness is the case with our tendency to believe in God.

Sociologist Christian Smith pointedly asks: "Why in a spiritless and godless world would people ever conceive of spirits and gods in the first place?" Why *voluntarily* sacrifice our lives for some intangible "super-empirical" realm? The reason humans persist in looking beyond the finite realm in search of the source of coherence, order, morality, meaning, and guidance for life is because this realm doesn't contain it. Humans, though embodied, are moral, spiritual beings with the capacity for self-transcendence and reflection upon our world and our condition;

this in turn enables us to search for a world-transcending God.[12] Naturalistic explanations that suggest that theology is a useful fiction—or, worse, a harmful delusion—fall short of telling us why this religious impulse is so deeply imbedded. If God exists, however, we have an excellent reason for thinking religion should exist.

Furthermore, if there is evidence for God's existence outside the mind through general and special revelation, then we should consider this as an *independent* indicator of God's presence rather than focusing solely on brain function.

Fifth, it would appear that the atheist must work harder to overcome the disposition toward the divine or transcendent. In light of the human disposition toward the divine, Barrett adds that if a person wants to be an atheist or to overcome this predisposition to being a theist, he should do the following: (a) sequester himself in urban settings and avoid the majesty, power, and beauty of nature; (b) avoid spending time with those who are religious believers and taking their experiences seriously; (c) avoid urgent or life-threatening situations (in which one might be tempted to call upon outside help such as a supernatural agent) or situations in which humans are regularly vulnerable and powerless (e.g., depending upon good weather for crops); (d) hole up in university or university-like settings, where atheists tend to congregate—not because they are more intelligent than theists, but because this setting allows for greater energy devoted to explaining away God's existence than under average circumstances.[13]

Sixth, where do we look for guidance about religious experience given the various conflicting religious viewpoints? Despite charlatans or well-intentioned—but partially informed—religious claimants, Jesus of Nazareth stands out as the authoritative model and touchstone over all other religious experiencers. No mere human teacher, this paragon and exemplar of religious experience testified that experiencing him meant experiencing God (John 14:9). Jesus speaks with all authority (Matt. 28:18), reveals God's wisdom (Matt. 12:42; cf. Matt. 11:19; 13:54), and bestows saving spiritual knowledge (Matt. 11:27–30). We are wise to contemplate Peter's insightful question of Jesus: "Lord, to whom shall we go? You have the words of eternal life" (John 6:68).[14]

Summary

- People can experience God, even if not savingly (e.g., having a profound sense of God's presence, holiness, transcendence). This phenomenon can contribute to a broader case for God's existence.

- Many people across religious lines have claimed to have *mystical* or *numinous* encounters with God; people have experienced God's nearness or transcendence. They can feel dread, awe, impurity, fascination. Religious experience can point us *beyond*—to a transcendent God.

- The Christian has come to know God through Christ; by God's Spirit the Christian is made aware of God's loving presence and fatherly acceptance (Rom. 5:5; 8:15; Gal. 4:6). Such genuinely saving experiences are life transforming and self-authenticating—not officially requiring evidence or argument (1 John 2:20, 27).

- Thoughtful Christians, though, must recognize the need to offer *public reasons* for belief to the questioning outsider. An argument from religious experience is only part of the broader explanatory case for our examinable faith.

- If something seems quite apparent to me, then I should take it seriously rather than dismiss it, unless there are very good reasons for doing so (the principle of credulity).

- People may misinterpret a religious experience, but this doesn't necessarily cancel out a legitimate aspect of that experience—or that the Christian's saving experience isn't genuine. (Remember the example of color-blindness.)

- People may and do "overreport" their religious experiences, but again, this need not negate their experience in its totality. The mystic (e.g., Meister Eckhart) may go too far in talking about absolute union with God. (Here God's nearness may be overemphasized.) Or she may "filter out" an aspect of God, such as God's infinity or power.

- Overreporting doesn't imply or favor a secularist's viewpoint—and *both* immanence and transcendence characterize the God of Scripture.

74

- Yes, delusional people may make religious-experience claims that are simply false. However, if the whole earth is full of God's glory, we shouldn't be surprised by people's encounters with God, however veiled.

- Genuine religious experiences (a) won't serve as the basis for an immoral lifestyle, (b) will be on the whole beneficial to the person, (c) will encourage love and self-sacrifice toward others, (d) won't be self-refuting (e.g., the Buddhist non-self doctrine), (e) will, if the Christian faith is true, match up with Scripture.

- Calvin's point about the *sensus divinitatis* (the sense of the divine) suggests that an encounter with God is properly basic. Proper basicality doesn't imply infallibility. Such a basic belief is warranted if (a) *conditions or circumstances are right*, (b) *my faculties—rational, emotional, spiritual—are properly functioning in the way they've been designed*, and (c) *these beliefs are successfully directed toward the truth*.

- Religious experience isn't reducible to brain activity. Rather, heightened brain activity during a religious experience isn't surprising if we've been made for the capacity to connect with a transcendent God. Evidence suggests that we are intuitive theists. Furthermore, apart from such activity, there are independent reasons (through general and special revelation) to believe in a personal God.

- Atheism, it appears, takes more effort to sustain since the evidence suggests we are naturally wired to connect with the divine.

- In the midst of various religious claimants, Jesus of Nazareth offers us guidance in this matter (John 6:68: "Lord, to whom shall we go?").

Further Reading

Alston, William P. *Perceiving God: The Epistemology of Religious Experience*. Ithaca, NY: Cornell University Press, 1991.

Barrett, Justin L. *Why Would Anyone Believe in God?* Walnut Creek, CA: AltaMira Press, 2004.

Corduan, Winfried. *The Tapestry of Faiths*. Downers Grove, IL: InterVarsity, 2002.

Davis, Caroline Franks. *The Evidential Force of Religious Experience*. Oxford: Clarendon, 1989.

Geivett, R. Douglas. "The Evidential Value of Religious Experience." In *The Rationality of Theism*. Ed. Paul Copan and Paul K. Moser. London: Routledge, 2003.

8

Does the Bible Condemn Loving, Committed Homosexual Relationships?

Sy Rogers, a former homosexual and (for one and a half years) transvestite, grew up in an abusive home and was tormented by his peers. In the midst of his homosexual struggles, he would pray, "Lord, I have these temptations in my life.... I have these desires in my life. But I want You more." He eventually married and became a father, and he is now a pastor and popular speaker on the topic of sexual temptation and wholeness.

Rogers tells audiences that when he was a practicing homosexual, "Christians tried to reach out to me." However, "they made a classic mistake; they tried to win a moral argument with me." Deep down Rogers knew that acting on his homosexual inclinations was wrong, and he was aware of what God had to say about it: "I believed in God and His son Jesus Christ, but I also believed that God hated people like me. I wonder where I picked that up"![1]

In this chapter we will look at the delicate and often emotional issue of homosexuality and the Bible. Some scholars, in the name of Christianity, have erroneously claimed that loving homosexual relationships are biblically permitted (e.g., Jack Rogers in *Jesus, the Bible, and Homosexuality*).[2]

Before I begin, I should say that I am not writing with some personal ax to grind, and I don't have some "agenda" for responding critically to the issue of homosexuality. All too often self-proclaimed "Bible-believing Christians" can act with a smug moral superiority toward homosexuals rather than extending friendship and Christ-like love to them. Let me say that I have a great appreciation and respect for the homosexuals I know, and I don't write this to "attack." However, this is an important issue—one that is often insensitively handled—and I am writing on it in response to questions I have been asked in classes, open forums, and seminars.

By focusing on homosexual *activity* (not homosexual *attraction*), I'm not singling it out as inherently worse than other sins. Unfortunately, many professing Christians focus on homosexual acts as the worst of sins. I disagree. Sadly, even as Christians may triumphalistically point to Romans 1, which describes humanity's "downward moral slide" illustrated by homosexual activity, they seem to stop reading at verse 27. However, verses 28–32 refer to the "depraved mind," leading to what is "not proper." This depravity sounds like what you might encounter in a lot of churches—greed, envy, strife, deceit, malice, gossip, slander, insolence, arrogance, boastfulness, disobedient to parents, lacking understanding, untrustworthy, unloving, unmerciful. Paul declares that *all* of this is worthy of God's judgment (v. 32)—not just homosexual activity.[3]

That said, let me respond to the false, but popular, belief in many churches that one sin is "just as bad as another." This is an abuse of Jesus' words in the Sermon on the Mount. Jesus did not teach that hateful anger is just as bad as murder, or that lust is as sinful as adultery (Matt. 5:21–30). They are equally *sin* (lust is wrong)—this is Jesus' emphasis—but they aren't equally *sinful* (adultery is lust taken to the extreme).[4] Scripture makes clear that there are degrees of sin—some sins are worse than others. Consider the distinction between *unintentional* versus *defiant* sins (Num. 15:24, 30), "greater" and "least" commandments (Matt. 5:19), "weightier provisions of the law" (Matt. 23:23), "the greater sin" (John 19:11), and the unpardonable sin (Matt. 12:30–32). And even though there are degrees of sin, Paul doesn't highlight homosexual acts as the worst of sins (more on this later).

In the next chapters, I'll address the issue of whether people are "born gay" as well as the subject of gay marriage. As the introduction to this chapter suggests, people who are gay/lesbian or transgendered (who have undergone a "sex change") or cross-dressers need to know first of all that they are deeply loved by God; that Christ has died for their—and our—forgiveness; and that the church has an obligation to express this love to them in appropriate ways.

First, while the church shouldn't affirm *homosexual activity (or adultery, idolatry, or greed, for that matter), it should* welcome *anyone—gays included—to discover who God is and to find his forgiveness.*[5] Lots of people wear WWJD (What Would Jesus Do?) bracelets and T-shirts, but they don't treat homosexuals as Jesus would. He wouldn't react in fear or avoid them; he would welcome them, sit with them, and tell them of God's deep interest in them. Many churches treat homosexuals as modern-day lepers—as outcasts; but Jesus came to heal, help, and set all people free to live for God.

Surely churches can welcome gays without condoning their lifestyle—just as they can receive adulterers and alcoholics. As my pastor, Bill Stepp, regularly says, "God *accepts* you the way you are, but he loves you too much to *leave* you as you are." It's strange that professing Christians single out homosexual activity as the most wicked of sins. Often those who claim to be saved by God's grace are amazingly judgmental, hateful, and demeaning (calling homosexual persons "fairies" or "faggots") rather than being compassionate and embracing. Professing Christians are often harder on homosexuals outside the church than they are with the immorality within the church (cf. 1 Cor. 5:9–13). New Testament scholar Bruce Winter writes with a prophetic voice, "The ease with which the present day church often passes judgment on the ethical or structural misconduct of the outside community is at times matched only by its reluctance to take action to remedy the ethical conduct of its own members."[6]

Second, the Bible doesn't condemn homosexual inclinations, but rather sexual activity outside of a marriage relationship between husband and wife. In fact, no writers of antiquity, including biblical ones, had any idea of "sexual orientation"; they talked about sexual behavior. When the Scriptures speak against immoral sexual relationships, the focus is not on inclinations or feelings (whether homosexual or heterosexual).[7] Rather, the focus is on *acting* out those impulses (which ranges from inappropriately dwelling on sexual thoughts—lusting—to carrying them out sexually). Even though we are born with a sinful, self-centered inclination, God judges us based on what we *do*.[8] Similarly, a person may, for whatever reasons, have same-sex inclinations, but God won't judge him on the basis of those inclinations, but on what he does with them.

A common argument made by advocates of a gay lifestyle is that the Bible doesn't condemn loving, committed same-sex relationships ("covenant homosexuality")—just homosexual rape or going against one's natural sexual inclination, whether hetero- or homosexual. Now, "the Bible doesn't say anything about ——" or "Jesus never said anything about ——" arguments can be tricky and even misleading. The Bible doesn't speak about abortion, euthanasia, political involvement, Christians fighting in the military, and the like. Jesus, as far as we know, never said anything about rape or child abuse. Nevertheless, we can get guidance from Scripture's more basic affirmations about our roles as God's image-bearers, about God's creation design, and about our identity and redemption in Christ, as we'll see below.

Like Jack Rogers, John Boswell, author of *Christianity, Social Tolerance, and Homosexuality*,[9] has claimed that today's concept of loving, committed homosexual relationships—foreign to the cultures of biblical times—are still permitted within the Christian tradition. His use of sources, however, is quite selective. For example, he omits important sources among the church fathers[10] and is otherwise hardly even-handed. New Testament scholar Richard Hays (Duke University) says this of Boswell's interpretation of Scripture and his rewriting of history: his view "has no support in the [biblical] text and is a textbook case of reading into the text what one wants to find there."[11] Authoritative Christian teaching has always maintained that homosexual activity is wrong. Furthermore, casual homosexuality, homosexual temple prostitution, pederasty (adult-child homosexual acts), and homosexual rape were carried out during biblical times in pagan cultures; so "committed, loving homosexual relationships between adults" would have been an option as well, but Scripture leaves no door open for "covenant homosexuality."[12]

Certain groups such as Evangelicals Concerned and the Metropolitan Community Churches claim to have a high view of Scripture while affirming the legitimacy of a gay/lesbian lifestyle. We can appreciate their concern to reach out and love gays and lesbians who are often shunned by many self-confessed "biblical" churches. Even so, the biblical evidence indicates that accepting their lifestyle as legitimate violates Scripture's teachings.

Third, the Old Testament begins with the affirmation of the creation order (the goodness of sexual pleasure within the context of a husband-wife relationship), and this creational order—as opposed to homosexual relationships—is appealed to by Jesus and Paul. Some gay sympathizers may appeal to examples from Scripture, claiming that David and Jonathan were gay, Ruth and Naomi lesbian. (For example, they embrace, kiss, and weep together—which, of course, is common in the Middle East today without any homosexual connotations!) Some have also severely strained to connect Jesus and "the disciple whom Jesus loved" to homosexual relations. Richard Hays, whom we cited earlier, calls such stretches "exegetical curiosities" that just aren't taken seriously by biblical scholars: these examples "can only be judged pathetic efforts at constructing [biblical] warrant for homosexual practice where none exists."[13] The Scriptures offer no indications—no stories, no metaphors—that homosexual relationships are acceptable before God.

Rather, the traditional understanding of marriage has been a husband-wife one-flesh relationship. Both Jesus and Paul appeal to God's design at creation ("from the beginning") in support of lifelong marriage between husband and wife as God's ideal and thus the context for human sexual activity (Matt. 19:3–12; Mark 10:2–12; Rom. 1:18–32; 1 Tim. 4:3–4). The redemptive movement of the biblical witness is uniform and unwavering: it offers no support for homosexual acts. The Scriptures not only present God's creational design for humans as heterosexual sex within marriage before the fall, but even given a postfall condition, the Bible regularly appeals to God's creational intentions.

In contrast to the ethical stance of Israel's neighbors, God lays down laws for his people that help them make dramatic moral advances in contrast to the surrounding societies. For instance, the king of the first Babylonian dynasty, Hammurabi, issued the first series of judicial codes in world history (second millennium BC), revealing the brutal power of this ruler. In historian Paul Johnson's words, "These dreadful laws are notable for the ferocity of their physical punishments, in contrast to the restraint of the Mosaic Code and the enactments of Deuteronomy and Leviticus."[14] And while the Law of Moses makes certain accommodations due to human hard-heartedness regarding divorce or slavery or polygamy (Matt. 19:8), the sweep of Scripture reveals an underlying spirit, a redemptive movement that *consistently affirms* the full humanity of slaves (e.g., Job 31:13–15) and eventually encourages slaves to pursue their freedom (1 Cor. 7:21) and declares that in Christ there is no difference between slave or free (Gal. 3:28). We see the same affirmations of the dignity of women.

The same cannot be said for homosexuality. *The underlying spirit and redemptive movement across the sweep of Scripture consistently prohibits homosexual activity.* New Testament scholar R. T. France writes that direct references to homosexual acts in Scripture are "uniformly hostile"; homosexual behavior—so common in surrounding cultures (ancient Near East/Greco-Roman)—was "simply alien to the Jewish and Christian ethos."[15]

Some people point out that less than two centuries ago Christians supported slavery in the South and denied voting rights to women. They go on to conclude that Christians must shed their prejudices about homosexuality as they did with slavery and women's suffrage. This, however, is a bad analogy. Homosexuality doesn't fit some "pattern of oppression" here. Scripture clearly affirms the equality of all *individuals*—blacks, women, slaves—because they are God's image-bearers. The same doesn't hold true for *sexual relationships*. Scripture's regular affirmations reinforced by the unfolding direction of Scripture reject any inherent legitimacy to homosexual relations. If one persists in trying to muster biblical support for homosexual relations, we could point out that the same argument could be extended to bigamy/multiple marriage, incest, or pedophilia—as the North American Man/Boy Love Association would favor.[16]

Of course, those committed to the pursuit of a gay lifestyle aren't going to be swayed by such appeals to biblical texts. Besides that, grace, kindness, and love tend to speak much more powerfully!

Nevertheless, it's important that we be aware of what Scripture says and how it can be misapplied by some claiming God's endorsement of "loving, committed gay relationships." Some pro-gay authors cite Galatians 3:28 ("[In Christ] there is neither male nor female") to support Christ's allegedly breaking down barriers of sexual orientation. As we'll see, however, (a) Paul had no category for "sexual orientation"; (b) he assumed the heterosexual creation design as normative in his writings; (c) he was speaking of social inequality between (generally heterosexual) males and females (the latter often being socially stigmatized or treated according to double standards favoring males). So Paul didn't say "neither gay nor straight," just as he wouldn't say "neither adulterer or faithfully married."[17]

Fourth, specific Scriptures uniformly reject the legitimacy of homosexual relations in favor of a one-flesh husband and wife union. We will explore the relevant biblical passages below.

1. *Genesis 19:1–29 (cf. the similar incident in Judges 19).* Gay sympathizers sometimes interpret God's judgment on Sodom as not being due to an association with homosexuality per se. After all, Gomorrah was also destroyed at this time. If anything, a mob wanted to homosexually *rape* Lot's two visitors—a terrible violation of the custom of hospitality. Or perhaps the Sodomites wanted to *forcefully interrogate* these strangers to "know [Heb., *yada*]" (v. 5) whether they were spies—to get acquainted but in an overbearing manner. After all, Derrick S. Bailey argues (with Boswell following) that the word "to know" occurs 943 times in the Old Testament but refers to sexual intercourse only 10 times (e.g., Gen. 4:1: Adam "knew" [KJV] or "had relations" with Eve, and she conceived).[18] Also, the argument continues, when the reasons for Sodom's condemnation are mentioned elsewhere in Scripture, they are *nonsexual sins*—arrogance and not helping the poor and needy (Ezek. 16:49–50; cf. Isa. 1:10; Jer. 23:14).

In response, we should pay attention to how Ezekiel does emphasize Sodom's neglect of the poor and needy. Maybe we Western Christians should be more careful about singling out homosexuality as particularly evil and take the logs out of our own eyes, as we so often neglect the poor—a serious offense indeed! Also, Gomorrah is punished by God along with Sodom for its basic wickedness; so divine judgment comes not merely because of an attempted gang rape. That said, ancient Jewish literature regularly connected Sodom and homosexual activity/rape[19] (the Sodomites "hated strangers and abused themselves with sodomitical practices" [Josephus, *Antiquities* 1.11.1, 3]).

Against Bailey's and Boswell's claims about Sodomites merely violating hospitality norms, the word translated "know" (KJV, RSV) in Genesis 19:5 (and Judg. 19:22) is clearly sexual, as the context indicates. (a) The words "wickedly," "lewd," and "disgraceful" (Gen. 19:7; Judg. 19:23; 20:6; cf. Gen. 13:13) don't sound like a mere breach of hospitality. (b) The offer of the *women* in both stories (Lot's daughters; the Levite's concubine) has sexual connotations. Why offer women if the Sodomites' intentions weren't sexual in nature? (c) Although the word *know* means "sexual intercourse" only ten times in the Old Testament, Bailey fails to mention that seven of those occurrences are in Genesis (4:1, 17, 25; 19:5, 8; 24:16; 38:26 KJV)! The Sodom story itself mentions Lot's daughters who had not *known* a man (19:8 KJV)—that is, virgins.[20] (d) One of Sodom's sins *is* homosexuality, as indicated both by 2 Peter 2:7 ("the sensual conduct of unprincipled men"; cf. v. 10: "who indulge the flesh in its corrupt desires") and Jude 7 ("indulged in gross immorality and went after strange flesh"). Again, this offense is more than just a breach of hospitality. (e) The Greek translation of the Old Testament (the Septuagint [LXX]) indicates that the translators understood *know* in this context as *sexual relations*; they used *syngenōmetha* (from *synginomai*)—the very verb used in Genesis 39:7–10, where Potiphar's wife wants Joseph to "lie with" (*syngenesthai*) her.[21]

2. *Leviticus 18:22 ("You shall not lie with a male as one lies with a female; it is an abomination")* and *Leviticus 20:13 ("If there is a man who lies with a male as those who lie with a woman, both of them have committed a detestable act")*: The claim by homosexual sympathizers like Boswell is that homosexuality is condemned in the Law of Moses because of its association with idolatry or cult prostitution (cf. Deut. 23:17) and/or because it is in the same category as other Levitical laws (e.g., kosher food laws prohibiting, say, shrimp or pork). But the Canaanites were punished because of *immoral acts*, not simply because they had certain dietary preferences. Also included in Leviticus 18—the same chapter as the verse on homosexual relations (v. 22)—are sins such as adultery (v. 20), rape, incest, child sacrifice (v. 21), and bestiality (v. 23). And even if the Canaanites didn't practice these things, such acts would have been

wrong for the Israelites. Adultery is wrong even if it's not committed with Canaanite cult prostitutes![22] We can't simply relativize all purity laws to the level of kosher foods and not planting two crops in the same field (which I've discussed elsewhere).[23] As we'll see (in 1 Cor. 6:9–10 and 1 Tim. 1:10), Paul speaks against homosexuality by using the very language used in Leviticus 18. Notice also that the *act* of lying "with a male as with a female"—not an *inclination* or *desire*—is emphasized.[24]

3. *Romans 1:26–27 ("For this reason God gave them over to degrading passions; for their women exchanged the natural function for that which is unnatural, and in the same way also the men abandoned the natural function of the woman and burned in their desire toward one another, men with men committing indecent acts and receiving in their own persons the due penalty of their error").* This passage is a clear text against homosexual relations. In 1:18, Paul speaks of the "unrighteousness" (*adikia*) of humanity in contrast to God's "righteousness" (*dikaiosynē*). Humans ignore the evidence of God in creation and turn to idolatry (1:23). Included in this turn away from God is the example of sexual perversion. Paul's argument is that sexual deviancy is the *result* of God's wrath, not the *reason* for it. It is a manifestation of God's judgment on a rebellious human race. So God "gave them up" to their idolatry and sexual sin. Along with idolatry and other symptomatic deviations from God's ordered creation, homosexual behavior is a clear indication of violating God's creational design of male and female as his image-bearers (Gen. 1:26–27). God commands them to be fruitful and multiply and to enjoy sexual relations within marriage (Gen. 2:18–24). Homosexuality is seen by Paul as a clear example of the rejection of God's created design—something that is against "nature [*physis*]" (Rom. 1:26)—that is, God's created ordering of things.

Of course, Romans 1–3 is making the argument that *all of us* are under God's judgment—whether an observant Jew or a morally reckless pagan, *everyone* is "without excuse [*anapologētos*]" (1:20; 2:1).

A common pro-homosexual argument is that homosexuality itself isn't being condemned, but when individuals go against their own natural sexual orientation ("exchanged the natural function for that which is unnatural," v. 26). So someone "naturally" homosexually inclined would go "against nature" by engaging in heterosexual relations. But this is commonly acknowledged to be anachronistic: "neither Paul nor anyone else in antiquity had a concept of 'sexual orientation.'"[25] "Sexual orientation" is a fairly recent category.[26]

Others might argue that Paul is really critiquing the wild sexual orgies of the pagans; that he simply opposes pederasty (adult male sex with boys); that he is just rejecting cult prostitution; or, finally, that this is part of his setup argument against Jewish hypocrisy (homosexuality goes against the Jewish holiness code but isn't necessarily sinful for Gentiles).[27] A few brief points are helpful here:

- We shouldn't discuss these matters *sociologically* (reasoning, "If Paul were alive today, he wouldn't say that acting on one's homosexual propensity is wrong"), but *theologically* (looking at God's original design that is regularly appealed to throughout Scripture).[28] Humanity *as a whole* was designed with the capacity for heterosexual marriage, and homosexuality and adultery are deviations from that design.[29]

- The logic of such arguments is that if someone had a "natural inclination" toward bestiality (being in a "loving relationship" with an animal such as one's pet) or necrophilia (sex with corpses), sadomasochism, pederasty (adult male sex with boys), or even rape,[30] that person can legitimately act on that orientation. If we're just talking about "consenting, committed adults," why can't we use the language of Jack Rogers and others to speak of "loving and faithful *incestuous*—or *multiple-partner*—unions"?

  One writer who claims homosexuality is consistent with the spirit of Christianity forcefully asserts, "Only a sadistic God would create hundreds of thousands of humans to be inherently homosexual and then deny them the right to sexual intimacy."[31] As we'll see in the next chapter, the notion of "inherent homosexuality" is questionable. More to the point, we're all born with a natural self-centered tendency, but that doesn't mean we should assume that we have a "right" to fulfill those inclinations. We hear plenty of self-centered slogans—"Look out for number one" or "Entertain me; I'm bored"—but it would be wrong to act on those tendencies. Whether we're homosexually or heterosexually oriented, we're *all* twisted in one way or another by the fall; we're not what God meant for us to be spiritually, psychologically, sexually, physically, or mentally. However, that doesn't mean that we should *act* according to our damaged inclinations. (Note that in Romans 1, the words "exchanged" and "abandoned" reflect not mere inclinations, but acting on them.)

+ Paul's contemporaries, Seneca and Plutarch, condemned homosexuality (and pedophilia); more significantly, sex between females was almost universally condemned.[32]

+ Boswell and others have attempted to relativize Paul's strong use of "against nature [*para physin*]" in Romans 1 by appealing to other uses of "nature" elsewhere. For example, Paul argues against long hair for men because that was against "nature [*physis*]" (1 Cor. 11:14–15).[33] The idea here, it is suggested, is that nature implies "culture"—hardly universally binding. However, although he had the creation of male and female in mind (Gen. 1:26–27), Paul wasn't specifying a universal male (short) hair length when he wrote the Corinthians. Rather, in Roman society, a male's long hair indicated a denial of masculinity—even advertised one's homosexuality—just as a woman's short hair/shorn head indicated adultery: "All first-century cultures possessed means by which the polarity of the sexes was defined by various conventions; hair length was one such feature in Roman Corinth, as [1 Cor.] 11:14–15 accurately noted."[34] So Boswell misunderstands Paul, who actually appeals to *creation*, not simply culture.

4. 1 Corinthians 6:9–10: "Or do you not know that the unrighteous will not inherit the kingdom of God? Do not be deceived; neither fornicators, nor idolaters, nor adulterers, nor effeminate [Gk., malakoi, cf. Lat., malacus], nor homosexuals [arsenokoitai], nor thieves, nor the covetous, nor drunkards, nor revilers, nor swindlers, will inherit the kingdom of God. Such were some of you." Although our topic is homosexuality, note again that we aren't singling this out in our list, as many Christians are wont to do. Paul includes heterosexual sin (fornication, adultery), sins related to possessions (thieving, coveting, swindling), and—here's a broad one that hits close to home—idolatry. Richard Hays points out the hypocrisy: "Some of the most urgent champions of 'biblical morality' on sexual matters become strangely equivocal when the discussion turns to the New Testament's teachings about possessions."[35]

Paul addresses Christians in Corinth, a Roman colony in which elite citizens were permitted to be the sexually "active" participants—leading partners—involved with male noncitizens (e.g., slaves).[36] It was not unusual for the *paterfamilias*—the male head of the Roman household—to buy male slaves to use for just this purpose (as passive sexual partners). Yet there was a double standard: while Roman law permitted this practice, it was a crime for a male to take sexual initiative with a male Roman citizen. Not surprisingly, the Romans didn't even come up with their own word for this despised passive activity, but their Latin word *malacus* was simply a transliteration of the Greek *malakos* (passive homosexual male).

Paul, however, speaks quite counterculturally: *both* homosexual participants are in the wrong: the socially despised *passively involved* ("effeminate") and the socially acceptable *actively involved* ("practicing homosexuals," TNIV).

Contrary to what some pro-gay interpretations claim, Paul is not speaking against male prostitution or pederasty (sexual molestation of underage boys by adult males). For one thing, Paul makes clear in Romans 1 that *all* homosexual relations are in view, including lesbianism. David Wright's article "Homosexuals or Prostitutes?"[37] also makes clear that Paul's language refers to *a male who lies with another male*. In fact, Paul, using the language of Leviticus 18:22 and 20:13, even *coins a new word* based on these passages—*arsenokoitēs* (from *arsēn* = "male" and *koitē* = "bed," which has sexual connotations [cf. Rom. 13:13: *koitē*, or "sexual promiscuity"; Num. 5:20 LXX]):

Leviticus 18:22: "You shall not lie with a male as one lies with a female [*meta arsenos ou koimēthēsē koitēn gynaikos*]."

Leviticus 20:13: "If there is a man who lies with a male as those who lie with a woman [*hos an koimēthē meta arsenos koitēn gynaikos*] . . ."

We have no ancient usage of this word prior to 1 Corinthians. Every usage of the word after Paul by the Christian church fathers indicates male homosexual activity, and it is frequently placed on their "vice lists."[38]

Here Paul's use of two words makes clear that *both* participants—the leading and the following partners—are in the wrong. So Paul, in faithfulness to the order God laid down at creation, wouldn't parrot what was acceptable in Roman society. Now if Paul was merely condemning male prostitution (as Boswell[39] and other pro-gay interpreters claim), he would have used the well-known masculine word *porneuōn* (a female prostitute is *pornē*, as in 1 Cor. 6:15, 16). This word for "male prostitute" is used in the LXX in Deuteronomy 23:17—"nor shall any of the sons of Israel be a cult prostitute." As Winter notes, if *arsenokoitēs* "had meant something other than an actual homosexual person, Paul would have been proscribing [prohibiting] only passive homosexuality and thereby would have reflected the values and attitude of Roman society on this issue."[40]

5. *1 Timothy 1:9–11: "... law is not made for a righteous person, but for those who are lawless and rebellious, for the ungodly and sinners, for the unholy and profane, for those who kill their fathers or mothers, for murderers and immoral men and homosexuals* [arsenokoitais] *and kidnappers and liars and perjurers, and whatever else is contrary to sound teaching, according to the glorious gospel of the blessed God, with which I have been entrusted."* Here Paul applies the Ten Commandments to his contemporary context, and he includes "immoral men [*pornois*]" and "homosexuals [*arsenokoitais*]," emphasizing the socially acceptable active (as opposed to passive) homosexuality.

Fifth, here are a few final reflections on the biblical material we've surveyed:

- *The Scriptures indicate that God is able to deliver people from a lifestyle of homosexuality (or adultery, greed, and so on).* Paul reminds the Corinthian believers, some of whom had been delivered from a homosexual lifestyle: "Such were some of you; but you were washed ... sanctified ... justified" (1 Cor. 6:11). For the homosexual to affirm, "That's just the way I am," reveals that deeply imbedded emotional longings can't readily be disentangled from his perceived self-identity. The homosexual's situation calls for compassion, not judgment. Yet the Scriptures indicate that God is able to deliver or help us live with our brokenness in a fallen world—the "but [*alla*]" in this passage suggests a strong contrast to a previous way of life. The Christian community should be available to those who struggle with care, friendship, and appropriate touch.

- *The Bible also insists that sexual gratification isn't a right. Self-control is called for whether one is heterosexually or homosexually inclined. We are to honor God in our bodies (1 Cor. 6:20); our bodies are "for the Lord" (6:13). In fact, one can serve God as an unmarried person, whether voluntarily single or not.* In a society that emphasizes "freedom" and "rights," we shouldn't neglect talking about personal responsibility in the sexual realm. God's salvation is from sin, from the bondage of doing what I want apart from God. Indeed, our highest calling is to love God. We are to find our identity in him—not in "finding" or "authenticating" ourselves. God requires us to do justice, love mercy, and walk humbly before him (Micah 6:8; cf. Deut. 10:12).

- *If a husband-wife marriage relationship is the only context in which a sexual one-flesh union should take place, and if one-flesh unions are possible only through heterosexual relationships, then it is in principle impossible to engage in a one-flesh union with a member of the same sex.* Sex between a man and woman is a deeply binding union, and so Paul says that a man shouldn't engage in sex with a prostitute since he binds himself to her (1 Cor. 6:16). Sex is reserved for marriage. The goal of a one-flesh union between husband and wife is a picture of marital *completeness* and *unity*, not simply a fulfillment of *sexual desires*.[41] If a marriage is a one-flesh union that's only possible between male and female, then "homosexual marriage" is a contradiction in terms. As theologian Stanley Hauerwas noted, "I do not believe in the category of homosexuality at all and think that we simply ought to talk about promiscuity and its problems."[42]

- *We must be careful not to exalt experience and preference above the Word of God.* Many arguments used by the homosexual community—"God made me this way" or "I was born this way"—could be used to justify *any* kind of behavior: incest, prostitution, pedophilia (a man might not intend to hurt a boy, and the boy might not perceive any harm; so why not?), bestiality, sadomasochism. In other words, "*there is ultimately no argument against pedophilia or any departure from heterosexual monogamy if individual experience is imposed on Scripture.*"[43] The Bible doesn't open the door for homosexual activity simply because one has certain motives: "it's not hurting anyone" (the "date-rape" drug may not *appear* to harm either party) or "it's between two consenting adults" (so is sadomasochism). While *motives* are important, Scripture takes *actions* very seriously.

  Consider the parallel of alcoholism. Some people struggle more than others with the temptation of drinking. But we don't want to affirm them by saying, "You were born this way." Rather, we want them to battle against this inclination by taking personal responsibility, showing self-control, and getting help from a loving community of family and friends. Or think of Paul's own "thorn in the flesh"—an affliction Paul prayed that God would remove. But Christ told Paul, "My grace is sufficient for you" (2 Cor. 12:7–9).

- *Our response to the gay community must be compassionate and loving, not self-righteous and judgmental.* Too many homosexuals don't feel safe coming to our churches. Many homosexual strugglers fear rejection by Christians if they open themselves to help and friendship. Christians have an exceptional opportunity to show Christ's love to, say, AIDS patients in the gay community, build bridges of understanding, and show a spirit of goodwill even if we disagree. Think of how Jesus treated the adulterous Samaritan woman (John 4). Though he didn't condone her sin, he acted lovingly toward her. How many people within our churches are struggling with homosexual desires? Are we providing them a safe, welcoming community to provide help and healing—or will they go somewhere else?

91

Summary

- The church should be *welcoming* to all, even if not all lifestyles/actions are *affirmed*. God takes us as we are but doesn't want to leave us there.
- Scripture doesn't highlight homosexual acts as the greatest wrong but includes them in lists of other sinful practices. (This isn't to deny Scripture's emphasis on *degrees* of sin, however.)
- The Bible speaks against homosexual *activity*, not *inclinations*.
- Homosexual acts are wrong because they violate the creational order (a one-flesh union of husband and wife in the context of marriage), which biblical writers continually appeal to as normative for sexual activity.
- If we justified sexual activity based on "natural attraction" or "That's the way I was born," all kinds of immoral activity could be justified (e.g., pedophilia, bestiality, necrophilia).
- The Bible uniformly rejects homosexual activity as legitimate (see comments on the various texts).
- Scripture affirms that those who have participated in homosexual activity—or other sinful acts—can be transformed by God's Spirit.
- Sexual gratification isn't a right. Scripture regularly exhorts us to act in a self-controlled manner.

Further Reading

Hays, Richard B. *The Moral Vision of the New Testament.* San Francisco: HarperSanFrancisco, 1996. Chapter 16.

Schmidt, Thomas E. *Straight and Narrow? Compassion and Clarity in the Homosexuality Debate.* Downers Grove, IL: InterVarsity, 1995.

Webb, William J. *Slaves, Women, and Homosexuals: Exploring the Hermeneutics of Cultural Analysis.* Downers Grove, IL: InterVarsity, 2001.

Winter, Bruce W. *After Paul Left Corinth: The Influence of Secular Ethics and Social Change.* Grand Rapids: Eerdmans, 1995. Pages 110–20.

Wold, Donald J. *Out of Order: Homosexuality in the Bible and the Ancient Near East.* Grand Rapids: Baker, 1998.

9

Aren't People
Born Gay?

Time magazine's cover story of July 26, 1993, made the pronouncement: "Born Gay? Science Finds a Genetic Link." An article in *Time's* June 12, 1995, issue was titled "Search for a Gay Gene"; it referred to an "orgy" of "gay" fruit flies in a laboratory—an observation that allegedly has implications for the naturalness of human gayness. Later on that year, an article in *US News & World Report* asked, "Is There a 'Gay Gene'?"[1] The impression often given by such popular news articles is that people are "born gay." In 1948, William Kinsey's report, *Sexual Behavior in the Human Male,* claimed that up to 10 percent of any given population may be gay.[2] This double-digit figure has been taken for granted by many and appears somehow to sanction homosexuality—"here is a trustworthy statistic, worthy of full acceptance"!

What *does* science tell us about homosexuality? Are people born gay? As we'll see, what some people call "proof" for homosexuality based on science is highly questionable. This is so not only because some of the research has been quite biased or slipshod, but it's not always clear what conclusions one should draw based on certain kinds of biological research. So on this emotional issue, we must be careful not to overdraw certain conclusions based on science; the issue is far more complex and nuanced than some elusive "gay gene."[3]

First, the first official "scientific" legitimization of homosexuality didn't come as the result of research; it came as a result of political pressure. Ironically, despite the claims that people are "born gay" and that homosexuality is "natural" and legitimate, the 1973 reversal of the American Psychiatric Association's position on homosexuality had nothing to do with advances in scientific research to support the biology of homosexuality. In fact, prior to this time, the APA had listed homosexuality in its *Diagnostic and Statistical Manual of Mental Disorders*, believing that homosexuals needed treatment. Its about-face was actually the result of strong political pressure from gay activists (the National Gay Task Force) to "legitimize" what was once considered a disorder. Even so, the APA vote was still far from unanimous. In fact, even in 1979, sex researchers Masters and Johnson said that homosexuals are "homosexually oriented by learned preferences," and, as late as 1985, declared the "genetic theory of homosexuality" to be "generally discarded today."[4]

We'll see below that the actual percentage of those who are consistently sexually attracted to the same sex is more like 2 to 3 percent. However, Christians shouldn't overplay the percentage game. Yes, an alleged double-digit (10 percent) homosexual representation in any given population may seem impressive to some, as though gay relationships somehow become legitimized and moral. But percentages themselves don't tell us about the rightness or wrongness of something. (Consider that a small percentage of any given population will be left-handed too!) So, in light of the previous chapter, even if 10 percent actually were born gay (as opposed to "created gay" by God), this would simply be further indication of the broken, fallen world in which we live. The same would be true if one could locate a "biological basis" for alcoholism, pedophilia, or violent behavior. In fact, 100 percent of the human race is fallen and in need of God's redemptive, re-creative work in Christ!

Second, the idea that "biology is fate" is actually demeaning to homosexual persons, who are much more than sexual (or biological) beings. This notion also assumes that having a sexual inclination entails that we carry it out in pursuit of sexual fulfillment. We are more than sexual beings, though. We are spiritual, creative, volitional, emotional, intellectual, and social beings as well. We should be cautious about reducing our status to that of "biological organism." A person shouldn't be defined by whom he sleeps with. Through love and grace, we should take pains to show that finding homosexual acts to be wrong doesn't imply a personal attack on or lack of respect for the homosexual.[5] *Respecting* someone with a different sexual orientation is not the same as *accepting* that homosexual relationship as legitimate. For example, Jesus' disapproval of the rich young man's idolatry didn't diminish his concern for that man (Mark 10:21: "Looking at him, Jesus felt a love for him").

Third, just because we're born a certain way doesn't mean that it ought to be affirmed—let alone that we're compelled to carry it out. We shouldn't make the mistake of moving automatically from "is" to "ought." In the preceding chapter, we explored this topic somewhat. What if people are "born with" a tendency toward aggression and criminal activity? What about those who claim their family has a tendency toward alcoholism? What if people have tendencies toward pedophilia, cannibalism, racism, rape, or substance abuse? Should we affirm this or seek to correct it? *Tendencies* don't necessarily tell us how we *ought* to live. Indeed, gene therapy attempts to correct genetically transmitted diseases, and if homosexuality is strictly genetic, another question emerges: should we view this trait as a genetic defect and therefore attempt to "fix" it? At any rate, presumed *explanations* for behaviors are not the same as *justifications* for those behaviors.[6] We know how we must regularly restrain our self-centered desires to do what is right; so if God has created us, we must live according to his intentions and designs for us.

Fourth, the scientific evidence for homosexual tendencies is hardly definitive, and the media tend to make inferences that are not warranted by the scientific data. A lot of people don't know that Kinsey's study was skewed—hardly a cross-section of the general population. For instance, 25 percent of his 5,300 male subjects were prison inmates, many of whom were sex offenders; 44 percent of these inmates had engaged in homosexual practices while in prison; some groups, such as church attendees, were hardly represented at all.[7] In fact, psychologist Abraham Maslow warned Kinsey about the misleading analysis, but Kinsey didn't listen to him.[8] (Even so, Kinsey actually claimed that 10 percent of white American males—and 5 percent of females—were "more or less" homosexual for at least three years of their lives between ages sixteen and twenty-five; and 4 percent of men and 3 percent of women were *exclusively* homosexual throughout their lives.)[9] Indeed, many studies—from the Alan Guttmacher Institute, the Batelle Human Affairs Research Center, the Radcliffe Infirmary (Oxford), and others—have shown that the number is more like 1 to 2 percent or perhaps slightly higher.[10]

That said, there are oft-touted studies that allegedly show a strong biological basis for homosexuality. Psychologist J. Michael Bailey and psychiatrist Richard Pillard did a study in 1991 involving identical twins (identically genetically coded) and fraternal twins (differently genetically coded), 161 of whom were gay or bisexual men. If an identical twin was homosexual, then the other's chances of being gay turned out to be three times higher. Does this suggest a "gay gene"? Even if this study were reliable, at most it would show a *predisposition*, not *inevitability*. Environment (e.g., similar relationships to fathers) could be just as significant a factor as certain biological predispositions. Why not argue for environmental factors? Why focus on genetics as opposed to environment? As it turns out, Bailey and Pillard used biased samples (having advertised in pro-gay magazines and tabloids).[11] In another study, two researchers interviewed forty-six homosexual twins who were reared apart from their counterparts after birth. None of the females (four pairs) shared a homosexual preference, and only one male pair did. The conclusion was that "genetic factors are insufficient explanation of the development of sexual orientation."[12]

Another study conducted by Simon LeVay involved examining the brains of thirty-five cadavers (nineteen of whom were homosexual males)—a small number of samples.[13] The hypothalamus (responsible for regulating pulse rate, body temperature, and hormone production, among other things) of the nineteen presumed homosexual men was less than half the size of that of the heterosexual men.[14] What should we infer from this? Many in the media concluded that homosexuality is rooted in biology. But there's more to the story: LeVay *presumed* that sixteen were heterosexual since their sexual orientation wasn't mentioned in their medical charts—another research mistake. All nineteen of the homosexual men died of AIDS after having been medically treated for HIV (both the virus and the medication could have affected the size of the hypothalamus). What's more, we don't know much about their sexual habits. In March 2001, William Byne attempted to duplicate LeVay's attempt at differentiating the hypothalamuses of homosexuals and heterosexuals, but without success.

Also, LeVay himself admitted that a small hypothalamus could have been the *result* of homosexual activity, not necessarily its *cause*:

> In the case of the hypothalamus, which I studied, there's no way of telling whether those structural differences are the cause of people's sex behavior or the consequence—or none of the above. It's possible that it's a "use it or lose it" phenomenon: If you don't practice straight sex you lose that part of the brain that's involved. I don't favor that explanation [LeVay is himself a homosexual], but it's a possible explanation.[15]

Further confirmation undermining the "born gay" thesis comes from puberty studies in different cultures showing that first attraction for those experiencing same-sex and opposite-sex attraction isn't biologically preprogrammed like puberty is. One's first memories of same-sex attraction don't warrant the conclusion, "I was born that way." Cultural and probably various random and unpredictable elements—"factors other than biological ones"—influence same-sex attraction.[16]

While there are further such examples (by geneticist Dean Hamer and others) that we can't explore, the list of biased, botched, and misinterpreted studies directed to support the "born gay" thesis is indeed long.[17] Such "homosexual by nature" claims tend not to be replicated in similar research. Indeed, what is commonly ignored is the "nurture" side of the debate.

Fifth, both sides must be careful not to commit the either-or fallacy ("it's either biology or environment; either nature or nurture, either determined or a choice"). Regarding homosexuality, it seems wiser—and clearer—to talk about influences *rather than* causes. *Homosexuality isn't reducible to mere genetics, but also includes environmental factors (family upbringing, childhood experiences, reactions and choices, and the cultural environment).* Most homosexuals don't see their sexual orientation as a choice but as a deeply embedded aspect of their identity. Therefore, if it's not a choice, then it's a legitimate part of the fabric of their lives. As we'll see shortly, homosexual inclinations may be *deeply* embedded, but that doesn't mean that they have to be *permanently* embedded.

A note of caution: Christians mustn't be so quick to claim that homosexuality is simply a *choice*—something individuals can "just say no" to. Homosexuals don't think to themselves, "I'll choose to be attracted to those of my own gender." Most of them didn't choose to be attracted to the same sex; such attraction is involuntary. Even if they go too far by asserting that same-sex attraction is an unchangeable part of their identity, we shouldn't simplistically resort to "homosexuality is a choice" claims.

Now, it may be true that effeminate males and masculine females are more likely to become homosexuals, but does this *cause* their homosexuality? For some people certain influences may contribute to the development of homosexual inclinations while for others the same sorts of influences don't lead toward homosexual attraction. Speaking from his own experience, Chad Thompson, an ex-gay and author of *Loving Homosexuals as Jesus Would*, points out that gay adults often seek love and affirmation from fellow males because they didn't receive those things growing up due to absent or emotionally distant fathers or a lack of male peers.

The scenario may look something like this.[18] A young boy doesn't connect emotionally with his father through affirmation, interest, and touch; he doesn't feel accepted by him or secure in his presence. (Note that boys typically start trying to attach to their fathers at two and a half; this is when they start to separate from their mothers and develop a sense of gender identity.) To make matters worse, the father may favor and affirm a more athletic son in the family rather than this boy, who may have been born slightly more effeminate and just isn't athletic. Or he simply has a strong interest in the arts or music. From age five and beyond, he starts to look for affirmation from his male peers. (Typically, this stage is when boys think girls have "cooties"! Then at puberty, after he has learned about and connected with boys, he starts to become interested in learning about girls.) This boy may miss out on physical contact through sports—with high-fives, pats on the back, hugs, and other nonsexual touch with his male peers. This artsy, nonathletic boy may be intelligent and sensitive, taking even the slightest rejections to heart. So when he's called a "sissy" and gets picked on by those of his male peer group, he withdraws to safer company.

This scenario illustrates how *a boy needs to be able to internalize a sense of his own masculinity*. When he does this, he's able to become interested in the opposite sex later on. On the other hand, a male who finds affirmation from his father and male peers early on is able to move from this identification and dis-identify with his gender group and cultivate relationships with females in the process of sexual maturation. When a boy doesn't have this early male affirmation, he detaches from his father and male peer group, *rejecting the masculinity he craves*. So if the need for emotional attachment to males is not met in these preadolescent years, the longing for bonding with males may become intertwined with sexual activity at puberty and beyond. While I am not ruling out homosexual inclinations through the influence of pornography, sexual abuse, or sexual experimentation at puberty or beyond, the above scenario tends to be common.

Lesbianism, though more complex, is often motivated by *seeking protection from unsafe men*—often because of sexual abuse or witnessing domestic violence. Such negative experiences with males may shape a girl's thinking that females are safer than males. Gender identification—perhaps among masculine tomboys who may not readily connect with girls in childhood—is just part of the issue. Women who identify with their mothers, though, will most likely become feminine-identified and heterosexual.

In one 1994 survey of 117 gay men, 86 percent said they spent little or no time with their fathers during childhood; 50 percent believed their fathers didn't love them; 45 percent said their fathers belittled or humiliated them; and only 18 percent said their relationships with their fathers were affectionate or warm. Many of these characterized themselves as sensitive (78 percent); only 8 percent enjoyed sports "very much." (A survey of homosexually oriented females indicated that almost 90 percent identified with *masculine* activities rather than feminine ones during childhood.)[19] In one study of 40 homosexual males by D. G. Brown (1963), not a single one reported having had an affectionate relationship with his father. In another study by Saghir and Robins (1973), only 13 percent of homosexual men identified with their fathers—in contrast to 66 percent of heterosexual men. The list of studies goes on.[20]

Dr. Elizabeth Moberly, who has been involved in ministry to homosexuals as director of Psychosexual Education and Therapy for BCM International, has observed this same pattern. She writes that the need for masculine love and affirmation that doesn't come in childhood may, with the onset of sexual maturation, "be inappropriately eroticized—with a pre-adult developmental lack carried into adulthood and inappropriately met with sexual activity. The adult homosexual does, of course, have choices—to remain celibate, to engage in sexual activity, or to seek therapy to resolve the unfinished business of childhood. But the homosexual orientation itself, though not innate, remains something the adult may not have chosen."[21]

Elsewhere, Moberly writes of one constant underlying principle that suggests itself: "that the homosexual—whether man or woman—has suffered some deficit in the relationship with the parent *of the same sex*; and that there is a corresponding drive to make good this deficit—through the medium of same-sex or 'homosexual' relationships."[22]

So we have a scenario in which both nature and nurture may *influence*—not determine—homosexual tendencies. Biology is not destiny, as it is with eye color or fingerprints. Nor is one's environment destiny either (e.g., a child's negative relationship with a same-sex parent may be a result of the child's willfulness and the ensuing relational rift). The influences that may lead to homosexuality often involve a *combination* of wide-ranging factors. On the *biological* side, males and females may come with certain natural dispositions and temperaments (e.g., athletic versus nonathletic, aggressive versus gentle/sensitive) and interests (sports versus arts and music). In addition, we should also include *psychological* and *sociological* (environmental) influences, including a cultural environment in which anything goes and any kind of sexual behavior is permitted. Such factors may *cumulatively* contribute to homosexuality. Any one of the following may be *weighted differently* depending on the person:[23]

- experiences, choices, reactions, and the moral cultural climate
- childhood trauma (e.g., loneliness following divorce)
- sexual experimentation/behavior with same sex
- sexual abuse or molestation
- persecution from same-sex peer group

- poor relationship with the father or mother
- passive, detached father
- controlling, interfering mother
- stiflingly close relationship to an opposite-sex parent

Psychologists Jones and Yarhouse argue that while people *don't consciously choose* their sexual orientation, science *doesn't eliminate responsibility* for sexual behavior: "There appear [sic] to be a variety of factors that provide a push in the direction of homosexuality, but *there is no evidence that this 'push' renders human choice utterly irrelevant.*"[24]

Thomas Schmidt, in his well-documented book *Straight and Narrow?* points out a combination of ranging factors that influence sexual orientation. One condition on the right side of the spectrum can flow into another condition or situation—without there being just one single factor to isolate and certainly nothing to override human responsibility:[25]

Aspect #1: BIOLOGICAL

    Normal   *genetic or hormonal difference*

                                ↓

Aspect #2: CULTURAL

    Clear gender roles   *societal or individual confusion*

                                ↓

Aspect #3: ENVIRONMENTAL

    Functional family   *family dysfunction*

                                ↓

Aspect #4: MORAL SETTING

    Responsible   *permissive*

                                ↓

Aspect #5: BEHAVIORAL

    Negative experience/ impression   *positive (homosexual) experience or impression*

                                ↓

Aspect #6: VOLITIONAL

    Refusal   *consent*

What some homosexual sympathizers call being "born gay" may be looking at things in reverse. Biology can be shaped by psychology! That is, our thoughts, choices, actions, and reactions—even if sub-conscious and early in life—can shape the neurological patterns within the brain so that they become deeply embedded. Eventually this leads to a restructuring or transformation of the brain. These patterns help shape the direction of our lives, reinforcing thought patterns, habits, and desires.

Dr. Jeffrey Satinover of Harvard Medical School speaks of these bio-neural processes that are shaped through habit formation.[26]

> The neocortex is the part of the brain that we might consider as the seat of the will. . . . It is also the part of the brain whose con-nections between the neurons will be slowly modified over time, strengthening some connections, weakening others, and eliminating some entirely—all based on how experience shapes us. This ongo-ing process embeds the emerging pattern of our choices ever more firmly in actual tissue changes. *These changes make it that much more likely for us to make the same choice with less direct effort the next time—and that much more difficult to make a different choice.*[27]

We could add that the life-shaping importance of the spiritual disciplines (as emphasized by Dallas Willard and Richard Foster) is part of this process of transformation.

Sixth, since homosexuality is not the result of genetic necessity but results largely from dysfunctional same-sex relationships in one's youth, this also signals the possibility of greater healing and wholeness, which thousands of ex-gays have found—another indication that people aren't "born gay." Plenty of homosexuals insist that gayness is just the way they are; they assume it can't be changed. Many in the gay community scoff—and even get angry—at the suggestion that homosexuals can become heterosexual. To be an "ex-homosexual" strikes them as dishonest.

They may quote the noted Evelyn Hooker study (1950s), which claims that the mental health of heterosexual men and gay men is virtually indistinguishable. Actually, hers was a *flawed, biased* study: she recruited homosexuals from pro-homosexual organi-zations and only those candidates who hadn't been hospitalized previously. Her article only refuted the claim that *all homosexu-als are manifestly disturbed*. She *didn't* prove that homosexuals are just as emotionally healthy as heterosexuals.[28] In fact, there are ample indications that homosexuals don't compare favorably to heterosexuals when it comes to mental health. Despite *Time* magazine's upbeat portrayal of gay teens (October 10, 2005), the indications are that gay teens are more significantly suicidal than their heterosexual peers.[29] Psychiatrists Jones and Yarhouse remark that one study that claimed to show no distinct psychopathologies in homosexuals as opposed to heterosexuals (Saghir and Robins, 1973) does just the opposite. Because the authors had screened out previously hospitalized homosexuals, if we include their number, the hospitalization rate for them would have been around 450 percent.[30] While I am not saying that there aren't fairly well-adjusted homosexuals, most psychiatrists around the world do not believe homosexuality to be normal but rather pathological. That said, even if there *were* no clinical evidence that showed this, homosexual activity would still be *morally wrong*.[31]

As we've seen, just because the APA's fourth edition of *Diagnostic and Statistical Manual of Mental Disorders* doesn't list homosexuality as a disorder, this doesn't mean that the homosexual doesn't need help in important areas. (And don't we *all* need help in many areas of our lives!) Indeed, there is strong evidence that homosexuality doesn't represent wholeness, but deep brokenness. As we saw in the preceding chapter, Paul's words to the Corinthians speak powerfully: "Such were some of you; *but* you were washed. . . ." (1 Cor. 6:11, emphasis added). Through conversion and prayer and the assistance of a Christian community, God offers hope for change. Such change can be realized as we not only *trust in* God but also *cooperate with* the way God has designed us to function. As Elizabeth Moberly notes, a person doesn't just "stop being a homosexual."[32] An important process of human growth and development has been blocked or bypassed by homosexuals, and these people are healed through nonsexual relationships—males with males, females with females.

In Chad Thompson's own experience of coming out of the gay lifestyle, the two key ways to find greater healing and to help decrease homosexual inclinations were through (a) committed same-sex *camaraderie* and (b) ongoing *nonsexual touch* from persons of the same gender.[33] Too often the lack of love from same-sex peers or a parent in childhood (not to mention being sexually abused) turns into a quest for sex in adulthood, but the need is still for love, and this need must be channeled in healthy, nonsexual ways toward members of the same sex—ways that weren't achieved in childhood. A homosexual, often unconsciously, charts a course that doesn't seek to receive love from a needed love source, and this can't be reversed by mere willpower. Whether a parent's failure is culpable or not, forgiveness is needed to overcome this, perhaps hidden, animosity, hurt, or loss. The defensive detachment must be overcome so that proper attachments *over time* can occur by learning to trust and receive love from the kind of source that can bring healing—supportive same-sex relationships—in the context of prayer and spiritual growth.

Ministries such as Exodus International (www.exodus-interna tional.org), Inqueery (www.inqueery.com), and the International Healing Foundation (www.Gaytostraight.org) offer support, help, and hope for transformation. The secular National Association of Research and Therapy of Homosexuality (www.NARTH.com) also offers important discussion and scientific research results on this topic. Indeed, thousands upon thousands have come out of active gay lifestyles and found significant help and healing—even to the point of marrying and having children. Christians shouldn't insist that homosexuals *have* to change, but that they can make significant strides if they *want* to.[34]

Ex-gay and founder of Genesis Counseling, Joe Dallas responds to the claim that even if gays change their behavior, they don't really change within. He compares this to saying, "A chain smoker may have stopped smoking cigarettes, but he still hasn't gotten rid of his cravings." Simply stopping certain activities may not go as far as one would like, but it is still a huge step forward. Furthermore, a person can move from saying "I'm gay" to saying "I'm a struggler," which can bring significant healing. He can also make progress from seeing another male and having a strong sexual attraction ("Whoa!") to a lesser reaction ("Oh."); and such steps are not insignificant. So it may be misleading to talk in terms of radical and immediate "conversion" from homosexual attraction to heterosexual attraction—though we shouldn't rule this out—but rather a *decrease* of one desire and an *increase* of another.[35]

In terms of our interactions with homosexuals, Dallas mentions three groupings of homosexuals and appropriate responses to them:[36] *militant* homosexuals, who are the minority—we can defend our positions without attacking; *moderate* homosexuals, who just want to live their lives but don't want to change—we should model God's love to them; and *repentant, struggling* homosexuals, who don't want to be gay—we can assist them in their pursuit of change by God's grace.[37]

Summary

- In the 1970s, political pressure by gay activists forced a change about the perception of homosexuality. It wasn't the result of "scientific" research; the medical community had previously considered it a pathology.

- Biology isn't fate. This is actually demeaning to homosexuals, who are much more than biological/sexual beings.

- Simply because we're born a certain way doesn't mean we ought to affirm it. Furthermore, just because we are born with certain inclinations doesn't mean we should carry them out (compare "tendencies" toward alcoholism, violence, pedophilia). We can't legitimately move from "is" to "ought."

- The scientific support for people being "born gay" is seriously lacking. The media tend to stretch the evidence beyond what the scientific data warrant.

- It's easy for both sides to play the either-or game ("it's either biology or environment, either nature or nurture, either determined or a choice"). The most appropriate and more obvious alternative is speaking of *influences* rather than *causes.* Homosexuality isn't reducible to mere genetics; it also includes environmental factors (family upbringing, childhood experiences, reactions and choices, and the cultural environment).

- Homosexuality is not the result of genetic necessity but results largely from dysfunctional same-sex relationships in one's youth (or, in the case of lesbianism, bad experiences with males who were abusive or violent).

- The fact that same-sex attraction is not biologically based suggests the possibility of healing and wholeness, which many have found.
- Changing from homosexual to heterosexual attraction tends to be gradual rather than immediate, but stopping homosexual activity in itself is a significant step forward—comparable to stopping smoking, even if the cravings are still there.

Further Reading

Jones, Stanton L., and Mark A. Yarhouse. *Homosexuality: The Use of Scientific Research in the Church's Moral Debate.* Downers Grove, IL: InterVarsity, 2000.

Kinnaman, David, and Gabe Lyons. *unChristian: What a New Generation Really Thinks about Christianity . . . and Why It Matters.* Grand Rapids: Baker, 2007. Chapter 5.

Nicolosi, Joseph. *Reparative Therapy of Male Homosexuality.* Northvale, NJ: Aronson, 1997.

Thompson, Chad W. *Loving Homosexuals as Jesus Would.* Grand Rapids: Brazos, 2004.

Wolfe, Christopher, ed. *Homosexuality and American Public Life.* Dallas: Spence, 1999.

10

What's Wrong
with Gay Marriage?

Part of the problem in the gay marriage debate is that emotions run high on both sides. Each side digs in its heels and refuses to budge in any way. Sometimes gays are vilified and misunderstood by traditionalists, but the reverse can be true as well. How do we handle this matter of defining (or changing the definition of) marriage in the public square? Are traditionalists discriminating against gays who believe they should have "equal rights under the law"?

First, Christians should seek to understand, show grace, correct misperceptions, and build bridges wherever possible when interacting with those who disagree about this emotional issue. Both sides ought to be committed to truth-seeking, not playing power politics. The term *homophobic* is commonly misused today: "If you don't *accept* homosexuality as legitimate, you're homophobic." Christians often are, but shouldn't be, homophobic—*afraid* of homosexuals. It's helpful to ask what people *mean* when they use this term. If they mean *nonacceptance* of homosexuality as a legitimate way of life rather than *fear* of homosexuals, then they are being inconsistent. In this case, they are being *homophobic-phobic*—not accepting the view of traditionalists as legitimate.

Both sides should be committed to fairness and truth-seeking. Elizabeth Moberly explains:

> Neither side should make inflated claims or distort data. Both sides need to be frank about their own shortcomings. Truth-seeking also implies an essential concern not to misrepresent others, and not to withhold research grants or publication from persons who hold other views. Genuine and principled disagreement needs to be respected, not dismissed as homophobia or bigotry. This debate is not an easy one. But if we all seek to act with integrity—if we promote truth-seeking and show real respect for those with whom we disagree—then we may realistically hope for the future.[1]

This pursuit of truth-seeking means that the gay community shouldn't use biased studies or the flawed 10 percent statistic to make their case. Nor should they ignore clinical studies that reveal genuine transformation from clients being homosexually inclined to becoming heterosexually inclined. In the same way, Christians shouldn't stereotype or generalize about homosexuals. For instance, Christians (or traditionalists) shouldn't assume that gays have no visitation rights or inheritance rights (more on this below). Nor should one assume that all gays are pedophiles. It is true, however, that pedophilia is "statistically more closely associated with homosexuality than heterosexuality," as psychiatrist Jeffrey Santinover of Harvard writes.[2] This may not be apparent at first, because approximately 35 percent of pedophiles are homosexuals. However, what the media don't report is that "homosexual pedophiles victimize far more children than do heterosexual pedophiles"—that is, "approximately 80 percent of pedophilic victims are boys who are molested by adult males."[3] While we ought to be on guard against pedophilia, whether initiated by heterosexuals or homosexuals, the point here is that *the majority of gay men aren't pedophiles.* Whatever side is taken on the issue, there should be a commitment to getting the facts straight and not stereotyping.

In a pluralistic society, both sides should be committed to fairness of access when it comes to sex education in public schools. The wishes and values of parents should be respected in public school sex education programs. (In this important area, my wife and I have undertaken to teach our children ourselves, having them excused from public school "sex ed" instruction.) That is, why assume that public school students should listen to pro-gay perspectives about sex in "health class"? If parents opt to have their children taught sex education, then they should have equal access to another track—a safe environment—that supports sex within the context of hetero-sexual marriage. And why shouldn't ex-gays be allowed to come to such a class to give another important perspective on this issue? School should allow their clubs and organizations to hold a spectrum of perspectives, not just a politically correct one.[4]

As Christians, we should speak the truth—but do so *in love*. Wouldn't it be a refreshing change to see Christians invite homo-sexuals to a safe support group; protest gay bashing, hate speech, and other forms of harassment toward gays; visit AIDS patients in a hospital; or defend the basic civil rights of homosexuals to pursue employment or to visit their partners in a hospital? Even as we disagree about gay marriage, we can show that our disagreement doesn't stem from hate or fear; we disagree in a spirit of love. As Chad Thompson reminds us: "whoever loves first wins."[5]

Second, the gay marriage debate, though invoking "fairness," tends to be rooted in moral relativism—"What's right for you may not be right for me." But if so, then why think humans have any rights—including a right to gay marriage—at all? If people insist on legaliza-tion of gay marriage as "inherently fair," one wonders on what basis. Where does the standard of fairness or human rights and human dignity come from? As I've argued elsewhere, it's hard to see how such moral standards could be grounded in anything apart from a good *Creator* who has made human beings in his image. And if that's the case, then we're back to God's original design for us at *creation*. Even when a person claims he can do "whatever makes me happy" without governmental interference, but then qualifies that statement by saying "just as long as it doesn't hurt anyone" or "but it should be between two consenting adults" or "just as long as you tolerate other views," we see a moral standard being slipped in. But why should relativists or hedonists (pleasure seekers) include such statements at all? Where does this requirement come from?

Moral relativism and rights don't mix. Relativism undermines any appeal to rights: If rights exist, relativism is false; if rights exist, where do they come from? Again, we're pointed in the direction of a good God in whose image humans have been made—and thus who sets the parameters regarding our sexuality.

Third, if we change the definition of marriage, why restrict it to two persons—or even to humans? If marriage is just socially constructed, then why should any marital arrangement be preferred over any other, and why should gays get preferential treatment over others? Hadley Arkes recounts an unusual "marriage arrangement" he had heard of: "Not too long ago, some friends in Denver brought the news of a man who showed up at the county office seeking a marriage license for himself and his horse. And the clerk found herself in the situation of one who applies the law but no longer remembers the reasons. I take some pride in reporting to you that, when the story was told to me, I did guess the reason that the clerk finally gave for refusing to issue the license: the horse was not yet 18."[6]

During the summer of 2004, I was listening to a radio talk show. A woman called in from Naples, Florida, to express her own marriage preferences—to her dog! Why couldn't the state recognize *this* union as legal?

Once we cast aside the time-tested male-female, one-flesh-union view of marriage in favor of marriage as individuals choose to define it, we have a grab bag of possibilities. Why not consider the following "marital arrangements" as having equal protections under the law?

- *Group marriage* (say, five men and three women or vice versa). Why define marriage as involving *two* persons "committed" to each other?
- *Incestuous marriage* (e.g., a father and a daughter, a mother with a son, a brother and a sister).
- *Bestial marriage* (e.g., a human with a dog, cat, or horse). Why think that humans can't marry nonhuman animals? This could be considered *speciesism*—inappropriately favoring your own species over others.
- *Pedophilia* (an older man marrying and having sex with a prepubescent child).
- *Polygamous* or *polyandrous marriage* (a man with multiple wives or a woman with multiple husbands).
- *Marriage to self.* A person may oppose "numbersism"—the prejudicial assumption that marriage must involve at least two persons.

- *Marriage with non-consenting adults.* Who says marriage has to involve consenting adults? Why not have a harem of sexual partners ("spouses") who are physically restrained from leaving?
- *Nonsexual marriage.* Why not call university fraternities or sororities or two brothers sharing an apartment a "marriage"?
- *Marriage to material objects.* Perhaps we can recognize a person for being married to his money, his job, etc.

If the government doesn't recognize any of these categories to be considered "marriages," is that "unfair" and "discriminatory"? If marriage is just a socially constructed arrangement as a result of human choice and preference, it's hard to see how *any* marital arrangement can rightly be banned.[7]

Fourth, the gay-marriage debate can't avoid questions about human identity and purpose. The attempt to redefine marriage away from a one-flesh union between husband and wife often reduces to a relativistic social construct—marriage (like all other standards) can be fashioned according to our individual preferences. To promote the legality of gay marriage isn't a neutral issue. It has widespread ramifications (adoption, child-custody laws, public and private school curricula, antidiscrimination laws based on marriage), and the government itself can't remain neutral. It will either continue with the assumed definition of marriage as the one-flesh union between husband and wife—or it will undo this, giving the message: "Marriage can be defined as we wish." In this case, marriage is based on nothing more than emotional and economic attachments.[8]

Are human beings just individualistic decision makers who live to "actualize" themselves through their preferred sexual expression? Are they just biological organisms? Or is there such a thing as a fixed *human nature* and so a *design* or *goal* for humans to pursue? These questions must be thoughtfully considered about so monumental a subject as marriage. A one-flesh union of husband and wife is more than just a sexual act; it is an expression of a deep interpersonal union that brings with it profound commitments and loyalties. This is not simply a matter of choosing one's own marital arrangements, some of which are better than others. On such an issue as this, the state has historically *recognized*—not *invented the idea*—that a husband-wife, one-flesh union reflects moral reality and human nature and the sexuality bound up with it.

Fifth, the state can't be neutral about the gay marriage issue. Even to say that "the state ought to be neutral about marriage" involves a moral standard. Lots of people say that government shouldn't take a stand on the definition of marriage. Instead of being "biased" toward heterosexual couples, the state ought to be neutral and unbiased toward couples, including gay couples.

However, those who think the government is morally obligated to be morally neutral about the definition of marriage are misguided. It is in fact a *moral position* to say the state has a *moral responsibility* to view the marriage question as *nonmoral*. As Princeton's Robert George says, "Neutrality between neutrality and non-neutrality is logically impossible."[9] The state will have to take a stand on the nature of marriage and family (e.g., are these just artificial social constructions?) and the basis of marriage (e.g., is it just two consenting adults?).

So if gay marriage is legalized, this won't simply be a neutral change. One can expect that principled disagreement of traditionalists who think gay marriage is a bad idea will lead to denunciations of their "hate speech" and intolerance. In fact, Christian groups (such as InterVarsity Christian Fellowship) on various university campuses (e.g., Tufts University) have been "de-funded" by the administration because they didn't allow gays in leadership positions (though the ruling didn't stand). This de-funding had been based on the claim that these Christian groups were bigoted and intolerant. No doubt, if present trends continue, similar pressures could well be applied to "intolerant" churches that do not accept homosexual activity as morally legitimate.

Sixth, a mother-father parenting arrangement is most beneficial for children and society, and public policy should support and assist this increasingly at-risk arrangement rather than contribute further to its demise. Church considerations aside, as marriages and families go, so goes the culture. A society will be as healthy and strong as the family units that constitute it. If families are fragmented and dysfunctional, societies will be as well

We must be careful about defining the ideal about marriage (or family) according to current cultural trends. Just because a third of all children in the United States are born out of wedlock, this is far from optimal. *Average* isn't *ideal* or *normal* (e.g., the *average* temperature of patients in hospital beds may be well above *normal*). That said, we should give credit and support to abandoned (or widowed) single mothers who raise their children alone or to grandparents who raise their grandchildren without the help of (perhaps) deadbeat parents. Nevertheless, it is the traditional two-parent arrangement that helps provide an important balance that other arrangements (including gay marriage) don't help promote.

Sociologist David Popenoe argues that fathers and mothers make complementary contributions to the lives of their children: "Children have dual needs that must be met [by the complementarity of male and female parenting styles]: one for independence and the other for relatedness, one for challenge and the other for support."[10] A child doesn't just need "parents"; she needs a mother and father, and must learn to relate to each in different ways. Maggie Gallagher argues in *The Case for Marriage* that cultures and communities die when the marriage idea dies out.[11] Gay marriage separates marriage and parenting, which marriage traditionally has not done: when you were ready to marry, you were ready to have children. In Scandinavia or the Netherlands, what cohabitation (and then legal equalization of marriage and cohabitation) began, legalized gay marriage expanded and reinforced. In 2000 the *Los Angeles Times* reported that Scandinavians have "all but given up on marriage as a framework for family living, preferring cohabitation even after their children are born."[12] For example, the number of children living with married parents dropped 16 percent from 1989 to 2002 (78 percent to 62 percent). With legalized gay marriage, which further reinforces the separation of marriage and children, the plummeting continues: "[Norwegians] started to shift from treating the first child as the test of a possible marriage, to giving up on marriage altogether. [13] A similar trend has taken place in Holland, as Stanley Kurtz has shown.[14] Furthermore, it is well-known that gay men tend to be more sexually promiscuous and more emotionally detached than women; this consideration alone does not encourage family stability. As gay marriage tends to diminish the family rather than reinforce it, we should be careful about rushing to legalize it and further destabilize the institution of marriage.

Seventh, we should consider how the push toward gay marriage involves the push toward pedophilia and lower age-of-consent laws. This fact should make us cautious about encouraging gay marriage and gay adoption. Organizations such as NAMBLA (North American Man/Boy Love Association), which advocate pedophilia and lowering the legal age of sexual consent, should be resisted. Although NAMBLA condemns sexual abuse and coercion, it asserts: "We believe sexual feelings are a positive life force. We support the rights of youth as well as adults to choose the partners with whom they wish to share and enjoy their bodies."[15] In a double issue of the *Journal of Homosexuality* (devoted to adult-child sex), one author approvingly refers to "social workers achieving miracles with apparently incorrigible young delinquents—not by preaching to them but by sleeping with them." This "did far more good than years in reformatories."[16] To make matters worse, the American Psychological Association (in its *Psychological Bulletin*) no longer views pedophilia as harmful.[17] There is even a (Dutch) journal, *Paedika: The Journal of Paedophilia*, whose premier issue began with the editorial acknowledgment: "The starting point of *Paedika* is necessarily our consciousness of ourselves as paedophiles."[18]

What is disturbing is the increased openness within the gay community about pedophilia and seeking to lower the age-of-consent laws. This, compounded by the much higher rate of sexual partnerships among gay men and the higher rate of pedophilia/child molestation by homosexuals, should raise warning flags about gay adoptions. Yes, many gays/lesbians can and do offer nurture and care to children, but this shouldn't be the basis for shaping public policy and revising our definitions of family and marriage.[19]

Eighth, many concerns that homosexuals raise can be addressed without having to change the definition of marriage. Homosexuals already have plenty of civic freedoms in the West. They are legally free to engage in homosexual sex, cohabit, hold down well-paying jobs, run for political office. And, yes, they have a right to marry heterosexually! A major barrier is whether marriage should be *redefined* to give homosexuals identical rights as a husband and wife have. For example, many homosexuals claim that marriage as presently defined means that homosexual persons will be deprived of inheritance rights, Social Security benefits, visitation rights in a hospital (e.g., visiting a gay partner who is dying of AIDS), acting as power of attorney, sharing insurance coverage, and the like. However, these sorts of benefits for homosexuals can be accommodated without having to change the definition of marriage. "Gay marriage grants no new freedom, and denying marriage licenses to homosexuals does not restrict any liberty. Nothing stops anyone—of any age, race, gender, class, or sexual preference—from making lifelong loving commitments to each other, pledging their troth until death do them part. They may lack certain entitlements, but not freedoms."[20]

A radical redefinition of marriage isn't needed; perhaps modifying some secondary laws is.

Ninth, Christians should be politically engaged and attempt to preserve certain important culture-sustaining conditions for the common good. But more important, the church must be the church. Believers, in dependence on God's Spirit, should live lives of truth and love rather than depending on government policies to set the moral tone of a nation. Of course Christians should vote, run for office, get involved with public school boards and curricula, and work hard to prevent marriage from being redefined and the age of consent from being lowered.

Too often, however, Christians respond to cultural decline with fear or attempt to take control of a culture through legislation. They cry, "Take back America!" or "Make America Christian again!" Such assertions are often motivated by *fear* of the loss of majority status and a desire for political influence and power.[21] We'd be wise to listen to the historian Tacitus (AD 55–120), who wrote of Rome: "The more corrupt the Republic, the more numerous the laws."[22] Many Christians have put their trust in changing laws rather than, with God's help, changing hearts of fellow sinners for whom Christ died (1 John 2:2). The church in America often depends on legislation to do the work that God calls his people to do. The Spirit's transformation of ourselves and of those around us comes when we love God and neighbor—the very core of our Christian commitment.

Summary

- Our first priority is to show grace and extend friendship to those who disagree with us on the emotional issue of gay marriage. We should try, however, to graciously address misperceptions (e.g., the "10 percent statistic"). Both sides should be committed to truth-seeking, not name-calling and playing power politics.

- The gay marriage issue, despite appeals to "fairness," is likely rooted in moral relativism ("What may be right for you may not be right for me"). This raises the question, Why think humans have any rights—including a right to gay marriage—at all? Moral relativism undermines any appeal to rights; if rights exist, relativism is false. If rights exist, where do they come from?

- Changing the standard definition of marriage leads us to ask, Why restrict marriage to two persons—or even to humans? If marriage is merely a socially constructed arrangement, why should *any* marital arrangement be preferred over any other, and why should gays get preferential treatment over others?

- Human nature/identity and purpose are a crucial and inevitable part of the discussion. Redefining marriage away from a one-flesh union between husband and wife tends to leave us with a relativistic social construct—marriage (or even human identity) is just a matter of personal choice, fashioned according to one's own preferences.

- A traditional model of mother-father parenting is empirically more beneficial for children and society. Public policy should support and assist this model that is being undermined rather than contribute further to its demise.

- We should take note that the push toward gay marriage moves us in the direction of pedophilia, and this should make us cautious about gay marriage and gay adoption.

- Homosexuals often raise certain "civil rights" concerns, but these can be addressed without having to change the definition of marriage.

- While Christians should be politically engaged and attempt to preserve certain important culture-sustaining conditions for the common good, the greater obligation is for the church to be the church. We should live lives of truth and love, depending on the power of God's Spirit rather than government policies to set the moral tone of our culture.

Further Reading

Beckwith, Francis J., and Gregory Koukl. *Relativism: Feet Firmly Planted in Mid-air.* Grand Rapids: Baker, 1998. Chapter 12, "Relativism and the Meaning of Marriage."

Ellison, Marvin M., et al. "The Same-Sex Marriage Debate." *Philosophia Christi* 7, no. 1 (2005): 5–58.

George, Robert P. *The Clash of Orthodoxies: Law, Religion, and Morality in Crisis.* Wilmington, DE: ISI Books, 2001.

Popenoe, David. *Life without Father.* New York: Free Press, 1996. Chapter 5, "What Do Fathers Do?"

Santinover, Jeffrey. *Homosexuality and the Politics of Truth.* Grand Rapids: Baker, 1996.

Wolfe, Christopher. *Homosexuality and American Public Life.* Dallas: Spence, 1999.

Part III

SLOGANS RELATED TO CHRISTIANITY

11

How Can the Psalmists Say Such Vindictive, Hateful Things?

When I was a boy, I would occasionally hear a Middle Eastern–sounding imprecation: "May the fleas of a thousand camels infest your armpits!" This "curse" would be uttered jokingly or playfully. Much more serious and severe, however, are the "imprecatory" psalms, which pray "imprecations"—the calling down of curses or judgments on someone (they include Psalms 7, 12, 35, 55, 58, 59, 69, 79, 83, 109, 137, and 139). An "imprecation" involves two elements: it is (1) a prayer or call to God who is being asked (2) to bring vengeance, curse, calamity, and judgment on the enemies of the psalmist/God.[1]

Psalm 137 is probably the harshest sounding of all the imprecatory psalms:

> By the rivers of Babylon,
> There we sat down and wept,
> When we remembered Zion.
> Upon the willows in the midst of it

We hung our harps.
For there our captors demanded of us songs,
And our tormentors mirth, saying,
"Sing us one of the songs of Zion."

How can we sing the LORD's song
In a foreign land?
If I forget you, O Jerusalem,
May my right hand forget her skill.
May my tongue cling to the roof of my mouth
If I do not remember you,
If I do not exalt Jerusalem
Above my chief joy.

Remember, O LORD, against the sons of Edom
The day of Jerusalem,
Who said, "Raze it, raze it
To its very foundation."
O daughter of Babylon, you devastated one,
How blessed will be the one who repays you
With the recompense with which you have repaid us.
How blessed will be the one who seizes and dashes your
   little ones
Against the rock.

A passage like this sounds shocking to our ears. Perhaps we shouldn't be surprised that the editors of certain psalter hymnals and prayer books have performed "psalmectomies," excising the last three verses altogether![2] Other psalms—not to mention other biblical poetry—contain prayers to God to break the arm of the wicked (10:15), to scatter their bones (53:5), or to slay those who oppose God (139:19). In his *Reflections on the Psalms*, C. S. Lewis declares that such imprecatory psalms are "terrible or (dare we say?) contemptible" prayers; they are "devilish," "profoundly wrong," and "sinful."[3] After all, they're a far cry from Matthew 5:43–48, which calls for a higher ethic—to *love* our enemies and *pray for* our persecutors.

How do we make sense of these strange, harsh-sounding texts? Are the psalmectomies performed on certain psalter hymnals or prayer books justified? Let's look at these issues in greater detail.

First, the outrage in the Psalms is an honest expression of anger at injustice and oppression, and we shouldn't be overly critical of those who are crying out to God in anguish and deep distress. Think back to Psalm 137. What is the background? The psalmist is exiled in Babylon. From 586/587 BC (Jerusalem's destruction by Babylon) to 535 BC (when Jews began to return to Jerusalem), the Jews were in great distress in their displacement from the city they had believed couldn't be moved (Ps. 46:5). For their amusement, the Babylonian captors would taunt the Israelites, forcing them to sing "songs of Zion." To add insult to injury, at Babylon's destruction of Jerusalem and the temple (the place of God's dwelling), Israel's brothers, the Edomites (who descended from Esau), joined in the destructive rampage and pillaging. They blocked fleeing Israelites from escaping, treacherously handing them over to the Babylonians (Obad. 11–14).[4]

This and other imprecatory psalms honestly portray the anguish of the psalmists—their moral outrage when injustice seems to prevail, when God's name is slandered, when God's people and king (who have been incorporated into God's saving purposes) are opposed. Imagine how you would react if a neighbor tried to give drugs to your child or attempted to seduce your teenage daughter. How would you feel? If your first impulse wouldn't be outrage and the urge to inflict bodily harm, something would be wrong with you. A hateful or outraged reaction is often "the first sign that we care," Eugene Peterson notes.[5]

In fact, *God's holiness* sets the stage for such expressions of outrage and revenge.[6] Even though C. S. Lewis wasn't completely accurate at this point (as we'll see below), he remarked, "If the Jews cursed more bitterly than the Pagans, this was, I think, at least in part because they took right and wrong more seriously."[7] These psalms reflect how any of us may honestly feel when we've been betrayed by a friend, mocked and humiliated, or violated. Whatever we think of these psalms, we can see the importance of pouring out our hearts before God (Ps. 62:8), of admitting how we're feeling, rather than suppressing or ignoring our emotions. These psalmists remind us to pray through our hateful feelings, to put our trust in God, and to be concerned about God's name and reputation.

Second, we should keep such imprecatory prayers in their ancient Near East context rather than impose modern standards on them. C. S. Lewis incorrectly believed that Israel was unique in its prayers of vengeance. He believed that Israel had "sinned in this matter worse than the Pagans" in that they "cursed more bitterly than the Pagans."[8] This is untrue. Consider a couple of ancient curses—curses that were standard fare in the "prayer books" of the ancient Near East.[9]

1. *The (Babylonian) Curse of Akkad* (or *Agade*). This curse reflects the injustices of an earlier war, in which the supreme god Enlil's temple-city of Nippur was devastated around 2400 BC:

> Enlil, may the city that destroyed your city, be done to as
>   your city.
> May the cattle slaughterer slaughter his wife,
> May your sheep butcher butcher his child,
> May your pauper drown the child who seeks money for
>   him!
> May your prostitute hang herself at the entrance of her
>   brothel,
> May your cult prostitutes and hierodules [slaves serv-
>   ing a deity in the temple], who are mothers, kill their
>   children!

2. *An Assyrian* text—a vassal treaty (from 672 BC):[10]

> May he [Ashur, king of the gods] never grant you father-
>   hood and attainment of old age.
> [May Sin], the brightness of heaven and earth, clothe you
>   with [a lep]rosy;
> [may he forbid your entering into the presence of the gods
>   or king (saying):
> "Roam the desert] like the wild-ass (and) the gazelle."
> [May Shamash, the light of the heavens and] earth [not
>   judge] you justly (saying):
> "May it be dark in your eyes, walk in darkness."
> [May Ninurta, chief of the gods,] fell you with his swift
>   arrow;
> [may he fill] the plain [with your corpses;]
> may he feed your flesh to the eagle (and) jackal.
> [May Venus, the brightest of the stars,]
> make your wives lie [in the lap of your enemy before your
>   eyes];

>   may your sons [not possess your house];
>   may a foreign enemy divide your goods.

Such harsh prayers weren't so startling in their ancient Near Eastern setting. They were quite common. While I am not justifying such prayers in all their stark harshness, I am saying that it is helpful to keep the use of them in perspective.[11] (Just consider how much calmer and more sedate Western funerals are compared to Middle Eastern ones. In the latter, one will witness loud wailing, women beating their breasts, and other expressions of anguish, which Westerners might consider excessive.)

Third, every biblical author's expression of moral outrage shouldn't be taken as a concrete desire; we are given the psalmist's emotional reaction, not his further reflections after cooling down. Think of the prophet Jeremiah. He had the thankless task of pleading with and warning God's hard-hearted and hard-headed people. In one instance, Pashhur the priest—a spiritual leader of the people!—had Jeremiah beaten and then placed in stocks (Jer. 20:1–2). In his distress, Jeremiah cursed the day he was born. He even cursed the messenger who announced his birth to his father. He wished he could have remained in his mother's womb until he died (Jer. 20:14–18). It's hard to imagine Jeremiah *literally* meaning these things. So what was going on? His soul was screaming out in anguish. He had been called by God to declare what God had told him, but he was rejected, opposed, and humiliated. So he expressed to God and to others the depths of his feelings. Now, he was not literally cursing the well-intended messenger. He wasn't literally wishing that his mother had been pregnant with him forever. He was expressing the depths of his anguish, and he wanted us to feel the emotion of it.[12]

We could also remember Job's situation: he experienced the loss of his children, a strained relationship with his wife ("My breath is offensive to my wife," 19:17; cf. 2:9–10), and the critical, cold, and cruel pat answers from his friends. Job cursed the day of his birth and often lashed out in his great dismay. Even Job needed to repent later on for his rash words and demanding spirit, though his friends were very clearly in the wrong (42:6–9).

In Psalm 137 the psalmist isn't talking dispassionately about what his cruel tormenters deserve ("the degree of suffering they've imposed is what they ought to get"). *We aren't given the psalmist's thoughts in his cooler moments, but when his emotions are white-hot.*[13] As Old Testament scholar John Sailhamer points out, "Biblical poetry, like most poetry, employs graphic imagery to portray and express its ideas. . . . This imagery [in Ps. 137:8–9] is no more intended to be taken literally than elsewhere in the psalms where the psalmists speak of rivers clapping their hands and mountains singing for joy."[14]

Fourth, these psalmists remind us to name or point out the evils we witness and to call the perpetrators to account, which is the first step toward making matters right and to finding healing. Those who have been sexually abused as children or who have been hurt by their spouses committing adultery often recognize that healing comes after they have sat down and articulated the pain they have felt. After horrific genocide in Rwanda or deep racial division in South Africa, it has been important for victims to name the evils done to them and to hold their persecutors to account. Through this process, some degree of healing has come. We can't love our enemies unless we are clear on who they are and what they have done to us.

Eugene Peterson reminds us that despite their good intentions, those who want to remove imprecatory psalms from Christian use are misguided:

> They are wrongheaded because our hate needs to be prayed, not suppressed. Hate is our emotional link with the spirituality of evil. It is the volcanic eruption of outrage when the holiness of being, ours or another's, has been violated. It is also the ugliest and most dangerous of our emotions, the hair trigger on a loaded gun. Embarrassed by the ugliness and fearful of the murderous, we commonly neither admit [nor] pray our hate; we deny it and suppress it. But if it is not admitted it can quickly and easily metamorphose into the evil that provokes it; and if it is not prayed we have lost an essential insight and energy in doing battle with evil.
>
> Dishonesty in prayer is already rampant enough without an assist from bleeding heart editors.[15]

Rather than trying to paper over the wrongs done, when we express our hate and anger, we are actually indicating that we care. So in a very real sense, hate and love may be less opposed to each other than indifference or apathy and love.

Fifth, the psalmists often reflect a personal concern for their enemies even when they call for God to deal harshly with them. One poet prayed: "Fill their faces with dishonor that they may seek Your name, O LORD" (Ps. 83:16). Remember that David treated Saul, Absalom, and others graciously even when he was being personally and physically attacked (2 Sam. 16:11; 19:12–13)—this psalmist who often wrote imprecatory psalms! David was outraged when someone claimed to have killed his enemy Saul (2 Sam. 1:1–16). Despite David's flaws, he showed amazing restraint and magnanimity when he could have retaliated, and he expressed moral indignation at the cruel acts of others—even when these acts could personally benefit him.[16]

In Psalm 35 the psalmist both (1) asks God to contend with those who contend with him (v. 1) and (2) reflects on how he shows kindness to his own enemies who "repay me evil for good." He had mourned, fasted, and prayed for them when they were sick. He treated them as a "friend" or "brother" (vv. 12–14; see also Ps. 109:4–5). These are the sorts of actions overlooked by Scripture's critics.

Sixth, the psalmists believe that their cause is also God's cause. Those who oppose God's purposes for Israel and for Israel's king and simply oppose what is good therefore oppose God. Hence, their indignation was not merely personal. God's plan to work through the call of Abraham and to establish a nation through which the Messiah would come (Gen. 12:1–3) implies that those who would attempt to thwart God's good purposes would set themselves up for judgment. Likewise, the psalmist is simply calling on God to take action for the sake of his own reputation.

In Psalm 139, David is angered by those who oppose God; so he sets himself up in opposition to them as well: "Do I not hate those who hate You, O LORD? And do I not loathe those who rise up against You? I hate them with the utmost hatred; they have become my enemies" (vv. 21–22). In the very next verses (vv. 23–24), David even declares, "Search me, O God, and know my heart; try me and know my anxious thoughts; and see if there be any hurtful way in me, and lead me in the everlasting way"!

127

Before we come down too hard on the imprecatory psalmists, we should first understand that they are concerned about God's reputation and purposes.

Seventh, the psalmists respond to God's own promises and predictions with respect to evil rather than out of personal hurt. The psalmists are calling on God to do what he himself has promised to do in the face of evil. It's fitting that God bring justice (Ps. 58:9–10). God is the judge of all; he will repay everyone according to what he has done; he doesn't ignore wickedness. For the psalmists, personal vengeance isn't the point. They're reacting to injustice, evil, and horror in the world. Even if they speak with uncomfortable harshness, we can be grateful that they are deeply stirred and outraged by human wickedness. We too should be morally outraged at rape, murder, or genocide; we should be concerned that justice be brought to the perpetrators, because they have violated the holy standards of God—even if we also hope for their repentance and salvation.

Eighth, the psalmists aren't self-righteous. They recognize that God's people aren't above God's righteous judgment if they rebel against him. To balance out the previous point, we should note that God isn't operating according to some double standard. In Psalm 89, God has "cast off and rejected" and is "full of wrath" against his "anointed" (v. 38). God's anointed king and people are themselves often the objects of God's wrath because they have opposed God's purposes.[17] God isn't playing favorites. He is doing to Israel exactly what he promised to do to the corrupt nations surrounding Israel: "As I plan to do to them, so I will do to you" (Num. 33:56).

Ninth, such biblical curses assume that if those under the threat of judgment repent and turn to the living God, the danger will be removed. Judgment or vengeance is secondary; God's mercy is primary. He is willing to relent if people turn to him. Think of Jonah, who didn't want to go to Israel's enemies in Nineveh. When God didn't send the threatened judgment (Jonah 3:10), Jonah was upset. Why? Because, as he told God, "I knew that You are a gracious and compassionate God, slow to anger and abundant in lovingkindness, and one who relents concerning calamity" (4:2; cf. Exod. 34:6). He just didn't want Israel's enemies to receive mercy. He had very strong reason to suspect God would show compassion.

God says the same thing to Jeremiah regarding *any* nation that turns in repentance to God: "At one moment I might speak concerning a nation or concerning a kingdom to uproot, to pull down, or to destroy it; if that nation against which I have spoken turns from its evil, I will relent concerning the calamity I planned to bring on it" (Jer. 18:7–8).

Then there is the evil king Manasseh, "who misled Judah and the inhabitants of Jerusalem to do more evil than the nations whom the LORD destroyed before the sons of Israel" (2 Chron. 33:9). When he was taken into exile by the Assyrians, he cried out to Yahweh, who had compassion on him: "When [Manasseh] was in distress, he entreated the LORD his God and humbled himself greatly before the God of his fathers. When he prayed to Him, He was moved by his entreaty and heard his supplication, and brought him again to Jerusalem to his kingdom. Then Manasseh knew that the LORD was God" (2 Chron. 33:12–13).

Tenth, we shouldn't forget the spirit of the Old Testament, which the New Testament emphasizes and builds upon. In the Sermon on the Mount (Matthew 5–7), Jesus tells his disciples to love their enemies and pray for their persecutors, to return good for evil. Paul picks up on this theme in Romans 12:17–20: "Never pay back evil for evil to anyone. Respect what is right in the sight of all men. If possible, so far as it depends on you, be at peace with all men. Never take your own revenge, beloved, but leave room for the wrath of God, for it is written, 'Vengeance is Mine, I will repay,' says the Lord. 'But if your enemy is hungry, feed him, and if he is thirsty, give him a drink; for in so doing you will heap burning coals on his head.' Do not be overcome by evil, but overcome evil with good."

Isn't this a radically new and improved ethic? Actually, it is taken from the Old Testament itself! In this passage, Paul is quoting Proverbs 25:21–22, which exhorts us to treat our enemies kindly. Again in Proverbs we're told not to rejoice when our enemy stumbles and falls (24:17). The Mosaic Law instructs Israelites (in Lev. 19:17–18) not to "hate your fellow countryman in your heart," not to "take vengeance, nor bear any grudge against the sons of your people, but you shall love your neighbor as yourself; I am the LORD." God commanded his people to return an *enemy's* ox or donkey if it should wander away—or to give assistance if his donkey is lying helpless under a heavy burden (Exod. 23:4–5).

Jesus further commands his followers to move beyond impreca-tion to desire the salvation of their enemies. In light of Christ's death and resurrection, we have a heightened new covenant emphasis on forgiveness, on blessing rather than cursing one's enemies. Jesus offers a better way than judgment and curse. He emphasizes bless-ing over cursing (Matt. 5:43–48), as do Peter (1 Peter 2:23; 3:9) and Paul (Rom. 12:14–21)—and we shouldn't forget that these bless-and-not-curse ideas are found in the Old Testament.

In the Sermon on the Mount, Jesus points to the very character of God, who *loves his enemies* by sending rain and sunshine on the just and the unjust. Disciples of Jesus aren't to be like the average sinner, who greets those who greet him and loves those who love him. They are to be like their Father, who loves completely. He lavishes love not only on the just, but on the unjust—a complete or perfect love. No wonder Jesus closes with this exhortation to be perfect or complete in our love/mercy, just as the Father is complete in his love/mercy (5:48). Yes, this love that prays for en-emies and does good to them is more difficult, but it reflects the very character of God. After all, God is constantly showing love to those who don't love him. Jesus let the rich man walk away from him because he loved his money more than he loved Jesus, but he "felt a love for him" (Mark 10:21). God loves the judgment-worthy world so much that he sent his Son to save it rather than condemn it (John 3:16–17).

Eleventh, the New Testament—not only the Old—also stresses the vengeance of God, and the severity of judgment is intensified because of the gracious gift of God in Christ. Jesus himself pro-nounced ultimate judgment on those who refuse to do God's will and who fail to show compassion to his followers, "the least of these My brothers" (e.g., Matt. 7:21–23; 25:40). Paul, who talked about loving enemies and praying for persecutors, wished that those who brought false teachings about circumcision would just go the whole way and emasculate themselves (Gal. 5:12). Paul wrote to Timothy: "Alexander the coppersmith did me much harm; the Lord will repay him according to his deeds" (2 Tim. 4:14). In Revelation 6:10, martyred saints cry out for justice from God, that he might avenge their shed blood: "they cried out with a loud voice, saying, 'How long, O Lord, holy and true, will You refrain from judging and avenging our blood on those who dwell on the earth?'"

In addition, when Christ returns, he will bring fierce and swift judgment. Revelation 19 uses military imagery to portray this event. Christ, seated on a white horse, is "clothed with a robe dipped in blood." He "judges and wages war." He will "strike down the nations"—those who oppose Christ and his people. He "treads the wine press of the fierce wrath of God, the Almighty." The judgment is complete, justice is done, and all rebellion—human and demonic—is put down (vv. 11–21).

Furthermore, Hebrews (2:2–3; 10:26–31; 12:25–29) and other New Testament passages (e.g., Matt. 11:21; Luke 10:13) make the following point: in light of the coming of Christ, to reject the good news of the gospel is to incur God's far more severe judgment. If God's judgment came on national Israel for being faithless to the covenant he made with them, how much more severe will the judgment be if we turn away from God's own Word, who took on human form and died a slave's cursed death to rescue us from our exile from God?

Twelfth, although we see glimmers of light in the Old Testament that direct us toward Jesus' emphasis on forgiving our persecutors, the New Testament makes clear that blessing instead of cursing, prayer instead of imprecation, is to characterize the believer's response to personal enemies. The psalmists' imprecations don't reflect literal wishes to bash infants' heads against the rocks, but there seems to be a movement in Scripture toward a clearer and cross-centered ethic rooted in what God has done for us in Christ. These prayers of the oppressed have justice at their heart—even if they are expressed less than perfectly. Perhaps an analogy would help: Slavery is permitted in the Scriptures due to human hardness of heart, but there are plenty of indicators in Scripture—from the image of God (Gen. 1:26–28) to our redemption in Christ, in whom there is neither slave nor free (Gal. 3:28)—that slavery isn't the last word. Similarly, there are plenty of hints in the Scriptures—including the Old Testament itself—that reinforce the point that Christians shouldn't literally pray for the skulls of their enemies' babies to be bashed in. We should desire our enemies' salvation. We should do good to them and pray for them. But we should also be people—like the martyrs in Revelation 6—who pray for God's righteous rule to be established, which will mean judgment on those who refuse to repent.

Although believers should desire the salvation of sinners, they must also desire their punishment if unbelievers refuse to repent. In fact, we should ask that God bring judgment to us if we bring shame to Christ's name, causing his name to be blasphemed by unbelievers (Rom. 2:24). We should not pray for God's justice to be done in a self-righteous manner, but pray that God would deliver *us* from ourselves so that we don't hinder his purposes. As John Stott wisely writes, "We cannot desire [sinners'] salvation in defiance of their own unwillingness to receive it. This is the heart of the matter."[18] Stott adds, "We should earnestly desire the salvation of sinners if they would repent and equally, earnestly desire their (and our) destruction if they (or we) will not."[19]

So our desire to see our enemies become part of God's family and be transformed by God's power *can be fulfilled only if they willingly receive God's grace.* Stephen's prayer while he was being stoned to death by his enemies was, "Lord, do not hold this sin against them!" (Acts 7:60). However, if his opponents didn't repent, then God would hold this sin against them.[20] Thankfully, at least one of Stephen's enemies who participated in this event (7:58; 8:1) later found salvation in Christ—the apostle Paul! So Stephen's prayer was marvelously answered in this particular instance.

Thirteenth, even though Christians shouldn't pray the imprecatory psalms in a literalistic sense, they can still benefit from them. Can we pray the imprecatory psalms today? Again, we certainly shouldn't literally wish that babies' brains be smashed—or that our enemy's children become fatherless and his wife a widow (Ps. 109:9). But neither should we excise such psalms from our psalter hymnals and prayer books, for, in addition to this being part of Old Testament Israel's—and thus our—story, there are some enduring aspects to these prayers from which we can benefit.[21] William Webb suggests that we can learn the following from the imprecatory psalms: how to be honest in prayer, how to express our genuine feelings to God, how to appeal for action on behalf of the powerless, how to cry passionately for justice in a painful world, and how to pray for salvation and blessing for our enemies. A prayer might look like this: "O Lord, "I certainly *feel* like the psalmist. . . . Bring *justice* to our world. . . . However, bring justice *your* way as *you* see fit. . . . Despite what these people have done and what I feel toward them, I pray for their *salvation* and *blessing.*"[22]

Fourteenth, the Christian can apply the imprecatory psalms not just to unbelieving human enemies, but to evil spiritual powers at work in the world as well. The church (the new and true Israel), unlike Old Testament (national) Israel, is non-nationalistic by design. Israel's enemies were often other nations (and the idolatry that went with them), and there was a deeply religious backdrop to the Israelites' devotion to their land, the city of Jerusalem, and the temple. They were God's chosen people in the land he had given them. So the psalmist is convinced that the wrong that has been done against God's purposes through Israel is ultimately against God. Therefore, when the exiled psalmist prays curses upon Babylon (and Edom), he is speaking from this profoundly religious framework.[23]

As we move from the Old Testament to the New, from Israel to the church (the new Israel in Christ), from a nation to an inter-ethnic fellowship, the "battle lines" shift. Previously God had helped Israel fight their battles against other nations (a topic I address elsewhere).[24] But God eventually made war on Israel for their abandoning the covenant God made with them. Nevertheless, he then promised a hero or warrior who would wage war against the enemies of God's people (e.g., Zech. 14:3).

When God incarnate came into the world, he fought not against Rome, but against the ultimate enemy of God's people, Satan. Jesus' ministry of casting out demons (Matt. 12:22–29) and his work on the cross reveal that Satan and his forces are doomed (John 12:31; 16:11—the ruler of the world is cast down). These evil powers can't last. Their time is limited (Col. 2:14–15).[25] The cross prepared the way for the final defeat of Satan and the forces of evil.

As Christians, we aren't ultimately fighting against fellow human beings, but against demonic powers determined to undermine God's kingdom purposes (Eph. 6:12). Unlike the national Israel, who fought against Gentiles opposed to God's purposes, Christians are not called to fight against non-Christians. We are to pray against Satan and his forces so that the gospel may spread and be boldly proclaimed (2 Cor. 10:4; Eph. 6:19; 1 Peter 5:8-9). As people respond to the gospel, they are set free from bondage to Satan.[26] We are to live godly lives, as lights in this world; in doing so, we help to set back the work of Satan as we colabor with God to advance his kingdom.

So, with certain qualifications, these psalmists were expressing what we ought to express—for God's just reign to be established, for all things to be made right: "Your kingdom come. Your will be done on earth as it is in heaven" (Matt. 6:10).

Summary

- The psalmists' outrage honestly expresses their anger at injustice and oppression. We shouldn't be too harsh on those who cry out to God in deep distress and anguish.
- We should understand the ancient Near Eastern context as we read these psalms rather than impose modern Western standards on them.
- Not every biblical author's expression of moral outrage should be taken literally—as a concrete desire; we should allow the psalmist to express his emotional reaction, which isn't the same as further reflections after having cooled down.
- These psalmists remind us to name the evils we witness and call perpetrators to account. This turns out to be the first step in making matters right and finding healing.
- Imprecatory psalmists often show deep personal concern for their enemies—even though they are calling on God to deal harshly with them.
- The Israelite psalmists believe that their cause (when righteous) is God's as well. Thus, those opposing God's saving purposes for Israel, Israel's king, and ultimately for the world are opposing what is good—indeed, God himself.
- The psalmists aren't responding to personal hurt; they are taking into account God's own promises and predictions with respect to evil.
- These psalmists don't react self-righteously. They're profoundly aware that God's people aren't above God's righteous judgment if they turn against him.
- Such biblical curses allow for repentance: if those threatened with judgment change their ways and/or turn to God, the danger will be removed. God's mercy is primary and judgment secondary. God relents when people turn to him.

- The New Testament, rather than being at odds with the Old Testament, emphasizes it and builds upon it.
- It's not just the Old Testament but the New as well that stresses God's vengeance. In fact, God's revelation in Christ increases the severity of judgment if people reject God's gracious gift of salvation.
- The Old Testament gives us many hints that point us to Christ's stress on forgiving persecutors. The New Testament, however, emphasizes that blessing instead of cursing and prayer instead of imprecation are to characterize the believer's response to personal enemies.
- While Christians shouldn't literally pray the imprecatory psalms (and it's doubtful that the psalmists would express such harshness in their cooler, more reflective moments), we can still benefit from them.
- Christians can apply such psalms not only to unbelievers or human enemies, but to evil spiritual powers at work in the world.

Further Reading

Kaiser, Walter C. *Toward Old Testament Ethics*. Grand Rapids: Zondervan, 1983. See pp. 292–97.

Kidner, Derek. *Psalms 1–72*. Downers Grove, IL: InterVarsity, 1973. See pp. 25–31.

Longman, Tremper, III. *Making Sense of the Old Testament: Three Crucial Questions*. Grand Rapids: Baker, 1998.

Peterson, Eugene H. *Answering God: The Psalms as Tools for Prayer*. San Francisco: HarperOne, 1989. Chapter 8.

Webb, William J. "Bashing Babies against the Rocks: A Redemptive-Movement Approach to the Imprecatory Psalms." Paper presented at the Evangelical Theological Society (November 2003), Atlanta.

12

Aren't the Bible's "Holy Wars" Just Like Islamic Jihad?

Part One

In his book *The Science of Good and Evil*, agnostic Michael Shermer refers to Israeli psychologist Georges Tamarin's 1966 study involving 1,066 schoolchildren ages eight to fourteen. These children were presented the story of the destruction of Jericho in Joshua 6 and then were asked, "Do you think Joshua and the Israelites acted rightly or not?" Two-thirds of the children approved. However, when Tamarin substituted "General Lin" for Joshua and a "Chinese kingdom 3,000 years ago" for Israel, only 7 percent approved while 75 percent disapproved. Apparently, approval ratings depend on who is the in-group or the out-group![1]

Is this a fair comparison? A lot hangs on whether God really commanded Israel to carry out such a task. One massive difference, however, is that Israel's history—unlike any other nation's—involves God's choosing theocratic Israel and using that country in an utterly unique way. The same is true when we compare Israel's emergence with that of Islam's. As Paul notes in Galatians 4, God was at work through the promised child Isaac in a unique manner. Ishmael, the father of the Arab people, was not the child of promise, as Muslims traditionally maintain. For my purposes, I won't offer reasons here for questioning the truth of Islam.[2] I'll take for granted that (a) God was genuinely working through national Israel, and (b) this fact places Old Testament Israel in a unique position—unlike any other nation or religion, such as Islam.

So what about Yahweh's command to Israel to kill the Canaanites? Is this scenario identical to what militant Islamic jihadists, from the time of Muhammad up to today, have been pursuing? I'll argue that God's commands for Israel to kill the Canaanites have a specific context and thus require nuancing.

In the next chapters, I'll address the question, "Is God's command to kill the Canaanites morally equivalent to Islamic jihad?" Before doing so, I'll look at "the Canaanite problem" briefly. Here I summarize—and add to—some material in *"That's Just Your Interpretation."*[3]

First, people who object to the command to kill Canaanites must first ask about the source of their moral standard; typically, this turns out to be the God of Scripture. As I've written elsewhere, the existence of genuine human rights and objective moral standards makes best sense if a good, personal God exists (as opposed to naturalism or nontheistic religions).[4] Without a good God, it is hard to see how valueless, unguided material processes could produce valuable, rights-bearing, morally obligated human beings. Historian Alvin Schmidt and others have documented how the biblical faith clearly shaped moral progress and the development of human rights in the West.[5] People who criticize Yahweh for such severe commands need to remember that it is God's character that is the ultimate moral standard—and that this standard, through Christianity's influence, has strongly shaped much of our moral understanding in the West. Ironically, this moral foundation is being criticized. As we'll see below, the Muslim understanding of God, who is *pure (arbitrary) will*, is far different from the God of Scripture, whose *nature* is good and serves as the moral context for his commands.

So, it's not just any military commander (e.g., "General Lin") who may be justified (or not) in killing a group of people; if God truly commands the killing of, say, the Canaanites, this command stems from his moral character and his sufficient moral purposes; such a judgment is justifiably executed. *Without* the backdrop of God's explicit commands and broader redemptive purposes, taking the lives of such people would *not* be justified. Also, unlike the "General Lin" case, the people who are to be killed aren't just any given population. The mission is aimed at those who are corrupted beyond moral repair.

Second, God's purposes are ultimately to bring salvation to all the nations through Abraham and his offspring (Gen. 12:3)—even if this involves punishment in the meantime. God's plan involved bringing just punishment on a morally perverse society so that his people would bring forth an appointed Messiah; to help accomplish this, God desired to protect his people from pagan religious influences. Christ would come to deliver Israel—and all humanity—from exile and alienation from God. As the true Son of God (that national Israel wasn't) and as the second Adam (in light of the first Adam's failure), Christ would bring about a new covenant people (through a new exodus) and a new humanity (through a new creation). God's saving purposes are global, but his plan to get to this point involves bringing punishment on a corrupt culture.

Third, war was a practical reality in the ancient Near East. Like all other nations back then, Israel had to fight to survive. Israel's world was one in which "peoples [took] away land from each other by force."[6] To keep their national identity, Israel would need to be prepared to do battle. Otherwise, they would not last.

Fourth, God, who is the author and giver of life, is cheating no one by taking his life up again. The suffering Job summarizes this nicely: "The Lord gave and the Lord has taken away. Blessed be the name of the Lord" (Job 1:21). It is God's prerogative to take the life he has given. He doesn't owe anyone seventy or eighty years of life. If God is punishing those who are corrupt and too far gone morally, God is not unjust in doing so.

Critics often assume that if God exists, he should have a status no higher than any human being. Thus, he has no right to give or take life as he determines. Yet we should press home the monumental difference between God and ordinary human beings: the Author of life shouldn't be held to standards of what is expected of humans, who don't have authority over human life.

What about infants and children? They would actually go to heaven and be delivered from this morally twisted culture. Adults are justly punished, and the young are ushered into God's presence and rescued from their culture's corruption. Sometimes it may be merciful for all concerned for God to simply wipe the cultural/moral slate clean and begin anew, despite the "collateral damage." Furthermore, those morally innocent who were killed would, in God's presence, agree that God's judgment was good and the final outcome outweighs anything they experienced on earth—even if it meant enduring moments of terror at the hands of Israelite soldiers. Notice, for instance, how Paul endures extreme hardships in 2 Cor. 11:22-28 while acknowledging earlier in 2 Cor. 4:17 that this is trivial—"momentary light affliction"—in comparison to the future weight of glory that surpasses all earthly hardships.

Fifth, in many cases, Israel's enemies struck first, not Israel. Many of Israel's battles were initiated by their opponents (see, e.g., Exod. 17:8; Num. 21:1, 21–32; Deut. 2:26-3:8; Josh 10:4; cf. Deut. 25:17–19; 1 Sam. 15:1–6). Other battles were a response to foreign attempts to deliberately lead Israel into immorality and idolatry (e.g., Num 25; 31:2–3, 16). Israel had to engage in ongoing battles with the aggressive, ravaging Amalekites (Exod. 17:8–16; Judg. 6:3, 33; 1 Sam. 15; 27:8; 30:1–18); this ongoing opposition of the Amalekites required fending them off generation after generation. Offensive battles clearly initiated by God were in fact quite limited. At other times, we're not told whether God endorsed a certain battle or not. In fact, Israel was to *avoid* engaging foreign armies altogether—such as Israel's avoiding battle with belligerent Edom (Num. 20:14–21) or King Josiah's going against Egypt (2 Chron. 35:20–24).

Sixth, because God is holy, there comes a time—whether in this life or in the life to come or in both—when God must deal with unrepentant, wicked persons for the sake of his righteous character. Yahweh wasn't wrong to bring judgment on corrupt Canaanite culture, and he was willing to receive any who would turn to him (as Rahab did). We must consider how he sought to accomplish his ultimate purpose of blessing *all* the nations (Gen. 12:3) through Jesus the Messiah (Gal. 3:8).

Moreover, we can easily misjudge what "fairness" should look like. Christopher Wright notes, "We are not so inclined to respond with 'That's not fair' when we enjoy gifts and blessings that others do not." Furthermore, we may protest when others have blessings we ourselves don't experience (cf. the parable of the vineyard workers in Matthew 20). Wright urges caution in assessing what is fair or unfair for God to do, as we can easily take on a skewed perspective.[7]

Seventh, Yahweh directly punished the morally corrupt cities of Sodom and Gomorrah (Genesis 19), but he indirectly punished the morally corrupt Canaanites by using Israel. While some may recoil at Israel's admittedly ghastly work, we must remember that God himself *directly* did the same sort of thing to Sodom, where he couldn't even find ten righteous people to save (Gen. 18:32). And God *directly* punished those whom Noah warned for 120 years but who still refused to listen (Genesis 6–7). In the case of the Canaanites, Israel was God's instrument to bring just punishment and to remove a dangerous theological and moral cancer from this region—after patiently waiting 430 years until the sins of the Canaanites had reached full measure (Gen. 15:16).

Perhaps the important question is this: wouldn't Israel's soldiers become morally damaged by killing women and children? Remember that in the ancient Near East, warfare was a way of life for survival; so perhaps we moderns are more sensitized to such concerns than the ancient world was. This aside, we shouldn't forget that *a good God gave a command to wipe out a morally corrupt culture, and this mission was not routine warfare; it was engagement in God's work.*

Eighth, besides these primary considerations, there was also a conventional warfare rhetoric common in the ancient Near East that is also used in the book of Joshua; the biblical text indicates that the conquest of Canaan was far less widespread and harsh than many people assume. Notice the sweeping language in Joshua 10:40: "Thus Joshua struck all the land, the hill country and the Negev and the lowland and the slopes and all their kings. He left no survivor, but he utterly destroyed all who breathed, just as the LORD, the God of Israel, had commanded." Joshua used rhetorical language, asserting that *all* the land was captured, *all* the kings defeated, and *all* the Canaanites destroyed (cf. 10:40–42; 11:16–20).

We know from Judges, however, which is literarily linked to Joshua,[8] that the task of "taking over" was far from complete. In

Judges 2:3, God says, "I will not drive them out before you"; earlier on, Judges 1:21–36 asserts that "[they] did not drive out the Jebusites"; "[they] did not take possession"; "they did not drive them out completely"; and so on. So isn't Joshua a bit misleading? We should be careful here: I am not saying that Joshua "gets it wrong" or intends to deceive. As Old Testament scholar Christopher Wright argues, this kind of language simply recognizes "the literary conventions of writing about warfare."[9]

Similarly, another Old Testament scholar, Gordon Wenham, comments on a presumed tension in Deuteronomy 7:2–5. While Yahweh tells Israel that they should show no mercy and "utterly destroy" the Canaanites, he immediately goes on to say: "Furthermore, you shall not intermarry with them; you shall not give your daughters to their sons, nor shall you take their daughters for your sons. For they will turn your sons away from following Me to serve other gods; then the anger of the LORD will be kindled against you and He will quickly destroy you. But thus you shall do to them: you shall tear down their altars, and smash their sacred pillars, and hew down their Asherim, and burn their graven images with fire." *So, if the Canaanites were to be completely obliterated, why is there any discussion about intermarriage or treaties?* The final verse commanding destruction of altars, images, and sacred pillars brings us to the important point of the passage: "It is evident that destruction of Canaanite religion is much more important than destroying the people."[10]

Ninth, the "military motif" may not be the only one to consider in Israel's taking Canaan; other factors may need to be considered. As biblical scholars look at Israel's relationship to the Promised Land and its inhabitants, many of them note a bigger picture than just a military campaign. They see the "conquest" as involving a combination of factors. We're familiar with *military onslaught.* But there is also some type of *infiltration* (e.g., Judg. 1:1–2:5). In addition, there is *internal struggle*: Israel goes through a not-always-successful process of overcoming idolatry and distinguishing itself from its pagan inhabitants. Scripture's realistic acknowledgment that the Canaanites continued to live in the land suggests that something more than a military campaign is taking place.[11]

Summary

- We should consider why killing of Canaanites is even an issue for critics. Presumably they are utilizing a moral standard, but their appeal to human rights and to moral obligations actually points us back to the God of the Bible, whose "compassionate and gracious" character is the source of all goodness. This is quite a contrast to the Qur'an, which portrays God as a pure arbitrary will that is not motivated by moral character.
- God's purposes are ultimately to bring salvation to all the nations through Abraham's offspring (Gen. 12:3), even if this may mean bringing just punishment to a morally depraved culture to pave the way for Messiah's world-saving mission.
- It's not just any military commander (e.g., "General Lin") who may be justified in killing certain persons; the command must come from the good God of Scripture, who has morally sufficient reasons for commanding this.
- It's not just any group of men, women, and children who are to be killed (cf. also the "General Lin" example), but those who are corrupted beyond moral repair.
- Israel had to fight for their very identity and survival in the ancient Near East; this was just a fact of life.
- God is the giver of life and can legitimately take it back again. Adults who are killed are justly punished, and infants and children are delivered from a corrupt religion and culture, and are ushered into God's presence. The morally innocent who are killed would come to agree in the next life that God was just and that the terror they experienced was trivial in comparison to God's glorious presence (cf. 2 Cor. 11:22–28 with 4:17).
- In Israel's early history, their enemies were often the aggressors.
- In the ancient Near East, overdramatized warfare rhetoric was common, which is what the book of Joshua uses.
- Israel's conquest wasn't as dramatic as the biblical texts themselves indicate. (For example, why were there prohibitions against intermarriage and treaties with the Canaanites they "completely" wiped out?)

- While the "military motif" is one factor in Israel's taking the land, other factors such as infiltration and internal struggle may be figured in as well.
- God's holiness requires that he must deal with the stubbornly unrepentant—whether in this life or in the life to come—or both.
- We may be skewed in our perspectives of fairness. We don't typically say, "That's not fair," when we're enjoying God's blessings, yet we protest when we don't have the blessings others have.
- Yahweh *directly* punished Sodom and Gomorrah (Genesis 19—not even ten righteous were there), but he used Israel to punish the morally corrupt Canaanites.
- God has the right to give and take life—and to show compassion.

Further Reading

Copan, Paul. *"That's Just Your Interpretation": Responding to Skeptics Who Challenge Your Faith*. Grand Rapids: Baker, 2001. Chapter 18.

Goldingay, John. *Old Testament Theology: Israel's Gospel*. Vol. 1. Downers Grove, IL: InterVarsity, 2003. Chapter 7.

———. *Theological Diversity and the Authority of the Old Testament*. Grand Rapids: Eerdmans, 1987.

Kaiser, Walter. *Toward Old Testament Ethics*. Grand Rapids: Zondervan, 1983. Chapter 11.

Wright, Christopher J. H. "Appendix: "What about the Canaanites?" in *Old Testament Ethics for the People of God*. Downers Grove, IL: InterVarsity, 2004.

13

Aren't the Bible's "Holy Wars" Just Like Islamic Jihad?

Part Two

Given the previous chapter's summary, let's try briefly to put some points into perspective in light of militant Islam and the post–September 11 world in which we live. I want to affirm that I have known many gracious, kind, and hospitable Muslims, in whose homes I have eaten and with whom I have attended mosques (as an observer). Indeed, I have come to know and love many dear Muslims. Further, I don't want to minimize in any way the remarkable achievements Muslims have historically made—in architecture, philosophy, music, literature, mathematics, and science. Nor do I want to diminish the tolerance Muslims have shown to non-Muslims. Our discussion, however, is focused on jihad, and I want to respond to the question about whether the killing of the Canaanites and Islamic jihad are virtually equivalent.[1] Before we make comparisons, some introductory comments are in order.

1. *We should observe the history of the word* jihad *itself.* The Arabic word *jihad* can have an "internal" sense of spiritual *struggling* or *exerting* oneself for Allah.[2] This could include intellectual or emotional aspects (sometimes called "greater jihad")—for example, believers who "strive with their wealth and themselves," as the Qur'an indicates (sura 8:72). However, jihad (especially in the late eighth century and beyond) has traditionally had militaristic connotations; this is called "holy war"—or "lesser jihad").[3] Today Muslim apologists to non-Muslim Western audiences typically downplay the militaristic dimension of jihad. Yet when Muslim scholars write to non-Western audiences, they tend not to refer to jihad as spiritual struggle but as physical fighting.

From the outset, Islam has had a militaristic impulse involved in its spread. According to the *Encyclopedia of Islam*, we read, "In law, according to general doctrine and in historical tradition, the jihad consists of military action with the object of the expansion of Islam and, if need be, of its defense."[4] Indeed, there is little support in the Qur'an and Hadith (early Islamic traditions) for the notion of jihad as internal struggle, as David Cook has argued.[5] In fact, the term *jihad* itself is used in the Qur'an (e.g., 2:216), and within the Qur'an we frequently read of physical *fighting* (*qitāl*) and a strong militaristic impulse ("whoso fights in the cause of Allah," 4:74; "those who fight in the cause of Allah with their . . . lives," 4:95; "[f]ight against those who believe not in Allah," 9:29). This fighting includes *terror*: "We shall cast terror into the hearts of those who disbelieve" (3:151); "strike terror into the enemy" (98:60). Furthermore, the Qur'an highlights *martyrdom* through fighting: "Those who believed . . . and fought in Allah's cause . . . with their lives" receive "everlasting delights" (9:20–22; cf. 9:111; 57:19). The Qur'an promotes *dawah* (inviting others to accept Islam through persuasion or defense of Islam [16:125; 28:87]).

Furthermore, the Hadith (early Muslim tradition) also connects *dawah* to violence when the invitation is rejected: "[Muhammad] . . . invite[d] them to Islam for three days before he was to attack them. . . . If they declined, he was to fight them. . . . so they accepted Islam." Again, "When you meet polytheists, summon them to Islam. . . . if they accept, refrain from further hostilities. . . . If they refuse to pay the tax [the second alternative], seek Allah's help and fight them."[6] In another passage in the Hadith, a man in an iron mask asked Muhammad if he should fight or embrace Islam first. Muhammad replied, "Embrace Islam first and then fight." So he "embraced Islam and was martyred."[7]

2. *The history of Islam has generally reflected a militaristic, oppressive stance toward non-Muslims.* Jewish Egyptian scholar Bat Ye'or has thoroughly documented the history of "dhimmitude" (the condition of Christians, Jews, and other non-Muslims [*dhimmis*] under Islamic law) in Muslim-dominated areas.[8] She argues that, yes, Muslims in the past have shown tolerance to Jews and Christians in their midst (Muslim apologists emphasize this side). This condition involved tribute (*jizya*) being paid to the reigning Muslims who compelled allegiance through compulsory religious war—jihad. However, any such tolerance was always under threat of Muslim jihad if tribute wasn't paid. Indeed, she thoroughly documents the oppression and even "open extermination of Christian populations and the disappearance of Eastern Christian culture."[9] Generally (though there were exceptions), non-Muslims could not freely practice their religion. They could not repair synagogues or church buildings; nor could they observe their religion in public. Despite Islam's "protection" of "People of the Book," so many humiliations and conditions were attached to their "legal standing" that dhimmitude took on the status of "oppression, deprivation and insecurity."[10]

According to Ye'or, the "myth of Muslim toleration" didn't exist before the twentieth century: "It is largely a modern creation. The West's obfuscation [or masking] [of Islamic intolerance] was a result of the political and cultural difficulties of colonialism." She adds: "France had North Africa, Algeria, Morocco, Tunisia, Syria, and Lebanon after World War I. England had a huge Islamic population in India and also in Egypt and Sudan, Iraq and Palestine. They didn't want to confront this population. They didn't want to protect the Christian minorities in these lands because they wanted to have an economically beneficial pro-Arab, pro-Islamic policy."[11]

So after colonial rule, Christians (predominantly) in these areas were forced to try integrating into Muslim cultures. They had no protection from the colonial powers who, for political and economic (mostly oil-related) reasons, didn't want to upset these Muslim countries: "As a result, they developed a whole literature praising Islamic tolerance toward Jews and Christians."[12] Even though we read in the Qur'an, "Let there be no compulsion in religion" (2:256), compulsion was part of the Muslim mind-set from the beginning, reinforced by other passages from the Qur'an.

3. *The Crusades and jihad in Islam make for an illuminating comparison.* We do not have much space to devote to the matter of the Crusades (1095–1291). These were fought in the name of Christ but, tragically, were inconsistent with the spirit of Christ, whose kingdom is not of this world. Even so, it is still instructive to note the contrasts between the Crusades and the growth of Islam.[13]

The Crusades	Jihad in Islam
The Crusades lasted about 200 years.	Jihad has been ongoing for more than 1,300 years.
The Crusades have been criticized as the beginning of "imperialism."	Muhammad's "imperialistic" jihad expeditions began more than 500 years prior to the Crusades.
The Crusades began as effort to recapture from Muslims land once occupied by Christians.	Jihad began with intent to take land never occupied by Muslims, to establish the *umma* (Islamic community).
Jesus, in whose name the Crusades were fought, did not teach or exemplify violence against those who refused his message.	Muhammad not only preached violence against nonbelievers; he engaged in it himself.

In the somewhat lengthy quotation below, the leading Western scholar on Islam, Bernard Lewis, nicely summarizes the key differences between jihad and the Crusades. He observes that, while both were waged as holy wars against infidel enemies for the true religion, there's a difference:

The Crusade is a late development in Christian history and, in a sense, marks a radical departure from basic Christian values as expressed in the Gospels. Christendom had been under attack since the seventh century, and had lost vast territories to Muslim rule; the concept of holy war, more commonly a just war, was familiar since antiquity. Yet in the long struggle between Islam and Christendom, the Crusade was late, limited, and of relatively brief duration. Jihad is present from the beginning of Islamic history—in scripture, in the life of the Prophet, and in the actions of his companions and immediate successors. It has continued throughout Islamic history

147

and retains its appeal to the present day. The word crusade derives of course from the cross [Latin, crux] and originally denoted a holy war for Christianity. But in the Christian world it has long since lost that meaning. . . . Jihad too is used in a variety of senses, but unlike crusade it has retained its original, primary meaning.[14]

Summary

- The word *jihad* itself can refer to an internal, spiritual struggle ("greater jihad") or to physical fighting ("lesser jihad"). After the late eighth century, jihad was more closely connected to the latter.
- The Qur'an and the Hadith (early traditions about Muhammad) have a strong militaristic bent.
- The treatment of non-Muslims under Muslim rule tended to be harsh and oppressive—though there are exceptions.
- Though the Crusades were carried out in the name of Christ, they weren't conducted in the spirit of Christ. Even so, the Crusades were still different from the military campaigns of Muhammad.

Further Reading

Ye'or, Bat. *The Decline of Eastern Christianity under Islam: From Jihad to Dhimmitude.* Teaneck, NJ: Farleigh Dickinson University Press, 1997.

———. *The Dhimmi. Jews and Christians under Islam.* Teaneck, NJ: Farleigh Dickinson University Press, 1985.

———. *Islam and Dhimmitude: Where Civilizations Collide.* Teaneck, NJ: Farleigh Dickinson University Press, 2002.

14

Aren't the Bible's "Holy Wars" Just Like Islamic Jihad?

Part Three

Now to our main question: How do Islam's holy wars/jihads compare to the Old Testament's "Yahweh wars"? As we'll see, the differences are far more significant than the similarities.[1]

First, Yahweh's command regarding the Canaanites was limited to a fairly small, specific geographic location, so that God could establish a religious culture from which a Messiah and universal Savior would come; militant Islam doesn't recognize geographical limits. The land of Israel (from the Mediterranean Sea to the Jordan) is about the size of Vancouver Island or slightly larger than New Jersey. In comparison to taking a specific, fairly small piece of land (and justly punishing a wicked people), the military spread of Islam was vast in its scope. The late scholar of Islam, Sir Norman Anderson, has commented that from earliest times, Islam has divided the world into two realms: *dar al-Islam/salam* ("the abode of Islam/peace"), where Islam dominates, and *dar al-harb* ("the abode of war"), where the rule of Islam should be extended—by war, if necessary. Islam is a *dominant* creed. Traditionally, the Muslim attitude toward non-Muslim has been *ruler* versus *ruled*, *victor* versus *vanquished*. Indeed, ancient Islam never gave thought to a Muslim living under a non-Muslim government.[2] For Islam, "church and state" are one; the public and private are blended together.[3] Islam is a *totalizing* religion—all must come under *submission* to Allah (which is what *Islam* means).

So, given this "abode of Islam" and "abode of war" distinction, any territory beyond the sway of Islam was "fair game." The rule of Islam was not geographically limited, as we'll see. Sadly, the military reach of Islam was so extensive that it overran many regions deeply influenced by Christianity and Judaism—monotheistic faiths! In contrast to the vast expanse of Islam through military aggression, the land of Canaan was miniscule by comparison. And as we'll see, the conquest of Canaan begun under Joshua wasn't even completed.[4]

Second, God's command was limited to a fairly narrow window of time—roughly a single generation surrounding the time of Joshua; this is different from Islam's lengthy history of aggression. We've noted that Israel needed to fight for its very survival, and military struggle was part of life during this time. Warfare was part of Israel's way of life in order to preserve its identity. However, God's specific command to kill the Canaanites was primarily directed to the generation of Joshua and a brief time thereafter. Furthermore, it was specifically directed toward wicked inhabitants of the land who were deserving of such punishment. Most of the book of Judges depicts Israel regularly trying to break free from enemy oppression rather than engaging in incursions into enemy territory. This is different from the history of Islam, which took an aggressive militaristic posture across its history.

Third, wars commissioned by Yahweh (in which Yahweh himself fought for or with Israel) were viewed as just punishment on a hopelessly corrupted culture (which engaged in infant sacrifice, temple prostitution, and the like), and this could negatively influence Israel. God waited 430 years for the "iniquity of the Amorite" to run its course (Gen. 15:16). Only then and not before—when the time was ripe—would Israel become an instrument of punishment—when "detestable things" were imbedded in the culture (Deut. 20:18; cf.

18:10). God displayed remarkable patience and longsuffering. In effect, the Canaanites had forfeited their right to live in the land because of their profound wickedness (Deut. 9:5).[5] Let's not forget that the same would prove true for Israel for their disobedience. The land was not a right, but a gift, which could be forfeited: ". . . so that the land will not spew you out, should you defile it, as it has spewed out the nation which has been before you" (Lev. 18:28; cf. 20:22).

God's command to lethally punish the Canaanites was a matter of *theological* principle (profound moral corruption, the dangers of idolatry), not an *ethnic* one; so this was far from "ethnic cleansing" or "genocide." As commentator J. A. Thompson writes, "If Israel had been dominated by any less tolerant attitude towards her pagan neighbours, she may well have been swallowed up by them."[6] Whatever would undermine allegiance to the covenant-making God had to be removed. Given Israel's track record of infidelity to God's covenant during the wilderness wanderings, Canaanite religion would have been a serious temptation to them.

Furthermore, we have indications from the Old Testament that God would be willing to preserve a wicked nation or a city (e.g., Sodom or Nineveh) *if* there was hope that it would turn from its wickedness. God was willing to preserve Sodom and Gomorrah for just ten righteous people in the city (Gen. 18:32), but they weren't to be found; the city was destroyed. We see God rescuing Rahab and her family from being destroyed with Jericho because of their responsiveness to the true God. Indeed, God's deliverance of Israel from Egypt and his help in defeating Israel's aggressors had become well-known in Canaan (Josh. 2:8–11; 9:9–11, 24; cf. Exod. 15:14–17; Deut. 2:25).

Later, in Jonah's day, God didn't punish the Ninevites as he threatened—to the disappointment of Jonah, who knew that this was the sort of thing God did: "I knew that You are a gracious and compassionate God, slow to anger and abundant in loving-kindness, and one who relents concerning calamity" (Jonah 4:2; cf. Exod. 34:6). Before God destroyed Sodom, Abraham confidently asserts that God would act justly (Gen. 18:25). But this city—as with Canaanite culture—was beyond hope. Unlike much of the forced conversion under Islamic aggression, God was simply demanding a turn away from moral decadence—not necessarily a conversion to worship the true God. It is this kind of profound corruption that brings punishment.

Keep in mind that *if* Israel turned from the God to whom they had attached themselves in a covenant relationship, they would become subject to the very same threats of punishment and judgment that their Canaanite predecessors had been under.

Also, remember God's overarching goal—to bring blessing to all the nations (Gen. 12:1–3). God worked one step at a time—to bring just punishment on a corrupt culture while establishing Israel in that land—so that the nations of the earth would come to be blessed with salvation and peace with God through Christ.

Fourth, the biblical God loves even his enemies and unbelievers (e.g., the Ninevites in Jonah), but the Islamic portrayal of God is one who loves only those who love him. Although the Qur'an refers to God as merciful and compassionate, he only loves those who love him: "God loves not the unbelievers" (3.25); "God loves not the prodigal" (6:140) and is "an enemy to unbelievers" (2:90; 5:82). Those who reject Islam are "the worst of creatures" (98:6). Here God's love is *conditional.*

By contrast, in the Old Testament, we see (from the story of Jonah) that God loves those who don't care at all for him. God intends to bless all the nations (Gen. 12:3)—even Israel's enemies. One of many passages is Isaiah 19, where God speaks of extending salvation to Israel's enemies—Gentile nations like Egypt and Assyria—which he calls "My people" and "the work of My hands" (v. 25). God cries out in compassion for the nation of Moab, whose people have become fugitives (Isa. 15:5; 16:9). When any nation—*whether Israel or not*—turns from its wicked ways, God will not send calamity (Jer. 18:7–8). What's more, God is regularly commanding the nation of Israel to look out for and love the "stranger" or "alien" in their midst because God himself *loves* them (e.g., Exod. 22:21; 23:9; Lev. 19:10; 23:22; Deut. 10:18–19; 14:21, 29; 23:7; 24:17, 19–20; et al.).

This theme of God's love for outsiders is carried over into the New Testament. God loves his enemies; in his mercy, he sends rain and sunshine on the just and unjust (Matt. 5:44–48). He sent his Son to die for his enemies (John 3:16–17; Rom. 5:6, 8, 10; Eph. 2:1, 4–7). God desires that none perish but that all come to repentance (2 Peter 3:9). We see Jesus extending kindness to a *Canaanite* woman (Matt. 15:22–28)—a clear indication that God's purposes had come full circle: God had punished the wicked Canaanites, helped establish Israel in the land, and paved the way of blessing for all nations—even Canaanites—through Israel's Messiah. People from all nations are now part of God's new community.[7]

Fifth, in Scripture, God's moral character furnishes the context for God's decrees and laws, whereas the Qur'an stresses God's arbitrary or capricious and unrestrained will as ultimate. For the Muslim, God is pure will. His will is more basic than considerations of morality and justice: "Whom Allah will He sendeth astray, and whom He will He placeth on a straight path" (16:39). How different is the biblical portrayal of God, who is by nature "compassionate and gracious, slow to anger, and abounding in lovingkindness" (Exod. 34:6)! God's commands are shaped and directed by his good character; they are not the product of whim and caprice.

Sixth, Christ, who is seen as fulfilling the Old Testament, engages Satan, the real enemy, rather than military enemies. Islam's call to military aggression is actually a reversion to the old order—setting back the clock on God's purposes.[8] The book of Hebrews presents Christ as fulfilling the anticipations and signs of the Old Testament—the priesthood, the sacrifices, the Day of Atonement. The least person in Christ's kingdom is greater than John the Baptist, the greatest of prophets under the old covenant (Matt. 11:11).

Jesus didn't think in terms of military conquest, viewing Israel's enemy as the dominating Roman power; he clearly rejected the violent "zealot" movement that viewed Rome's overthrow as the solution to their problems. Rather, Jesus saw his kingdom as a *spiritual* one (John 18:36) that utilized different tactics in fighting— prayer, holy living, proclaiming the gospel, practicing acts of love and service—the battle against Satan and his hosts (Eph. 6:10–18). So for Muhammad to engage in military battles in the name of God again is a *regression*—a *reverting back* to an old order of things that were fulfilled in Christ.

Seventh, Israel's fighting against the Canaanites was unique rather than normative and ongoing; the Qur'an, however, seems to suggest "holy war" as a standing obligation. Even aside from the New Testament, which affirms that the new and true Israel is the inter-ethnic community of believers headed by Jesus Christ, the Old Testament speaks of a unique, unrepeatable situation for national Israel. For instance, Israel wasn't on a mission to take over all outsiders. Israel was not allowed to fight Edom, Moab, and Ammon (Deut. 2:4–5, 8–9, 19)—even when one of them sought confrontation with Israel (Num. 20:14–21). Elsewhere, God reminded Israel that he gave various enemies of Israel *their* land—the *Philistines* and *Arameans*—just as he gave the Israelites *their* land: "'Are you not as the sons of Ethiopia to Me, O sons of Israel?' declares the LORD. 'Have I not brought up Israel from the land of Egypt, and the Philistines from Caphtor and the Arameans from Kir?'" (Amos 9:7).

Eighth, God demands different things of Israel at each stage of its history, but only one of these stages includes "Yahweh wars." With each step of Israel's history, particular ethical obligations arise that are not uniform throughout. Old Testament scholar John Goldingay ably shows how Israel's changing historical contexts call for varied ethical responses. These corresponding ethical responsibilities suggest that we not turn these particular required responses into timeless moral truths—even though the Old Testament does furnish us with permanent moral insights as well.[9]

Goldingay presents the very simple progression: Israel moved from being an ancestral wandering clan (Heb. *mishpachah*, Gen. 10:31-32) to a theocratic nation (*am*, Exod. 1:9; 3:7, or *goy*, Gen. 12:2; Judg. 2:20) to a monarchy, institutional state, or kingdom (*mamlakah*, 1 Sam. 24:20; 1 Chron. 28:5), then an afflicted remnant (*sheerith*, Jer. 42:4; Ezek. 5:10), and finally a post-exilic community/assembly of promise (*qahal*, Ezra 2:64; Neh. 13:1).

Along with these historical changes came differing ethical challenges. For example, during the wandering clan stage, Abraham and the other patriarchs had only accidental or exceptional political involvements. And even when Abraham had to rescue Lot after a raid (Genesis 14), he refused to profit from political benefactors. Through a covenant-bond, Yahweh was the vulnerable patriarchs' protector and supplier.

Then, after Israel had to wait over 400 years and undergo bondage in Egypt while the sin of the Amorites was building to full measure (Gen. 15:16), God delivered them out of slavery and provided a place for them to live as a nation. They became "a political entity with a place in the history books," Goldingay observes. Yahweh had now created a theocracy—a religious, social, and political environment in which Israel had to live. Yet she needed to inhabit a land, which would include warfare. So Yahweh fought on behalf of Israel while bringing just judgment upon a Canaanite culture that had sunk hopelessly below any hope of moral return (with the rare exception of Rahab and her family)—a situation quite unlike the time of the patriarchy.

Enduring insights derived from the wandering clan stage include the commitments of mutual love and concern and the importance of reconciliation in overcoming conflict. We see a people in between promise and fulfillment, dependent upon God who graciously initiated a covenant and then calls for full trust as he leads and guides through unforeseeable circumstances. At the theocratic stage of Israel's history, enduring insights include acknowledgment that any blessing or prosperity comes from the hand of God, not as a right but as the result of grace. The people of God must place their confidence in God rather than themselves or their holy calling. They must remember that "it is the rebellious nation that cannot exist in the world as a theocracy because of its sin."[10]

So we see that Israel at different stages of development faces various challenges that require distinct responses. However, the biblical narrative presents permanent insights for the people of God that rise above the historical particularities. Warfare is far from God's ideal—and we could add divorce, slavery, polygamy, and male dominance (cf. Matt. 19:8). Many ethical problems that emerge in the Old Testament involve God's accommodating between the ideal and the actual; God works in incremental steps to bring Israel out of their morally-inferior conditions of ancient Near East culture toward God's obscured creational standards for all humans (Gen. 1:26-27; 2:24). During this time of Israel's history, God endured human hard-heartedness and sinful social structures, overlooking these times of ignorance until the coming of his Son (Acts 17:30; Rom. 3:25). In the meantime, the Mosaic Law brought dramatic rights for slaves and women unheard of in the ancient Near East while certain embedded social structures were limited and restrained by legislation.[11]

So the Canaanite question turns out to be, in the larger picture, a "side issue" in Israel's practical politics rather than a dominant theme.[12] The Old Testament doesn't celebrate war but looks forward to Yahweh's establishing peace for all the nations (Isa. 2:2–4; 11:1–10; Micah 4:1–4). David, because he is a "man of war"

(1 Chron. 22:8; 28:3), isn't allowed to build the temple; Solomon (meaning "peaceful") is to establish it (1 Chron. 22:8–9)—even though David's military strength helped bring political peace to the region.[13] The Old Testament's word on war is far more nuanced than some people will allow, but the Bible hardly justifies "holy war" as an enduring standard; this is different from the Qur'an. As Kenneth Woodward wrote insightfully in *Newsweek*:

> The Bible, too, has its stories of violence in the name of the Lord. The God of the early Biblical books is fierce indeed in his support of the Israelite warriors, drowning enemies in the sea. But these stories do not have the force of divine commands. Nor are they considered God's own eternal words, as Muslims believe Qur'anic verses to be. Moreover, Israeli commandos do not cite the Hebrew prophet Joshua as they go into battle, but Muslim insurgents can readily invoke the example of their Prophet, Muhammad, who was a military commander himself. And while the Crusaders may have fought with the cross on their shields, they did not—could not—cite words from Jesus to justify their slaughters.[14]

Ninth, Islam's history, beginning with its founder, has been an aggressive and militant movement (to which the Crusades were a response). Muslims commonly point out that the Crusades, carried out in the name of Christ, were morally offensive. Christians can certainly agree. But as we have seen, a little context helps to give us a clearer picture: the Crusades were a response to a centuries-earlier forceful Muslim military aggression that swept across a significantly Christianized Middle East and North Africa. This was the region where theologians such as Clement of Alexandria, Tertullian, Cyprian, and Augustine had lived. Islam came to dominate four out of five chief centers of Christianity ("pentarchies"): Jerusalem, Alexandria, Antioch, and Constantinople (with Rome being the fifth). Prior to Constantine's making Christianity the "official" religion of the empire, the Christian faith had grown through persuasion and deeds of love in Jesus' name—not through military conquest or political power. This is a marked contrast to the spread of Islam, which advanced into and settled in Spain and several times threatened to overrun European Christendom (e.g., a Muslim advance stopped by Charles Martel at the Battle of Tours in 732; other thwarted attempts were made by the Ottoman Turks to capture Vienna in 1529 and again in 1566). Not only did Muslims aggressively exert military muscle; they also subjected Christians, Jews, and other non-Muslims to humiliation and oppression. And failure to pay tribute meant the threat of Islamic jihad.

Yes, Muhammad had initially been friendly toward fellow monotheistic Jews and Christians: "Dispute ye not with the People of the Book. . . . Our God and your God is one; and it is to Him we bow" (sura 29:45). When Jews didn't convert and even mocked Muhammad, he (in AD 627) killed more than seven hundred Jewish men and had their wives and children sold into slavery. He had come to despise Jews, demeaning them with insulting names, such as "pigs" and "apes" (2:65; 7:166; et al.).

It is estimated that Muhammad fought in more than sixty military campaigns. In Turkey's Topkapi Palace, the militaristic spirit of Islam's founder is evident: its "Chamber of the Sacred Relics" contains not only Muhammad's extracted teeth, beard hair, and soil from his grave; it also houses his swords decorated with precious stones, his bamboo bow, and the swords of the first four caliphs and other Islamic leaders.[15] Muhammad's career involves aggressive military campaigns that led to the forceful expansion of Islam.

Tenth, the Qur'an's militancy has been taken as justification for aggression throughout Islam's history up to the present; the Old Testament picture, however, is different. Muslim moderates like to cite the Qur'an's prooftext of religious toleration: "Let there be no compulsion in religion" (2:256). However, much in the Qur'an speaks to a militancy and aggressiveness. Muhammad would command his followers:

- "Fight those who believe not in God" (9:29; cf. 9:14) and "strike terror into (the hearts of) the enemies of God and your enemies" (8:60).[16]
- "I [Allah] will instill terror into the hearts of the Unbelievers: Smite ye above their necks and smite all their finger-tips off them. . . . The true believers fight for the cause of God, but the infidels fight for the devil. Fight then against the friends of Satan . . ." (4:74, 76).
- "Slay the idolaters wherever you find them, kill them, seize them, besiege them, lie in ambush everywhere for them. If they repent and take to prayer and render the alms levy; allow

them to go their way" (9:5). Note that unlike Israel's/God's commitment to the (deceptively-conceived) Gibeonite treaty under Joshua, Allah allegedly gave this command to Muhammad once a treaty with the polytheists expired (9:1–2).

- "Not equal are those believers who sit (at home) and receive no hurt and those who strive and fight in the cause of Allah with their goods and their persons. Allah hath granted a grade higher to those who strive and fight with their goods and persons than to those who sit (at home): unto all (in faith) hath Allah promised good: but those who strive and fight hath He distinguished above those who sit (at home) by a special reward" (4:95). Here, Muslims who fight rather than stay at home are of higher rank.

- "Make war on them until idolatry shall cease and God's religion shall reign supreme" (8:39).

This is no "just war" or a defensive measure against attack. Further, it is noteworthy that the common Islamic interpretation of the "tolerant" and "militant" Qur'anic verses is that the tolerant passages precede the militant ones, which are from Muhammad's later career; thus the earlier passages are overridden ("abrogated") by the later militant ones, which take priority and have normative status.[17]

We observed Islam's traditional distinction between the abode of Islam/peace and the abode of war (where the rule of Islam should be extended—by war, if necessary). This kind of mind-set continues into the present. The annual "Freedom in the World" survey by Freedom House[18] lists countries as "free," "partly free," and "not free." These categories are based on individuals' participation in the political process, free elections, freedom of assembly, and equal rights under the law. Virtually every predominantly Muslim country is either "not free" or "partly free"—with exceptions being Mali and Senegal. Despite the frequently cited Qur'anic passage that says there is "no compulsion in religion," Muslims are often not free to convert out of Islam to a non-Islamic religion in many predominantly Muslim nations (see 4:137) without suffering many hardships and ostracism.

Eleventh, unlike Old Testament Israel, Islam under Muhammad and beyond promoted fighting against all who disagreed theo-

logically and often pursued compulsory conversion (or the imposi-tion of heavy taxes). Israel did not fight to convert non-Israelites at sword point and coerce them to embrace Israel's religious beliefs and way of life. God used the Israelites to punish a very wicked culture, which had practiced "abominable customs" that had "defiled" the land so that the land "spewed out" the nation that it could no longer tolerate (Lev. 18:27–28, 30). We read of no attempt at *conversion* of the Canaanites—who were beyond hope—but of their *removal* from the defiled land. By contrast, the Qur'an affirms that Mus-lims should "[f]ight those who do not believe in Allah, nor in the latter day. . . ." (9:29). Military force from the very beginnings of Islam was a primary means of spreading Islam. In fact, today in many Muslim countries, the "law of apostasy" (for "those who reject faith after they accepted it"—sura 3:86–89) permits capital punishment for those who leave Islam—or, less severely, social ostracism and excommunication from their families.

We often hear the slogan "Islam is a religion of peace." Certain Muslim countries such as Mali and Senegal reveal that Muslims can be peace-loving, and we can be grateful that most Muslims are. But it might be more accurate to say "there are many peace-loving Muslims" rather than Islam intrinsically being a "religion of peace." After all, Islam's *founder* and his *immediate successors* engaged in aggressive military campaigns—in Judaized and Christianized areas (the "people of the Book," the Qur'an calls them). The Qur'an lends further support to Islamic militarism that has pervaded the religion's history and the current political climate where Islam is dominant.

The differences between "Yahweh wars" and Islamic jihad are quite apparent and should not be lumped together. To do so would be unwarranted and inaccurate.

I want to end where I began. I am writing in response to the Canaanite-jihad comparison. I do not address this question with the mind-set that Muslims are enemies nor do I deny that most Muslims are peace-loving. They are—like each of us—people for whom Christ died, people in need of forgiveness and of knowing the reality of God's presence in their lives. Ultimately, Christian arguments and debates with Muslims are far less fruitful than the practical demonstration of Christ's love to them.

Summary

"Yahweh War" vs. "Jihad"

Yahweh War in the Old Testament	Islamic Jihad
Geography: War is geographically limited to the Promised Land.	There are no geographic limitations to jihad. The non-Muslim world is the "abode of war."
Historical length/limit: Limited primarily to one generation (around the time of Joshua).	There are no historical/temporal limitations to jihad.
Objects of war: War is to punish a hopelessly corrupted culture (morally and theologically)—not because they were non-Israelites or even because they didn't worship Yahweh. This punishment came after a period of 430 years, waiting for the Canaanites' sin to ripen fully.	Aggression/war is directed toward non-Muslims (including Christians and Jews).
Objects of God's love: Yahweh loves even his enemies/those who don't love him (cf. Gen. 12:3; Jonah).	God loves only those who love and obey him.
Standard of morality: God's "compassionate and gracious" *nature* is the source of God's commands.	The Qur'an stresses God as sheer *will* (as opposed to a morally good nature), who commands whatever he likes.
Fulfilling God's plan: The Messiah's kingdom is to be characterized by peace (Isa. 9:6; 11:1–10). In the New Testament, Jesus' task would be to undermine the true enemy—Satan and his hosts (John 14:30; Eph. 6:10–18; Col. 2:15)—not Israel's political enemies.	Muhammad's military aggression is seen as legitimate (which sets the clock back on what the Messiah came to fulfill, undermining God's purposes). Note: Qur'anic "tolerant" verses are earlier and outweighed by the later more "militant" verses.
Normativity of war: Fighting against Canaanites was not intended to be normative (having the force of divine commands) but unique; the new covenant direction (Jer. 31; Ezek. 37) is where God is heading with his people.	The military aggression of Muhammad (founder), supported by the Qur'an's militarism, Islam's aggressive history, and present political realities in many Muslim countries suggest an intrinsic pattern.

Further Reading

Answering Islam website. http://www.answering-islam.org/.

Cook, David. *Understanding Jihad*. Berkeley: University of California Press, 2005.

Copan, Paul. "Is Yahweh a Moral Monster? The New Atheists and Old Testament Ethics." *Philosophia Christi* n.s. 10/1 (2008).

——. *"That's Just Your Interpretation": Responding to Skeptics Who Challenge Your Faith*. Grand Rapids: Baker, 2001. Chapter 18.

Geisler, Norman, and Abdul Saleeb. *Answering Islam: The Crescent in Light of the Cross*. Grand Rapids: Baker, 1993.

Goldingay, John. *Old Testament Theology: Israel's Gospel*. Vol. 1. Downers Grove, IL: InterVarsity, 2003. Chapter 7.

Jabbour, Nabeel T. *The Crescent Through the Eyes of the Cross*. Colorado Springs: NavPress, 2008.

Kaiser, Walter. *Toward Old Testament Ethics*. Grand Rapids: Zondervan, 1983. Chapter 11.

Wright, Christopher J. H. "Appendix: What about the Canaanites?" in *Old Testament Ethics for the People of God*. Downers Grove, IL: InterVarsity, 2004.

Was Jesus Mistaken about an Early Second Coming?

Part One

In his book *Why I Am Not a Christian*, Bertrand Russell claims that Jesus, if he existed at all, got things quite wrong about his second coming.

> I am concerned with Christ as he appears in the Gospels, taking the Gospel narrative as it stands, and there one does find some things that do not seem to be very wise. For one thing, he certainly thought his second coming would occur in clouds of glory before the death of all the people who were living at that time. There are a great many texts that prove that. He says, for instance, "Ye shall not have gone over the cities of Israel till the Son of Man comes into his kingdom"; and there are a lot of places where it is quite clear that he believed his second coming would happen during the lifetime of many then living. That was the belief of his earlier followers, and it was the basis of a good deal of his moral teaching.[1]

Does Russell have a point? Don't the following passages suggest that Jesus would soon "come"?

- Jesus commissioned his disciples to proclaim God's in-breaking reign ("kingdom") to the nation of Israel. "You shall not finish going through the cities of Israel until the Son of Man *comes*" (Matt. 10:23, emphasis added).

- Later Jesus addressed his disciples again: "There are some of those who are standing here who will not taste death until they see the Son of Man *coming* in his kingdom" (Matt. 16:28, emphasis added).

- In like manner, Jesus declared, "Whoever is ashamed of Me and My words in this adulterous and sinful generation, the Son of Man will also be ashamed of him when He *comes* in the glory of his Father with the holy angels" (Mark 8:38; Matt. 16:27; Luke 9:26, emphasis added).

- At his trial, Jesus affirms to the high priest that he is indeed "the Christ, the Son of the Blessed One," and that "you [plural] shall see the Son of Man sitting at the right hand of Power, and *coming* with the clouds of heaven" (Mark 14:61–62; Matt. 26:64; Luke 22:69, emphasis added).

In these passages, the "coming" (the Greek verb is *erchomai* = "[I] come") is expected *within* Jesus' own "adulterous and sinful generation." Something dramatic will apparently take place in the near future. Of course, this has led some critics to assert that Jesus "got it wrong." After all, Jesus didn't return in "this generation"; things seemed to be going as they always had.

As a result, the argument goes, the embarrassed early church had to revise its views on Jesus' second coming. According to certain critics, Jesus was an enthusiastic but misguided self-proclaimed prophet who fully expected the coming of God's eschatological (end-times) kingdom to be established on earth. By the time 2 Peter[2] was written, the early church's tune changed as the first generation of Christians and Jesus' original disciples were starting to die off ("ever since our fathers died," 3:4 NIV). Things seemed to be "business as usual" from creation up to the time of 2 Peter. Now scoffers were asking when Jesus was going to come back ("Where is this 'coming' [*parousia* = presence, visitation] he [Jesus] promised?" 3:4, NIV). So instead of an eager expectation of Jesus' return, the early church created a "delay" strategy—that God can take his time and is in no hurry. Crisis resolved![3]

Well-known theologians have held to a "delay of the parousia" (or, if you want to get fancy with some German, *Parusieverzöge-rung*). Prominent theologians and biblical scholars, such as Albert Schweitzer (in 1906), C. H. Dodd (in 1936), Oscar Cullmann (in 1951), and John Robinson (in 1957) referred to this notion in one form or another. For example, one suggestion is that with the delay of Jesus' return, the *Jewish* "apocalyptic" emphasis on the imme-diacy of Jesus' breaking in and bringing an end to evil (in the near future) gave way to a *Hellenistic* notion: rather than focusing on a historical, end-times return, the increasingly Gentile Christian community stressed its spiritual union or "presence" (*parousia*) with Christ.

Is this true? Did Jesus get it wrong about his own return during the lifetime of his hearers? Did his prediction fail to come true, ren-dering Jesus another well-meaning but misguided religious leader who embarrassed the church into coming up with an alternative "delay strategy"?

In this chapter, I will focus on this alleged problem; and then in the next chapter, I will look specifically at Matthew 24/Mark 13 (cf. also Luke 21).[4]

First, 2 Peter 3 isn't a hasty attempt to make sense of why Jesus hadn't yet returned; rather, it reflects Jewish apocalyptic tradition that exhibits the tension between immediacy (imminence) and delay. Between the early second century BC and the second century AD, Jews (and then later, Christians) engaged in writing apocalyptic literature—with its use of cryptic, highly symbolic language that portrayed the battle between good (God) and evil as being on the verge of the end. God would then break into history, rescue his people, judge the wicked, and usher in an age of peace and righteousness.

In the Jewish apocalyptic tradition, there's a tension: God is on the brink of breaking in (*imminence, immediacy*) but there is also room for *delay*, which is part of God's sovereign plan.[5] This tension—not contradiction—is evident in the Old Testament verse commonly cited by apocalyptic authors: "For the revelation *awaits* an appointed time; it speaks of the end and will not prove false. Though it *linger, wait* for it; it will *certainly come* and *will not delay*" (Hab. 2:3 NIV, my emphasis). Also, Daniel spoke of both immediacy ("Do not delay," 9:19) and delay ("How long . . . ?" 12:6). The Apocalypse of Baruch (late first/early second century BC) portrays the immediacy of God's acting in history: "The advent of the times is very close. . . . life approaches its end" (85:10)—immediacy— and "in its time" (5:2; 12:4; 13:5; et al.). As Psalm 90:4 emphasizes, a thousand years for God is like a day—another verse that was used in apocalyptic contexts.[6] So, "soon" could simply mean that God might act decisively and suddenly if he chooses to, but there was plenty of room for delay, as the early church recognized (cf. 2 Peter 3:8–9).

Following in this grand apocalyptic tradition, Jesus himself spoke both of immediacy (as we've seen) but also of delay—of the need to be prepared but also to expect delay. Jesus blends well into this prophetic and apocalyptic landscape.

Even in Revelation we see this tension—again, without any attempt to resolve it: On the one hand, Jesus is "coming quickly" (2:16; 3:11; 22:7, 12, 20), and "the time is near" (1:3); on the other hand, the martyrs cry, "How long?" (6:10) and they're told, "A little while longer" (6:11). On the one hand, "there will be delay no longer" (10:6); on the other, God *delays* the end so that the church's mission to every tribe, tongue, and nation can be completed (11:1–13).[7] As Richard Bauckham observes, "The problem of delay did not discredit or destroy the apocalyptic hope" for early Christians.[8] So the claim that Jesus—and early Christians—got things wrong about "the end" *overlooks the fact that from the beginning, apocalyptic literature was characterized by both imminence and delay.* God is sovereign, and thus the final victory is certain and could come in the near future (immediacy). But because God is also merciful in his sovereignty, he determines the time of the end and allows people to respond to his claim on their lives (delay).

Second, there are other reasons to reject the notion of the "embarrassed church's delay strategy." We can certainly acknowledge that the early church was hopeful and even expecting that Jesus would return soon after he had ascended (e.g., Paul, when he said, "we who are alive, and remain until the coming [*parousia*] of the

Lord" [1 Thess. 4:15]). Any generation could be "the last" before the end comes.

However, the New Testament writers didn't presume or teach that this *would* happen—only that it *could*. In fact, certain events had to take place before Jesus would return—for example, the temple/Jerusalem would fall (Matt. 24:1–3), Peter would die (John 21:22–23), and a "man of lawlessness" would appear (2 Thess. 2).

Below I respond briefly to this potentially embarrassing "delay of the parousia" strategy in reaction to Jesus' failure to return in good time.

1. *If Jesus (mistakenly) believed he was speaking of the end of history (when the temple will be destroyed), why would he speak of a "great tribulation" of AD 66–70 (Matt. 24:21) as he did?* He claimed that this destruction would be the worst calamity "such as has not occurred since the beginning of the world until now"—and he added—"nor ever will." Jesus was assuming that earthly human history would continue after Jerusalem fell.

2. *The dual position presented below—that Jesus "comes" up to God's throne for enthronement, vindication, and judgment during "this generation" (in AD 70) and that he will ultimately arrive (the* parousia*) at an unknown time in the future—avoids any potential embarrassment that Jesus appears to have gotten things wrong.* We can take at face value his predictions of something momentous happening to his generation.[9]

3. *Even though early Christians spoke of the Lord's coming being "near" or "at hand," these same writers noted that delay is inevitable.* We've already seen this tension played out in Revelation, which follows the tradition of Daniel and Habakkuk. Furthermore, Paul wrote that the fulfillment or "ends [*ta telē*] of the ages" had come upon Christians (1 Cor. 10:11)—a *present* reality. But he also wrote of a *final* "end [*telos*] of all things" in the same letter (1 Cor. 15:24). Indeed, he told the Thessalonians (around AD 50) that an apostasy and the appearing of a "man of lawlessness" had to take place before the parousia. James expressed this tension when he urged believers to "be patient . . . until the coming [*parousia*] of

the Lord" (5:7), and in the next verse he affirmed that "the coming [*parousia*] of the Lord is near."

4. *At times New Testament writers were correcting misperceptions that the end (or parousia) had already come.* In 1 and 2 Thessalonians, the "delay of the parousia" isn't a problem at all, but rather the opposite! Some Christians were assuming that the final day had already arrived (e.g., 2 Thess. 2:1–2)![10] Furthermore, some of the Corinthians were assuming that the end had already come—even to the point of denying a final resurrection (1 Cor. 15:12).[11] Interestingly, even with the chief "delay" text of 2 Peter 2:4, Peter didn't even mention an "apostasy" or the appearance of a "man of lawlessness," as Paul did in 2 Thessalonians 2. Why then not mention preliminary signs, as Paul did? This would completely overcome the alleged problem. Instead, Peter simply wrote that the Lord would come "like a thief" (2 Peter 3:10) and that believers were to look forward to "new heavens and a new earth, in which righteousness dwells" (v. 13).[12]

Biblical scholars have recognized that this "delay of the parousia" question that allegedly perplexed second- or third-generation Christians is to make mountains out of molehills. Any such evidence is, in fact, flimsy upon close inspection. What was true back then applies to us as well: each generation of believers must live as if theirs is the last—with patient faithfulness.[13]

Third, if we see that Jesus was speaking of two distinct events—answering two questions—in Matthew 24 and Mark 13, the alleged conflict is resolved. Jesus' disciples were admiring the temple precincts, and he told them of a cataclysmic event that would soon take place: "Do you not see all these things? Truly I say to you, not one stone here will be left upon another, which will not be torn down" (Matt. 24:2)—an impressive prediction, given that each stone weighed several hundred tons![14] His disciples then asked, "Tell us, when will *these things* happen?" (That is, when will the temple be destroyed?) But they go on to ask, "and what will be the sign of Your *coming* [*parousia*], and of the end of the age?" (24:3, emphasis added). Jesus told them that "these things" would be destroyed (v. 2). So the disciples wanted to know when "these things" would take place (v. 3). (Keep in mind that because Matthew follows Mark—the first gospel written—and elaborates on Mark's simpler account, we'll follow Matthew 24 in this chapter and the next. Also, since this view is not the traditional view preached from many pulpits in America, my approach may seem a bit foreign—but not to biblical scholars, among whom this view has generally been well-received. So in these two chapters I'll be doing a bit of repeating and perhaps overemphasizing to drive my point home!)

Plenty of preachers and popular authors on the "end-times" declare that the famines, earthquakes, false prophets, gospel proclamation to the ends of the earth, and even the darkening of the sun and moon refer to a time just before Jesus' second coming. If, however, we take this passage in context and view it through *Jewish* (Old Testament) eyes, we can see that Jesus was speaking of Jerusalem's destruction—an event that would take place during the disciples' lifetime (AD 70).

A close look at Matthew 24 shows that Jesus was answering two questions (the second question is implied in Mark 13). Jesus *knew* the answer to the first: "this generation will not pass away until all *these things* take place (v. 34, emphasis added). But he *didn't know* the answer to the second: "But of that day and hour [of Jesus' parousia or second coming] no one knows, not even the angels of heaven, nor the Son, but the Father alone" (v. 36). The first part of Matthew 24 (vv. 4–35) addresses the events of the near future. The second part of Matthew 24 (vv. 36–51) speaks of a more-distant future event—Jesus' ultimate return.[15]

Although the disciples asked for a "sign" of Jesus' parousia (v. 3), Jesus told them there wouldn't be a sign for the parousia, which would be unexpected. The only sign would come in light of the fall of Jerusalem in AD 70 (v. 30). This is when the Son of Man would come to God's throne to receive authority and vindication. This *heavenly* act was evidenced *on earth* by two things: the fall of Jerusalem and the gathering of the people of God from the nations.[16]

Part I: Matthew 24:4–35	Part II: Matthew 24:36–51
Question: When will the temple/ Jerusalem be destroyed? 24:2–3: "... *these things.... When will these things be ... ?"*	**Question:** When will Jesus return at the end of the age? 24:3: "*... and what will be the sign of Your coming [parousia], and of the end of the age?"*

Part I: Matthew 24:4–35	Part II: Matthew 24:36–51
The answer (which Jesus knew): The destruction of temple/Jerusalem (and all the signs leading up to it) would take place within a generation (AD 70). Jesus could confidently say that this event was *expected* and datable—within "this generation" (v. 34).	**The answer (which Jesus didn't know):** The parousia/the end of the age will be unexpected and cannot be dated. Not even Jesus knows this: "But of that day and hour [the parousia and the end of the age] no one knows" (v. 36).
A sign? The disciples ask for a "sign" of Jesus' parousia (v. 3).	**A sign, but . . . :** Jesus indicated that there *won't* be a sign for the parousia, which will be unexpected. Rather, any sign would be associated with the fall of the temple/Jerusalem. The only "sign" (v. 30) would come in AD 70—when the Son of Man came to God to receive authority and vindication. This heavenly act was evidenced on earth by the fall of Jerusalem and the gathering of the new Israel.

Fourth, to more clearly understand the thrust of Matthew 24, we should distinguish two words translated "coming" (parousia *versus* erchomenon*).* The disciples asked when Jerusalem and the temple would be destroyed and what the sign of Jesus' parousia ("presence, arrival, coming, visitation") and the end of the age would be. The word *parousia* (presence, coming)—a word used for the "arrival" of a dignitary or for the manifestation of a divine figure—occurs four times in Matthew 24, and these are the only occurrences in the Gospels. Matthew uses this word quite purposefully.[17] It refers not to AD 70, but to an unknown time of return:[18]

- v. 3: "what will be the sign of Your *arrival/coming . . .* ?"
- v. 27: "so will the *arrival/coming* of the Son of Man be"—that is, the parousia of Christ will be obvious—not a matter of guesswork, as with these misleading messianic pretenders before the fall of Jerusalem
- v. 37: "the *arrival/coming* of the Son of Man will be just like the days of Noah"
- v. 39: "they did not understand until the flood came and took them all away; so will the *arrival/coming* of the Son of Man be."

A different word is used in verse 30—*erchomenon*: "all of the tribes of the earth . . . will see the Son of Man *coming* on the clouds of the sky with power and great glory." Though this word is used for Christ's final return elsewhere in the New Testament, Matthew is specifically using it here to speak of Jesus' coming not *to earth* (which would be the parousia), but *to God* to be enthroned and vindicated as Messiah at the judgment on Jerusalem (in AD 70).

The passage quoted here is Daniel 7:13–14, where the "Son of Man" comes on the clouds to the "Ancient of Days" (i.e., God the Father) to receive authority from God as the confirmed king: "I kept looking in the night visions, and behold, with the clouds of heaven one like a Son of Man was coming [the Greek Septuagint uses *erchomai*, 'come'], and He came up to the Ancient of Days and was presented before Him. And to Him was given dominion, glory and a kingdom, that all the peoples, nations and men of every language might serve Him. His dominion is an everlasting dominion which will not pass away; and His kingdom is one which will not be destroyed." The verse Jesus quoted (Dan. 7:13) refers to the Son of Man coming *to God*—not to earth—on clouds; he receives the authority of a ruling king—dominion, glory, and a kingdom.[19]

Fifth, Jesus was speaking to his own generation as those who would witness the Son of Man's coming to his Father ("the Ancient of Days"). In Matthew 16:28, Jesus speaks of a "coming" of "the Son of Man" in the near future: "there are some of those who are standing here who will not taste death until they see the Son of Man coming in His kingdom." It would happen within a generation; some of Jesus' disciples would live to see that day. Likewise, Jesus told the Jewish leaders who tried him that he was indeed "the Christ, the Son of the Blessed One," and that "you [plural] shall see the Son of Man sitting at the right hand of Power, and *coming* with the clouds of heaven" (Mark 14:62/Matt. 26:64; Luke 22:69). Most scholars agree that this isn't the parousia ("second coming") but something Jesus' own generation would see. Jesus was speaking to the high priest and (as implied by the plural) the rest of those who condemned him. He said that although they accused and condemned him, they would soon see that he has become Lord and King.[20]

The same can be said for our passage (Matt. 24:30/Mark 13:26): *the majority* of interpreters see this as referring to Jesus' enthrone-

ment, not his parousia.[21] And this fits with what Jesus said elsewhere, using the same verb "come [*erchomai*]":

- Matthew 10:23: "You shall not finish going through the cities of Israel until the Son of Man *comes*."
- Mark 8:38; Matthew 16:27; Luke 9:26: "Whoever is ashamed of me in this adulterous and sinful generation, the Son of Man will also be ashamed of him when he *comes* [*elthē*, from Gk. *erchomai* ('come')] in the glory of his Father with the holy angels."

Jesus warned *his own generation* ("this generation"), which was ripe for judgment (i.e., AD 70). His first-century Jewish audience naturally would have understood Jesus' claims in light of Daniel 7:13–14—the Son of Man who "comes on the clouds" *to* the Father ("Ancient of Days") for exaltation, vindication, and heavenly enthronement, taking his co-regency and authority over the nations, surrounded by an angelic court. To "come in the clouds" is to be "seated at the right hand of God."[22] (It would be strange for Jesus to come *to earth* in a seated position!)

When Jesus was being condemned, he announced to those judging him that "[f]rom now on" (Matt. 26:64 NRSV) they would see him—the Son of Man—coming on the clouds, seated at God's right hand. The implication of the phrase *from now on* is that within their lifetime, these leaders would see this vindication in at least three ways: Jesus' resurrection and ascension, the spread of the church throughout the entire (civilized) world (Matt. 24:14), and the destruction of Jerusalem and the temple.[23]

Part I (Matt. 24:4–35; Mark 13:4–31)	Part II (Matt. 24:36–51; Mark 13:32–37)
Erchomenon (from the verb *erchomai* ["come"]) refers to Jesus' "coming" to God for his enthronement, authority, and vindication at the judgment on Jerusalem around AD 70.	*Parousia* refers to the "return" or "presence" of Christ as his second coming at the end of the age.
Jesus knew when *these things* would take place (i.e., within "this generation").	Jesus *doesn't know* when the parousia will take place ("But of *that day* and hour no one knows," emphasis added).

Many popular interpretations of Matthew 24 ignore the language and context of Daniel 7 as well as Jesus' use of this passage to his contemporaries.[24] Jesus' audience would have understood his reference to Daniel 7 as the Son of Man not descending to earth, but *coming up* to the Ancient of Days for exaltation and setting up a new kingship to replace the failed earthly empires.[25] The scene is a heavenly, not earthly, one.[26]

Summary

- The "delay of the Parousia" strategy isn't the result of an embarrassed early church's grappling with misguided promises from Jesus about his return. Jewish apocalyptic tradition exhibited the tension between *immediacy* (imminence) and *delay*—which is evident in Daniel, Habakkuk, Revelation, and elsewhere.

- The New Testament writers presume that several things would have to take place before the parousia: for example, the fall of the temple and Jerusalem (Matt. 24:1–3), Peter's death (John 21:22–23), and the appearance of a "man of lawlessness" (2 Thessalonians 2).

- Jesus didn't believe that his vindication ("coming" to God for enthronement) at the destruction of the temple (in AD 70) would usher in the end of history as we know it. He (hyperbolically) asserted that no calamity could be worse than this "great tribulation"—"nor ever will [be]." He assumed earthly history would continue after this.

- Early Christian writers used apocalyptic terms and utilized tensions of the Lord's being "near" or "at hand" while simultaneously noting that delay is inevitable. For example, Paul wrote to the Thessalonians that a man of lawlessness would appear before the parousia but urged them to "be patient" while asserting that the parousia was "near" (2 Thess. 5:7–8).

- New Testament writers at times corrected the misperception that the parousia had already come (e.g., 1 Thessalonians 4; 2 Thessalonians 2; 1 Cor. 15:12). However, the New Testament suggests that the parousia could take place within any generation and that believers must be spiritually and morally prepared.

• The two-staged position I have advocated—of (1) Jesus' "coming" (*erchomai/erchomenon*) to God for enthronement, vindication, and judgment in AD 70 ("this generation") and (2) ultimate arrival (the parousia) at an unknown future time—avoids any potential embarrassment that Jesus appears to have gotten things wrong. We can take seriously his claims about something dramatic happening within his own generation.

• Certain gospel passages speak of the "coming [*erchomenon*]" of the Son of Man to the Father ("the Ancient of Days")—a reference to Daniel 7—within his generation. Most New Testament scholars take passages such as Matthew 16:28 and Mark 14:62/Matthew 26:64 and Luke 22:69 as references to AD 70—not some distant "second coming."

Further Reading

France, R. T. *The Gospel of Matthew*. New International Commentary on the New Testament. Grand Rapids: Eerdmans, 2007.

———. *Jesus and the Old Testament*. Reprint edition. Vancouver: Regent College Publishing, 1992.

———. *Matthew*. Tyndale Commentary. Revised edition. Downers Grove, IL: InterVarsity, 1985.

16

Was Jesus Mistaken about an Early Second Coming?

Part Two

Having looked at some of the background to this passage, let's look at the specific text of Matthew 24. I hope it will become clear that Jesus is answering two distinct questions—one dealing with the near future (AD 70) and the other with the distant future.

First, Jesus at the outset specifically answers the disciples' question about Jerusalem's destruction, giving signs of what will take place in the near future—not at the second coming. Jesus implies that the disciples themselves will attest to the truth of Jesus' prediction. I have vivid memories of attending "end-times" conferences in my youth. Speakers and preachers would commonly refer to Matthew 24. They would invariably talk about the current increase of earthquakes and other natural disasters, international tensions (especially in the Middle East), societal breakdown, false prophets, and persecution. All of these were interpreted to be "signs of the end-times" just before Jesus' (secret) return. As it turns out, this isn't the message Jesus intended to communicate—and it's not what his first-century audience would have understood.

I've also attended missions conferences that emphasized the "promise" of Matthew 24:14—that the gospel had to be preached in all the world, and then the end would come. While missions work is certainly important, we will see that the fulfillment of this promise comes in the first century!

As a teenager, I would read this biblical passage and wonder why Jesus seemed to be addressing his disciples ("*you* will be handed over," v. 9 NIV; "when *you* see," v. 15; "if anyone says to *you*," v. 23 [emphasis added to all]); it appeared that *they themselves*, not some distant generation, would experience or be able to attest to these things. Of course, that would be a lot less sensationalistic than what many modern-day end-times popularizers would have us believe—namely, that Matthew 24 is being fulfilled on today's front pages![1] A closer look reveals that the events mentioned by Jesus leading up to Jerusalem's destruction are the same kind mentioned by the first-century Jewish historian Josephus (*Antiquities* [*Ant.*] and *Jewish Wars* [*Wars*]).[2] So let's take a look at this and other considerations from Matthew 24, as we examine this passage one step at a time.

- *False prophets/messiahs coming, saying, "I am the Christ"* (vv. 5, 11; cf. vv. 23–24). False messiahs and would-be saviors were plentiful in the first century, and Josephus lists only some of them, implying that these were just the tip of the iceberg.[3] Here is a sampling: Theudas (*Ant.* 20.97–99; cf. Acts 5:36); the sons of Judas of Galilee (*Ant.* 20.102); "the Egyptian" (*Ant.* 20.169–72); Menahem, son of Judas of Galilee, who came into Jerusalem (AD 66) "as if he were really a king" (*Wars* 2.433–48, esp. 434); Simon bar-Giora, who won the obedience of his fellow citizens "as to a king" (*Wars* 4.503–44, esp. 510); various unnamed impostors (*Ant.* 20.167–8, 188); and "deceivers and impostors, under the pretense of divine inspiration" (*Wars* 2.258–59). Even John the apostle would write that "many antichrists" had already come in *his own* day (1 John 2:18; 2 John 7).[4] These impostors weren't necessarily claiming to act on Jesus' authority, but they were seeking to usurp the place that was rightfully his.[5] In verses 26–27, Jesus tells his disciples that the appearance of would-be messiahs shouldn't fool them into thinking that the parousia (second coming) is near; this fact confirms that Jesus is not describing his parousia in verses 4–35.

- *Wars and rumors of wars* (vv. 6–7). The Jewish war with Rome (AD 66–70) was preceded by rumors of war incited by anti-Roman zealots. Those living in Palestine would have heard about Rome's border clashes and wars in Parthia (AD 36) and with the Babylonians. They would have known of the sporadic wars between Herod Antipas and the Nabatean king Aretas (which involved Rome in AD 36–37).[6] In AD 68–69, Rome experienced its own civil war during the "year of the four emperors," at which time the Julio-Claudian line of emperors came to an end. Furthermore, some messianic pretenders created local uprisings in Judea, which were put down by the Romans. The "Jewish revolt" (AD 66) eventually led to a civil war in Jerusalem itself as different Jewish groups struggled to gain control—with the temple at the center of the conflict.[7] Josephus wrote that just before AD 70 (during which time there was infighting and a quick succession of emperors after Nero's death), "every quarter of the world beneath [Rome's] sway was seething and quivering with excitement" (*Wars* 7.4).

- *Famines and earthquakes* (v. 7) were not at all unusual in the first century. Acts 11:28 mentions a famine during the reign of Claudius, which was widespread or empire-wide (see also *Ant.* 3:320; 20.51–3, 101). Under Nero's rule, there was rioting in Rome because of food shortages. Regarding earthquakes, Josephus mentioned one that took place around AD 45–47 (*Ant.* 20:51–53). Another hit Laodicea in AD 60–61 and Pompeii (which was partially destroyed) in AD 62. An earthquake occurred in Philippi (Acts 16:26). In AD 67 Jerusalem experienced an earthquake as well.[8]

Such initial *birth pangs* (v. 8) involving deceivers, wars, famines, and earthquakes use the language of the Old Testament; there they refer to national crises and suffering: Babylon (Isa. 13:8), Judah/Jerusalem (Jer. 6:24), Lebanon (Jer. 22:23), Judah/Jerusalem (Micah 4:9–10). The Israel of Jesus' day faces a looming crisis. But it is these birth pangs that precede the return of God's people from exile (Micah 5:3–4)—the in-gathering of Jews and Gentiles as God's new community in Christ.

- *Persecutions* (v. 9). In Acts we see the disciples and God's people persecuted by Jewish leaders on the Jewish ruling council, the Sanhedrin (e.g., 4:5–22; 5:27–41; 6:12; 22:30; 23:1; 23:30; James, Jesus' brother, also appears before this council [*Ant.* 20.9]). They are opposed in synagogues. Gentile rulers and kings get in on the interrogation as well (Acts 24:10–27; 25:1–12; 25:23–26:32). The book of Acts illustrates the official opposition to those who are promoting the gospel (cf. the beatings and stonings in Acts 5:40; 7:58; 14:19; 16:19–23, 37). Paul frequently wrote about opposition to his message.[9] Christ, anticipating the giving of the Spirit at Pentecost (Acts 2), promised that the Spirit would give Christ's followers wisdom to speak when called to account or when on trial (cf. Acts 2:4; 4:8, 13–14, 31; 13:9).

- *Apostasy/turning away from the faith* (vv. 10–13). Jesus' first coming ushered in "the last days" (Acts 2:17; Heb. 1:2); this is a new era of God's work of re-creation (e.g., John 3:3; 2 Cor. 5:17; Gal. 5:22–23) and bringing about a new exodus in Christ (1 Cor. 5:7–8). But it is also a period of apostasy along with false teaching, as New Testament writers make clear (cf. Matt. 7:15/Acts 20:29–30 ["ravenous/savage wolves"]; 1 Tim. 4:1–3; 2 Tim. 3:1–5; 4:10–15; 2 Peter 2:1; 1 John 2:18–19; et al.). Mark 13:12 emphasizes disciples being betrayed and opposed by family members. This is the very thing Jesus said his first coming would bring. He noted this in Matthew 10:34–35, citing Micah 7:5–6, which interestingly leads into discussion of God's gathering his elect people scattered among the nations (Micah 7:12–15). Micah's context fits nicely with what follows—the gospel being preached to the world (Matt. 24:14) and the gathering of God's elect people (24:31). Keep in mind that "lawlessness" isn't just criminal activity, but religious hypocrisy—a word Jesus applied to the scribes and Pharisees (Matt. 23:28).[10]

- *The gospel preached in the whole world* (v. 14). The worldwide proclamation of Christ to the Gentiles was to occur before the temple's destruction. Did this happen? Yes! Keep in mind that the phrase in Matthew 24:14, "the whole world [Gk. *holē tē oikoumenē*]" is the same one used for the extent of the famine in Acts 11:28 and the extent of Artemis worship in Acts 19:27. So by the mid-50s, Paul could rightly declare that he had "fully preached the gospel" in Asia and Europe (Rom. 15:19) and that the gospel had gone out "into all the earth" and "to all the nations" (Rom. 10:18; 16:26). Yes, the gospel had spread throughout the Roman Empire, the Mediterranean world. This gospel was proclaimed "in all creation under heaven" and bearing fruit "in all the world [*kosmos*]" (Col. 1:23, 6). A significant, empire-wide, inter-ethnic people of God—the new Israel—had come into existence well before AD 70.[11]

This spreading of the gospel was anticipated by the prophets. They spoke of the proclamation of "good news ['gospel']" of "salvation" to "all the nations" (Isa. 52:7–12). The Spirit would be poured out upon "all mankind" (Joel 2:28—a passage, Peter declared, that had begun to be fulfilled at Pentecost [Acts 2:16–21]). At any rate, this particular text shouldn't be taken by us as a motivation for missionary activity or starting a church for each of the earth's ethnic groups— as important as this task is! As R. T. France explains, such questions are irrelevant since "the event before which it must have happened has already taken place more than nineteen centuries ago."[12]

Second, Jesus then speaks of the siege of Jerusalem and a profound crisis with unprecedented suffering (vv. 15–28). The end of the temple still looms. The reference to the abomination of desolation (*to bdelygma tēs erēmōseōs* [v. 15] and slight variations) is originally mentioned in Daniel 9:27; 11:31; 12:11. Compare "the sin of desolation" (*hē hamartia erēmōseōs*) in Daniel 8:13 (my translation from the Greek); it is a reference to some coming sacrilege—namely, the "Maccabaean crisis" of 167 BC (as N. T. Wright and numerous other scholars argue).[13] Indeed, Daniel 9–12 is centered on this crisis, which lasted three years. The pagan ruler Antiochus Epiphanes, the "king of the north," set up a statue of Zeus in Jerusalem's temple and killed a swine on the altar, thus desolating temple worship. This desecration is confirmed by the book of 1 Maccabees (1:54, 59): "They erected *the abomination of desolation/desolating sacrilege* [the same phrase Daniel used] on the altar of burnt offering . . . [and] offered sacrifice on the pagan altar which was on top of the altar of the Lord." Jesus is reminding his disciples to look out for the same kind of sacrilege as in 167 BC.[14]

So what could this new sacrilege or "abomination" refer to? There seem to be a couple of options. (1) The temple's desecration took place when murderous Jewish zealots established a fake high priest (in the winter of AD 67–68) and angered Jewish crowds, which led to fighting in the temple itself (*Wars* 4.388). (2) The Roman army (in AD 70) brought its military standards, with a silver or bronze eagle over the emperor's bust, and even offered sacrifices before them; these soldiers highly revered—and nearly worshiped—these standards, which Jews considered idolatrous.[15] The point of sacrilege or "devastating pollution" is probably more general—an "ever-present threat once the Roman invasion had been provoked."[16]

Notice the details of the crisis (vv. 16–21), which aren't world-wide, but are confined to the culture and geography of Judea (e.g., praying that the flight might not be on the Sabbath or during the rainy winter season, fleeing into the hills, etc.). There is no reason to think this scenario goes beyond Palestine or AD 70.

In verse 27, Jesus says that this isn't the period of the parousia (second coming), which will be obvious—like the lightning that brightens the sky. Furthermore, the gathering of vultures clearly indicates the presence of a carcass (v. 28). It is the time of the "end [*telos*]" for Jerusalem (24:6), though not the "end [*synteleias*] of the age" (24:3).[17] This is the only mention of parousia when Jesus answers the first question. He is trying to dissociate it from the events leading up to the temple's destruction.

When we're told (v. 21) that *there will be a great tribulation, such as has not occurred since the beginning of the world until now, nor ever shall*, does this point to something worldwide? Surely, one might argue, the Holocaust was worse than this. Now the siege of Jerusalem was horrific—with cannibalism, starvation, disease, and a proportionately large percentage of deaths in the city (*Wars*

5.420–38).[18] The destruction of Jerusalem and the temple signaled the demise of the old order—a powerful theological sign of national Israel's collapse as the people of God. National Israel as the people of God was forever finished, and a Jewish-Gentile church emerged as the new Israel (see, e.g., Rom. 2:28–29; Gal. 6:16; 1 Peter 2:5, 9–10). In addition, Jesus is speaking *hyperbolically*—in keeping with apocalyptic language (e.g., Dan. 12:1; Joel 2:2; Rev. 16:18)—to depict horrible suffering and tragedy.[19] And he speaks hyperbolically elsewhere of the mustard seed being "the smallest of all your seeds" (Matt. 13:32); though not literally true, you get the point. We read the same sort of (hyperbolic) claims in the Old Testament: King Hezekiah trusted in the Lord "so that after him there was none like him among all the kings of Judah, nor among those who were before him" (2 Kings 18:5); but a few chapters later, we read of King Josiah that "before him there was no king like him who turned to the LORD with all his heart . . . nor did any like him arise after him" (23:25).

Third, the dramatic apocalyptic language of Matthew 24:29–31 isn't referring to Jesus' second coming (parousia) and "the end of the world," but (following the Old Testament) it indicates a geopolitical calamity in AD 70—the disastrous fall of Jerusalem. Although end-times popularizers commonly assert that these verses refer to Jesus' return and "the end of history,"[20] the more natural reading (following Daniel 7 and other Old Testament passages) suggests that they speak of something else. Consider the following five matters:

1. *The phrase "immediately after the tribulation of those days" rules out the traditional end-times interpretation*—namely, reference to a remote event (the parousia) at the end of the age; it must refer to AD 70. Certain commentators and many Christian popularizers don't properly handle the words "immediately after."[21] There is no gap between the distress of "those days" in AD 70 and the calamitous fall of Jerusalem and the coming of the Son of Man (vv. 29–30). As R. T. France notes, the most natural interpretation presents a "formidable problem" to the traditional view.[22] After all, Jesus didn't finally return *immediately after* the difficulties of AD 70. France rightly affirms that probably the only reason people don't recognize this simple chronology (i.e., the temple's destruction

and then the collapse of Jerusalem and the coming of the Son of Man) is due to the incorrect assumption that verses 29–31 refer to the parousia, not the temple's destruction. But there simply is no delay here.

2. *The quotation "The sun will be darkened, and the moon will not give its light," is taken from several Old Testament references, and all of them are figurative and refer to historical political upheavals.* None of them refers to a natural disaster or cosmic upheaval, but to national or political calamities—to the upheaval of kingdoms or empires. N. T. Wright observes that these words are "typical Jewish imagery for events within the present order that are felt and perceived as 'cosmic' or, as we should say, 'earth-shattering.'"[23] That is, the lights of the centers of political power are going out, and a new world order is emerging. God is altering the world political structures, and the geopolitical scene is being changed.[24] Note these Old Testament passages where such "cosmic signs" are metaphorical.

- *Isaiah 13:10 (Babylon's* doom predicted): "For the stars of the heaven . . . will not flash forth their light; the sun will be dark when it rises and the moon will not shed its light."
- *Isaiah 34:4–6 (Edom's* doom predicted): "All the host of heaven will wear away, and the sky will be rolled up like a scroll; all their hosts will also wither away."
- *Jeremiah 4:23 (Judah's* doom/exile predicted): "I looked on the earth, and behold, it was formless and void [or, better, NET, 'empty wasteland"]; and to the heavens, and they had no light."
- *Ezekiel 32:7 (Egypt's* doom predicted): "I will cover the heavens and darken their stars; I will cover the sun with a cloud and the moon will not give its light."
- *Joel 2:10 (Judah's* doom/exile predicted): "Before [the destructive armies] the earth quakes, the heavens tremble, the sun and the moon grow dark and the stars lose their brightness." (See also 3:15–16.)
- *Amos 5:18–20 (Israel's* doom/exile predicted): "Alas, you who are longing for the day of the LORD, for what purpose will the day of the LORD be to you? It will be darkness and

not light. . . . Will not the day of the LORD be darkness instead of light, even gloom with no brightness in it?"
• *Amos 8:9* (*Israel's* doom predicted): "I will make the sun go down at noon and make the earth dark in broad daylight."

These passages clearly use symbolic language to speak of social and political (and moral or spiritual) catastrophes created by the fall of these significant societies, which are being judged by God. This apocalyptic language used by the prophets fits very well with the collapse of Jerusalem and the end of national Israel as God's chosen people. A new world order has come. The centrality of the temple and of Jerusalem (Israel) is being replaced—a decisive, catastrophic event—and a new community (the new Israel) is being formed. The old order is done; a new one has begun, focused on the Son of Man as king and a new community as his subjects. So it's quite appropriate that Peter in Acts 2:17-21, now that "the last days" had begun, similarly describes what is happening at Pentecost in apocalyptic, earth-shattering terms. Citing Joel 2:28–32, he refers to "wonders in the sky above. . . . The sun will be turned into darkness and the moon into blood." A new order had begun with the Christ-event.

3. *The climactic "coming" of the Son of Man in Matthew 24:30 (citing Dan. 7:13) fits an AD 70 setting.* As we've seen, the Son of Man's "coming" is an *ascent* to the Ancient of Days (for kingly authority, enthronement, and vindication), not a *descent* to earth. He comes on clouds, which often symbolize power in judgment (see, e.g., Pss. 18:12–14; 97:2–3; 104:3; Isa. 19:1; Nah. 1:3). A new king is coming to replace the failed kingdoms of the past.[25] This is what Jesus, at his trial, tells the high priest he will see—"*From now on* you will see the Son of Man seated at the right hand of Power and coming on the clouds of heaven" (Matt. 26:64 NRSV, emphasis added). R. T. France reminds us that this passage and Matthew 24:30 are "now widely recognized" as being "enthronement texts" and not end-times, second coming passages.[26]

Again, this "coming" in kingship and judgment fits nicely with passages such as Matthew 10:23; 16:28; Mark 8:38; and

14:62 (which also use the word *erchomai* ["come"]). The reigning Jesus comes to receive vindication as "this generation" of antagonistic Jewish leaders is judged, bringing their rule to an end. As the vindicated Son of Man, forgiveness proclaimed to all nations would come through *him*, not through the now-destroyed temple (Luke 24:47). God's earthly purposes will be advanced by the true Israel—the international community of Jesus' disciples—who will be a light to the nations that national Israel failed to be (Isa. 42:6; 49:6; Matt. 5:14–16; cf. John 8:12).

The disciples asked for a "sign" of his parousia, but Jesus, instead, gives them a *sign* related to the temple's destruction and the Son of Man's vindication (v. 30). There is no sign for the parousia since this is unexpected—the timing of which Jesus himself doesn't know (v. 36). So if the Son of Man's coming to God *in heaven* is a sign, how will this be known *on earth*? Jesus' vindication and authority before God will be evidenced by two things: (a) the destruction of the temple and of the old order of national Israel and (b) the ingathering of Jesus' new Jewish-Gentile community (the new Israel); the next verse makes this clear, as we'll see.

So despite the popular end-times interpretation of this verse as a "second coming," Jesus' hearers would have understood this passage quite differently. Knowing well the Old Testament context from which Jesus spoke, they didn't have the "baggage" of more recent theological interpretations and modifications.

4. *The quotation from Zechariah 12:10–13 refers to a national mourning of the Jews in Palestine, who see the words of Jesus coming true in the destruction of the temple.* This passage is typically translated "all the tribes of the earth [Gk., gē]." However, it is better translated "land": the mourning takes place in "Jerusalem," according to Zechariah. The original context also refers to Israelite "tribes" or "houses" (clans) of David, Nathan, Levi, and Shimei specifically; they are not the tribes of the whole world. (This word gē also refers to the land of Palestine in Matt. 27:45; Mark 15:33; Luke 4:25; and 21:23. It can refer to a territory or region such as Judah/

Israel [cf. Matt. 2:6, 20].)[27] So this is a *Jewish* mourning, not an international one.

This Old Testament citation perfectly suits this Matthew 24 setting—namely, the context of Jerusalem's destruction. As the king with full authority, Jesus will judge those who have rejected him. Such judgment would bring mourning and wailing from those who rejected him.[28] Again, Jesus' vindication and judgment would be seen in a dramatic reversal of fortunes: not only in the destruction of the temple and the destruction of national Israel by their pagan enemies, but in the spread of Christ's church to the ends of the earth. These events give further indication of Jesus' supreme rule and his vindication in AD 70.[29]

5. *The gathering of the elect, the new Israel, is appropriately placed within a pre–AD 70 setting.* What are we to make of the angels that gather God's elect from the four winds (v. 31)? Some end-times popularizers might see this passage as problematic for the position I've taken. However we navigate this interpretation, it's still quite clear that Jesus is talking about what will take place within "this generation." Also, the Old Testament indicates that God will restore his people, gathering those who have been scattered to the "ends of the earth," the "four winds/corners," or "four winds," and to "every side" (Deut. 30:3–4; Isa. 11:10–12; Ezek. 37:9, 21; cf. Jer. 31:7–8). The New Testament makes clear that this gathering of the elect from among the nations began in the first half of the first century: "now in Christ Jesus you who formerly were far off have been brought near by the blood of Christ" (Eph. 2:13).

Indeed, the language of God's *gathering* his *elect/chosen* fulfills what the Old Testament anticipates. For example, the Septuagint (not the Hebrew) anticipates in Zechariah 2:6, "I will gather you from the four winds of heaven." This is precisely what Jesus himself speaks of in Matthew's Gospel. We've already seen that national Israel would mourn at the judgment that came to them in AD 70. Furthermore, God's *elect* or *chosen*—the new, true Israel comprised of Jews and Gentiles in Christ—will receive the kingdom of God that has been taken from national Israel, which Matthew has already mentioned (cf. Matt. 8:11–12; 21:43; 22:14; cf. 24:22, 24). A new Israel under Christ's rule is being reconfigured, and it will include the ingathering of the Gentiles—the vindicated King gathering together his new subjects. This theme permeates the New Testament. Note the significance of Jesus' selecting twelve apostles or the celebration of a second Passover (1 Cor. 5:7) with a slain Lamb of God who leads his people into a second exodus out of slavery. The ingathering of God's new chosen people who have been aliens and exiles scattered among the nations are being gathered into God's household. We get a foretaste of this ingathering at Pentecost, when people from "every nation under heaven" gathered in Jerusalem (Acts 2:5), and many received Messiah's salvation. In this "new covenant," those from the "house of Israel" and the "house of Judah" include Gentiles (see Hebrews 8). We've already noted the empire-wide spread of the gospel in our discussion of verse 14.

Here in Matthew 24, we read that God will *gather* (the word is *episynagō*) his elect—an inter-ethnic community in Christ—because the Jewish nation that Jesus longed to *gather* to himself (the same word is used in Matt. 23:37–39) turned away from him. National Israel had failed to be a light to the nations and had become absorbed with preserving their own national identity to the exclusion of gathering in the Gentiles. Thus Jesus tells Jerusalem that its house would be left *desolate* (Matt. 23:38), which connects neatly to the abomination of *desolation* of AD 70 (24:15).

This quotation in Matthew 24:31 is taken from Isaiah 27:13 (see also Deut. 30:4; Zech. 2:10); it refers to the final regathering of Israel in the last days. This "gathering of Israel" language is used by the New Testament to refer to the Gentiles who are being incorporated into the people of God; they are now the true Israel (cf. Matt. 8:11; Eph. 2:19–22; James 1:1, where the church is "the twelve tribes who are dispersed abroad"; 1 Peter 2:5, 9–10, where the Gentile church [cf. 4:3–4] is called a "royal" and "holy priesthood" as national Israel had been [Exod. 19:5–6] and is charged to live uprightly "among the Gentiles" [i.e., nonbelievers (2:12)]. In Acts 15:16–18, James cites Amos 9:12, indicating God's plan that "the rest of mankind may seek the Lord . . . all the Gentiles who are called by My name"; this same point is made earlier in 13:46–48, where Gentiles are "appointed" or elected to receive salvation, citing Isa. 42:6; 49:6). The "gathering of the elect" is simply the inclusion of all nations into the people of God, which is no longer national/ethnic Israel,[30] and this ingathering is taking place before the fall of Jerusalem.

The trumpet call here is figurative, just as in Isaiah 27:13; it's simply a call to "gather" those who are "scattered" among the nations to "come and worship the LORD." Trumpet calls were typically a summons to assemble or to make war. Here the summons is for the Gentiles to believe in Christ. Again, this happens before AD 70.

How are *angels* involved? We could readily see that angels are assisting in the early church's missionary activity, supporting Christian efforts directed toward the ingathering of God's people; elsewhere angels are described as "ministering spirits" of those who "inherit salvation" (Heb. 1:14). That is, spiritual power is involved in human evangelization,[31] just as there are spiritual powers that attempt to thwart it (e.g., Eph. 6:12).

So the preliminary signs of Matthew 24:15–25 (like the tender shoots of the fig tree [v. 32] in March–April) indicate that the fall of Jerusalem is near (as the summer harvest—May–June—is close at hand). These early signs clearly reveal that the end of national Israel with the vindication/"coming" of the Son of Man is sure to follow. Thus, "all these things" (v. 33)—namely, the destruction of Jerusalem (Matt. 24:1–3/Mark 13:4)—will take place within "this generation" (v. 34): that is, Jesus' own day. So, the "fig tree" is not Israel's becoming a nation in 1948, as popular evangelical opinion holds. Indeed, earlier reference to the "fig tree" in Mark 11:11–13 refers to the Israel of Jesus' day, which bore no spiritual fruits of obedience and thus was cursed and cut down.[32]

Some may appeal to a final restoration of national Israel when "all Israel will be saved" (Rom. 11:26). But Paul tells us at the beginning of this section in Romans that "they are not all Israel who are descended from Israel" (Rom. 9:6). Paul is distinguishing between two "Israels"—those who are the redeemed people of God in Christ ("all Israel") and those who are unbelieving ethnic Jews ("descended from Israel"). No, there aren't two peoples of God—national/ethnic Israel and the church. God's plan moves from national Israel, which finds its permanent fulfillment in a multiethnic community of Jews and Gentiles in Christ. To go back to a national Israel as God's people is to turn back the clock on the completion of God's purposes. Paul has already said in this letter that the true Jew is one who has been transformed inwardly by faith (Rom. 2:25–26; cf. Gal. 6:16; Phil. 3:2–11).[33]

So when Jesus says that *his* generation wouldn't pass away until "all these things" would take place, the natural interpretation is that he is speaking of the temple's destruction in AD 70. In fact, *everywhere* Jesus says "this generation," he refers to his contemporaries (cf. Matt. 11:16; 12:39, 41–42, 45; Mark 8:12, 38; Luke 11:29–32, 50–51; 17:25; et al.).[34] Again, this mention nicely parallels the other "coming-within-this-generation" passages noted earlier in the Gospel (Matt. 10:23: "You will not finish going through the cities of Israel until the Son of Man comes"; 16:28: "There are some of those who are standing here who shall not taste death until they see the Son of Man coming in his kingdom"). Indeed, with the coming of AD 70, national Israel is no longer the people of God. King Jesus and his church are the true Israel.

Fourth, with Matthew 24:36–51, we now shift to a different subject—the answering of the second question—namely, Jesus' unexpected parousia. This new section answers the second part of the disciples' question—about "the sign of Your coming [*parousia*], and of the end of the age." Verse 36 shifts the emphasis: "But of that day and hour no one knows." In contrast to the events of AD 66–70 (described as "all these things" and "those days" [vv. 8 and 22; cf. Mark 13:17, 19, 20, 24]), the phrase "that day" is newly introduced. The new parousia section in Mark (13:32) begins, "But of that day." This verse requires the beginning of a new subject since no singular "day" has been mentioned up to this point.[35]

There is a difference between Matthew and Mark, however. Mark, the original gospel, presents the disciples asking one question (when the temple would be destroyed)—with Jesus answering it and going beyond the question to address *another implied* question (about his parousia). Matthew draws out Mark's subtly introduced second question; he presents the disciples as asking two questions with Jesus giving two clear and distinct answers.

Why doesn't Mark present a context? The chief reason is because "that day" is a commonly understood phrase throughout the New Testament—often without any context given. As R. T. France notes, the final day of judgment is simply assumed in many places (Matt. 7:22; Luke 10:12; 17:31; 21:34; 2 Thess. 1:10; 2 Tim. 1:12, 18; 4:8). In places such as Matthew 7:22; Luke 10:12; and others, the commonly understood eschatological ("end-times") phrase "that day" is presented without any context—just as it is in Mark 13:32. France explains: "Mark could thus expect his readers to detect in the use of this phrase a shift from the historical events of the Jewish War to a more ultimate perspective, without having to spell this out. Any readers/hearers who managed to miss this idiom would quickly realize the change of subject when they heard in vv. 33–37 what the coming of [*that day*] was to be like."[36]

Mark's Gospel	Matthew's Gospel
Mark 13:33: "But concerning *that day.*" This is a new subject since no singular "day" has yet been mentioned. The second question is *implied*.	*Matthew 24:36*: "But of that day and hour no one knows." The second question is *clearly indicated*.
Mark begins with only *one* question (the temple's/Jerusalem's destruction). Yet Jesus speaks of *two* events—the destruction of Jerusalem (within "this generation") and the unknown day ("that day"), which Christ does not know.	*Matthew* introduces *two* questions—when the temple will be destroyed and when Christ's parousia/end of the age will be.

From this point (Matt. 24:36) and beyond (into Matthew 25), we are dealing with the parousia, and Jesus affirms that he does not know the day or the hour of his "arrival." This is unlike the detailed timetable he had given in addressing the first question—the destruction of the temple. For this second event, no one can set a timetable or date. One must simply be prepared by living a faithful, obedient life of discipleship—rather than calculating the days. There is a different feel and approach between these two sections. While "the period preceding the fulfillment of Jesus' prediction of the destruction of the temple will call for a cool, level-headed refusal to become excited too soon, the expectation of the unknown day and hour of the parousia demands constant alertness."[37]

So, as this time is unknown, many people will be unaware and unprepared as they carry on with everyday life—eating, drinking, marrying (v. 38), but they will still be "taken away" (v. 39) *in judgment* (not in some "secret rapture") at Christ's return. Jesus calls us to be "on the alert" (v. 42). This doesn't mean quitting our jobs and pitching tents on mountains to "wait" for Jesus' return. After all, remember that the *wise* bridesmaids (Matt. 25:1–13) who brought oil *still fell asleep* while waiting for the bridegroom! But when he appeared, they were prepared for him and joined in the celebration. Being alert has nothing to do with being aware of times and dates, but with living morally and spiritually alert lives (24:45–51). That is what it means to be watchful.

So we see that Bertrand Russell and other critics got it wrong about Jesus getting it wrong about his return! Jesus expected vindication of his claims—a "coming" to God's throne—within his generation. But that is distinct from a much later, undatable parousia.

Summary

- Jesus begins by talking about the initial birth pangs and signs of what will first take place before the temple is destroyed (Matt. 24:1–14). Jesus implies that the disciples themselves will experience these events that will take place in the near future.
- Famines, earthquakes, wars, and even the gospel's proclamation to the whole world aren't signs pointing to Jesus' "second coming." These events took place in the first century before AD 70.
- Still answering the first question, Jesus tells of the horrible, calamitous event of Jerusalem's siege and suffering (vv. 15–28). The "abomination of desolation," referring back to Daniel's reference to Antiochus Epiphanes and the Maccabean crisis (167 BC), is an appropriate metaphor for the temple's desecration that would take place around AD 70.
- The dramatic apocalyptic language of verses 29–31, referring to Daniel 7, isn't about "the end of the world" or the parousia.

It comes "immediately after" the events just mentioned—all before AD 70.

- The horrific fall of Jerusalem is a geopolitical calamity like the fall of ancient kingdoms in the Old Testament, and the prophets would use images of the sun being darkened and the moon no longer shining—supremely appropriate for Jerusalem and the end of national Israel as God's people.

- The coming of the Son of Man isn't to earth but to the Father/"Ancient of Days" for vindication and enthronement, as Daniel 7 makes clear.

- Those who mourn at the fall of Jerusalem are the tribes from the "land" of Israel—not the whole "earth"—as the context of Zechariah 12 makes clear.

- God's elect are gathered from the four winds—a reference to the incoming of God's true people (Jews and Gentiles alike) and the new Israel, who replace national Israel.

- In verses 36–51, Jesus answers the disciples' second question—the timing of the parousia. Unlike the detailed answer to the first question, Jesus says he doesn't know the day or the hour of his parousia. There is no sign for it. Nevertheless, he calls his followers to be morally and spiritually prepared.

Further Reading

Caird, G. B. *The Language and Imagery of the Bible.* Philadelphia: Westminster, 1980.

France, R. T. *The Gospel of Mark.* New International Greek Textual Commentary. Grand Rapids: Eerdmans, 2002.

———. *The Gospel of Matthew.* New International Commentary on the New Testament. Grand Rapids: Eerdmans, 2007.

———. *Matthew.* Tyndale Commentary. Revised edition. Downers Grove, IL: InterVarsity, 1985.

Pitre, Brant. *Jesus, the Tribulation, and the End of the Exile.* Grand Rapids/Tübingen: Baker Academic/Mohr Siebeck, 2005.

Tasker, R. G. V. *Matthew.* Tyndale Commentary. Grand Rapids: Eerdmans, 1961.

17

Why Are Christians So Divided? Why So Many Denominations?

A man was walking along a high bridge over a river when he saw a woman about to jump off. He ran up to her, trying to dissuade her from committing suicide. He told her simply that God loved her. A tear came to her eye.

He then asked her, "Are you a Christian, a Jew, a Hindu, or what?"

"I'm a Christian," she replied.

He said, "Me, too! Small world! Protestant or Catholic?"

"Protestant."

"Me, too! What denomination?"

"Baptist."

"Me, too! Northern Baptist or Southern Baptist?"

"Northern Baptist."

He remarked, "Well, *me, too*! Northern Conservative Baptist or Northern Liberal Baptist?"

She answered, "Northern Conservative Baptist."

He said, "Well, that's amazing! Northern Conservative Fundamentalist Baptist or Northern Conservative Reformed Baptist?"

"Northern Conservative Fundamentalist Baptist."

"Remarkable! Northern Conservative Fundamentalist Baptist Great Lakes Region or Northern Conservative Fundamentalist Baptist Eastern Region?"

She told him, "Northern Conservative Fundamentalist Baptist Great Lakes Region."

"A miracle!" he cried. "Northern Conservative Fundamentalist Baptist Great Lakes Region Council of 1879, or Northern Conservative Fundamentalist Baptist Great Lakes Region Council of 1912?"

She said, "Northern Conservative Fundamentalist Baptist Great Lakes Region Council of 1912."

He then shouted, *"Die, heretic!"* and pushed her over the rail.[1]

Perhaps we laugh with some degree of discomfort at such a joke. After all, many people associate Christianity with division and religious rivalry. And the track record hasn't always been good. Indeed, things used to be much worse—when denominational differences were a matter of life and death. Sixteenth- and seventeenth-century Europe experienced severe religious conflict—indeed, warfare— often between Protestants and Catholics. In the Peasants' Revolt of 1524–25 in Germany, the Protestant peasants opposed their Catholic overlords. Over the next decade or so, tens of thousands of Anabaptists were killed by Catholics, Lutherans, and Zwinglians. The St. Bartholomew's Day Massacre of 1572 brought the slaughter of a hundred thousand Protestants. The Thirty Years' War (1618–48), which ended with the Treaty of Westphalia, involved fighting between Catholics and Protestants. England's two civil wars (1642–45 and 1648–49) involved Oliver Cromwell's leading the Puritan revolt against King Charles I and his Anglican and Catholic supporters, resulting in the king's execution. The list of examples goes on. This era of religious intolerance and warfare has certainly damaged many people's perceptions about the Christian faith.

Doesn't Jesus pray to his Father that his followers "may be one, even as We are" (John 17:11, 22)? Doesn't Paul write that "God has so composed the body, giving more abundant honor to that member which lacked, so that there may be no division in the body, but that the members may have the same care for one another" (1 Cor. 12:24–25)? Though the early Jerusalem church "had all things in common" (Acts 2:44), what has happened to this ideal? We live in a more tolerant age, but some Christians argue that the existence of Christian denominations—Baptists, Pentecostals, Presbyterians, Methodists, and so on—is shameful and sinful. Denominations seem to indicate Christian disunity and thus diminish our witness for Christ in the world.

But is this necessarily so? How should we think about Christian denominations? Here are some considerations.

First, not all who declare themselves Christians are true or consistent followers of Christ. A lot of things that have been done in the name of Jesus—the Crusades, the Inquisition, anti-Jewish persecution (pogroms), neglect of social responsibility, hatred of homosexuals—hardly resemble the attitude of Christ or reveal the Spirit's fruit (Gal. 5:22–23). In the Sermon on the Mount, Jesus said, "You will know them by their fruits" (Matt. 7:16). He goes on to say, "Not everyone who says to Me, 'Lord, Lord,' will enter the kingdom of heaven, but he who does the will of My Father who is in heaven" (v. 21). Just because people *call* themselves "Christians" doesn't mean they truly are.

Across the Christian denominations, there will be people who bear a certain label but whose lives haven't been transformed by God's Spirit. There are *Christian* Baptists, *Christian* Methodists, and *Christian* Pentecostals, and there are *non-Christian* Baptists, *non-Christian* Methodists, and *non-Christian* Pentecostals.

What's more, sometimes Christians, who have God's Spirit, simply may not be living consistently with their calling and the provision God has made for them. Think of the Corinthians: though they were "spiritual" (having God's Spirit), they lived as "natural" (Spirit-less) persons (1 Cor. 3:1–3; cf. 2:10–15).

On top of all this, hypocrisy doesn't *disprove* a viewpoint. Just because a child may see professing Christian parents act hypocritically does nothing to logically undermine or refute the truth claims of Jesus and his exemplary moral character. If hypocrisy disproved a viewpoint, we would have to reject any belief system, because hypocrites—those who flagrantly resist practicing what they're preaching—will be found within any of them.

Second, denominations remind us of a common denominator—a "mere Christianity" that different Christian groups share. I've been asked by Muslims, "Why do Christians have so many denominations?" Of course, the same could be asked about Muslims, who are divided into groupings such as Sunni, Shi'a, Ismaili, Sufi, Ahmadiyya, Wahhabi, and others. But for our purposes, this is beside the point.

When people ask about *denominations*, I use the illustration of fractions—as opposed to "factions"!—and the notion of the *common denominator*. You can have 3/16, 5/16, or 13/16, but the denominator is still the same—16. "Denomination" actually represents *unity* rather than *disunity*. Christian churches can enjoy fellowship (*koinōnia* = communion, commonality) without compromising the fundamentals of the faith.

When we recite the Apostles' Creed or appreciate books like C. S. Lewis's *Mere Christianity*,[2] John Stott's *Basic Christianity*,[3] and N. T. Wright's *Simply Christian*,[4] we're reminded of the basic commonalities that Christians share—despite differences in secondary doctrines. As the obscure writer Rupertus Mendelius nicely put it:

> In essential matters unity.
> In non-essential matters liberty.
> In all things charity.[5]

During the fifth century, Vincent of Lérins affirmed that Christian basics are what have been believed "everywhere, always, by all" (Lat., *ubique, semper, ab omnibus*).[6] Such a standard has merits, although it shouldn't be slavishly followed, as we must not close ourselves off from fresh discoveries and insights and applications from God's Word that have gone unnoticed in the past.[7] There were periods of church history when certain important themes in Scripture were diminished or eclipsed—the priesthood of all believers, the emphasis on grace and faith, or the Jewishness of Jesus, for instance. It seems Mark Twain was on to something when he (purportedly) said, "It ain't those parts of the Bible that I can't understand that bother me; it is the parts that I do understand."

Third, denominations don't imply disunity (and uniformity doesn't equal unity). Denominational affiliation is not division. Indeed, a spirit of unity and charity that goes beyond external labels is to permeate our dealings with fellow Christians. Paul chided the Corinthian church for its divisiveness: some aligned themselves with Paul, others with Cephas, still others Apollos, and apparently the "super-spiritual" ones with Christ (1 Cor. 1:10–17; 3:1–9). Paul urged them that "you all agree and that there be no divisions among you" (1 Cor. 1:10). The problem was not really doctrinal emphases, but the prideful *attitudes* that Paul criticizes. In Romans 14–15, Paul addresses those strong and weak in conscience: although he points out that eating and drinking are theologically neutral issues, he addresses attitudes and expresses concern for their building up one another. He tells the strong of conscience not to flaunt their liberty or look down on the weak; he tells the weak not to judge the strong. Paul isn't so much concerned about doctrinal or organizational uniformity in these disputed areas, but he is concerned about spiritual unity.

I was in Moscow in October 2002. During that time I was speaking at an American club where Russian speakers would come to practice their English. I spoke on the topic of truth and relativism. Afterward, a young man, who had been listening attentively, approached me and asked me what my "religion" was. I replied, "Christian."

He answered, "Yes, I know, but what kind of Christian?"

"Isn't the important thing that we are obedient followers of Christ?"

"Yes, but what kind of Christian are you?"

"I prefer to think of myself—in the words of C. S. Lewis—as a 'mere Christian,'" I responded.

"But are you Protestant, Catholic, Orthodox?" he persisted.

"If you want to label me, I identify myself as a Protestant," I told him.

"Why are you coming here to bring division? We are Orthodox in Russia!"

I replied, "I haven't been the one trying to divide. It seems that you are dividing by putting a label on me!"

This incident illustrates how having a certain denominational label doesn't guarantee a spirit of unity. A Christian can affirm the faith of fellow Christians from other denominations with charity and grace.

Think of organizations such as InterVarsity Christian Fellowship, Campus Crusade for Christ, or the Navigators that serve on university campuses—or, for that matter, the Veritas Forum held on many university campuses each year. These can serve as a focal point for fellowship, ministry, and outreach for Christian university students who recognize that Christian unity can be evident despite secondary doctrinal differences. One need not abandon denominational distinctives in favor of a "generic" church.

Fourth, it is believers' union with the triune God in Christ that links them with "the communion of saints" (living and dead)—not affiliation with a certain denomination. Christian unity isn't found in the apostolic succession of authority through popes or bishops. The church's unity is rooted in the unity of the triune God. Unity is a gift from God as well as a human response to God's calling upon us. That is, we are to be "diligent to preserve the unity of the Spirit in the bond of peace" (Eph. 4:3). Christians should seek to make visible the invisible unity of believers in God: "since God has created one church of Christ on earth, let Christians live up to that fact in empirical life."[8] This is clearly displayed by Christians *loving* one another (John 13:35).

So Christians can allow for *degrees* of visible unity and there can be *difference* in the midst of unity. In Philippians 1, Paul affirms the authentic faith of Christians with wrong motives. Though certain local Roman Christians don't like him, Paul rejoices that the gospel is still being proclaimed through them (Phil. 1:15–18). The union of believers, as Donald Bloesch writes, is inward and spiritual, not outward or denominational.[9]

Fifth, denominations serve as a call to humility rather than pride, and we should be willing to learn from Christians of other denominations, of other cultures, and throughout church history. Let's be clear: Not all denominations will be correct in their unique doctrinal emphases; *they can't all be right!* For example, either infant baptism is biblically permissible or it is not. Either the Reformed view of election/predestination is correct or it is not. Either it is or isn't true that all genuine believers can never fully and finally fall away from their faith. Some denominations may better reflect biblical truth in some areas but less so in others. From this perspective, denominations are not ideal given the fact that secondary doctrines of one denomination clearly conflict with those of the next.

On the other hand, certain Christian denominations can offer different emphases that enhance and bring illumination to other Christian groups. Let's be clear on this as well: *No one Christian denomination will fully capture the totality of the Christian faith in its particular denominational expression.* While we are part of what some have called the "universal" or "invisible" church, God works in the world through *particular expressions* of his worldwide church. As C. S. Lewis said, denominations and local churches are "the only way of flying your flag."[10] That is, we show our identification with Christ's church by being part of a local body or denomination. So, given the fact that we're part of a localized community in this place and culture and at this period of history, we should take seriously the task of humbly learning from and appreciating important focal points found within various other denominations and cultures.

1. *Other Christian denominations.* We can benefit from the Eastern Orthodox emphasis on the Trinity as a communion of three persons in one being—a valuable doctrine for individualistically minded Americans! Also, this tradition has much to teach us about the place and importance of beauty in Christian life and worship. The Reformed/Calvinist churches' stress on the majestic glory of the sovereign God reminds us that there is no dichotomy between sacred and secular, since all belongs to God. Mennonite and other Anabaptist traditions can serve as models for social involvement and community. Pentecostal and charismatic churches emphasize the power of prayer, expectant faith, and the centrality of the Spirit's life-giving power. "Free" churches can derive much benefit from liturgical ones: utilizing many centuries-old Christian creeds and liturgies can give us a greater sense of stability and rootedness as we connect with the church past and present—and a greater sense of God's transcendence, which tends to be lost in many contemporary American churches.

2. *Christians in other cultures.* I once asked a Nigerian seminary student named Joseph how he would compare the church in America with the church in Nigeria. He told me, "There are two areas of difference. The American church is unaware of spiritual warfare, and it is prayerless." We could add that the Western churches characterized by individualism could learn some helpful lessons from Christians in non-Western, more community-oriented cultures. Also,

Western Christians have tended to interpret Scripture in ways that minimize passages on justice, poverty, evil social structures, love of wealth, and the like. Another interpretive blind spot stems from the West's emphasis on "guilt" rather than "shame," which communal Oriental or Middle Eastern cultures more readily understand; a deeper understanding of Scripture's cultural context notions of shame and honor helps illuminate our reading of the text.

3. *Theological discussion and doctrinal development throughout church history.* By understanding the development of Christian doctrine over the ages, Christians can learn how to avoid error and guard orthodoxy. This doesn't mean that we should be blind traditionalists, but rather appreciators of the heritage we have as Christians. As the late Jaroslav Pelikan has written, *traditionalism* is "the dead faith of the living," whereas *tradition* is "the living faith of the dead."[11] As we recite the Apostles' Creed, Pelikan points out, we affirm the universality of faith across *space* as well as *time.* We identify with what Christians worldwide affirm each Sunday—and what Christians over the centuries have as well. We confess that we are part of a historic community, and such a creed helps sustain us through the fluctuations of our individual feelings, historical limitations, doubts, and questions.[12]

Christians can become myopic by reading Scripture through their own cultural or denominational or contemporary lenses. So we are wise to humbly listen to the experiences of fellow Christians from other *denominations, cultures,* and *eras.* We need the enrichment of a global, cross-denominational, and historical perspective to enhance and deepen our discipleship. We can be enriched in our understanding of God and assisted in our Christian pilgrimage by giving heed to fellow travelers. As New Testament scholar Ernst Käsemann once said, "In scholarship as in life, no one can possess the truth except by constantly learning it afresh; and no one can learn it afresh without listening to the people who are his companions on the search for that truth. Community does not necessarily mean agreement."[13]

Sixth, an awareness of one's own traditions and denominational distinctives may better help to guard against false teachings or heresies that can creep into the church. When churches emphasize their doctrinal distinctives, they will more likely be more in tune with possible heresy and doctrinal deviation when hiring pastors or tracking their denomination's seminaries. This may be more difficult for a more "generic" or "independent" church.

Seventh, admittedly there are risks, challenges, and tensions in showing "theological hospitality."[14] As Christians interact theologically with fellow Christians from other denominations, there is a "risk" that one's doctrinal thinking will be changed or at least challenged. Some Christians will recoil out of fear or because of a lack of confidence in their own theological beliefs. In such cases, one's denomination may be more like a self-protective *fortress* rather than an inviting *home.*[15]

Changing one's denominational allegiance is different, though, from abandoning the Christian faith for a non-Christian movement such as Mormonism or the Jehovah's Witnesses. While we can and should interact with Mormons and Jehovah's Witnesses, we should not widen the tent so much that groups denying historic, scripturally rooted Christian creeds and doctrines are included as fellow Christians. The Scriptures have plenty to say about heresies—even if many churches seem to have forgotten this. We shouldn't overlook doctrinal error at the expense of "getting along with everyone." In fact, *compromising on Christian fundamentals is the surest way to create disunity.*[16]

*Eighth, the Protestant/evangelical commitment to "Scripture alone" (*sola scriptura*) is not a negation of tradition, but stresses Scripture's primacy over tradition.*[17] I have stressed that wise Christians will take tradition seriously and not neglect its direction in church history and its influence on us today. But let me say something here about the relationship of Scripture and tradition.

Protestant Christianity has stressed the *"solas"*: Christ alone (*solus Christus*), by Scripture alone (*sola scriptura*), by faith alone (*sola fide*), by grace alone (*sola gratia*), to God alone be the glory (*soli Deo gloria*). One "sola" that has been misunderstood has been *sola scriptura*, and a brief discussion may be helpful. Protestantism has denied what the Roman Catholic Church has affirmed—that the church "does not derive her certainty about all revealed truths from the holy Scriptures alone. Both Scripture and tradition must be accepted and honored with equal sentiments of devotion and reverence," as the *Catechism of the Catholic Church* affirms.[18] Rather, the Scriptures alone are the infallible guide and norm for our faith and practice.

However, we shouldn't *interpret sola scriptura* too narrowly—as though it *excludes* the role of tradition or experience or reason. There is truth outside of Scripture since all truth is God's truth. Remember Luther at the Diet of Worms speaking of being persuaded or "convinced by the testimonies of Scripture *or evident reason.*" Tradition is to be respected and studied, but church traditions or creeds (e.g., Apostles' or Nicene) have authority precisely because they are rooted in the Scriptures. Church tradition doesn't have equal authority with Scripture. Also, John Calvin could "willingly embrace and reverence as sacred" the "ancient councils [Nicea, Constantinople, Ephesus, Chalcedon] . . . in so far as relates to the doctrines of faith, for they contain nothing but the pure and genuine interpretation of Scripture," which Calvin gave "the highest place." Calvin pointed out the error of the second council at Ephesus, which accepted the false teaching of Eutyches, who rejected Christ's two natures in favor of one. Calvin boldly declared that "the Church was not there."[19]

Some maintain that the Scriptures themselves don't teach *sola scriptura.* However, we can draw this inference from Scripture just as we can about the Trinity and the incarnation. In Matthew 15:1–9 and Mark 7:1–13, when push comes to shove, we should opt for the Scriptures over tradition. We should guard against what may be "invalidating" the Word of God—of what may "add to" or "subtract from" Scripture (Deut. 4:2; 12:32; Rev. 22:18–19; cf. Matt. 15:3–6). The 2 Timothy 3:16–17 reference to the Scriptures doesn't mention any other source of authority: "All Scripture is inspired by God and profitable for teaching, for reproof, for correction, for training in righteousness; so that the man of God may be adequate, equipped for every good work."

While the church/tradition isn't a standard with equal authority to the Scriptures, claiming the Scriptures are the standard won't mean much without the church's living in dependence on the Spirit of God. And while we are wise to study and learn from church tradition, we must acknowledge that the church and tradition have gone wrong. But doesn't the Reformation's emphasis on the "priesthood of all believers" lead to individualism, division, and pride in one's own "authoritative" interpretation of Scripture? Not necessarily. The corrective to such abuses is not an authoritative magisterial interpreter for all Christians (e.g., a pope or council); rather, the corrective is a *humble* interpreting of Scripture *in community* with fellow Christians—*with an awareness of history and tradition.* The Christian who deliberately ignores such a path is acting foolishly and dangerously.

Again, we shouldn't take the *solas* too narrowly. When we say *solus Christus*, we're not ignoring Father and Spirit. When we say *sola scriptura*, we're not rejecting tradition ("no tradition"). Wesleyan theology has helpfully emphasized "the Quadrilateral"—the important role of Scripture, tradition, reason, and experience for the Christian. This isn't to say that all four are on the same level; Scripture is ultimately the norm for faith and practice. However, all have value in a well-balanced Christian community.

In the end, the church itself should be an *interpretation of authoritative Scripture*: "You are our letter, written in our hearts, known and read by all men; being manifested that you are a letter of Christ, cared for by us, written not with ink but with the Spirit of the living God, not on tablets of stone but on tablets of human hearts" (2 Cor. 3:2–3). The church should be, as Kevin Vanhoozer writes, a commentary on God's Word and a witness to Scripture that is lived before God and a watching world.[20]

Summary

- Not all professing Christians are genuinely or consistently Christian. What kind of fruit is borne through their lives?

- The *truth* of a position isn't undermined just because a person acts hypocritically. These are logically distinct issues. Besides, if we reject a philosophy of life based on hypocritical adherents, we'd believe nothing!

- Think in terms of "common denominator"—that is, a "basic Christianity" that different denominations share (unity in essentials, liberty in nonessentials, charity in all things). Denominations don't necessarily suggest disunity.

- Believers are connected through their union with the triune God in Christ, not a denominational label. Christians should seek to make visible this invisible unity.

- The existence of many Christian denominations reminds us to be humble rather than arrogant. Not all denominations can be right in their unique doctrinal emphases. There are genuine doctrinal conflicts, and not all of them can be right.

- Since no one Christian denomination will fully capture the totality of the Christian faith in its particular denominational expression, we should humbly learn from Christians of other denominations and cultures and from church history.

- An awareness of our own traditions and denominational distinctives may give us a clearer idea of what is heresy and what is not. Error may be more difficult to detect for a more "generic" or "independent" church that does not stress doctrinal distinctives.

- "Theological hospitality" toward other denominations may involve challenges and tensions.

- The (Protestant) evangelical commitment to "Scripture alone" (*sola scriptura*) isn't a rejection of tradition (consider the Wesleyan "Quadrilateral"); rather, it emphasizes Scripture's primacy *over tradition*.

Further Reading

Boyd, Gregory A., and Paul R. Eddy. *Across the Spectrum: Understanding Issues in Evangelical Theology*. Grand Rapids: Baker Academic, 2002.

Buschart, W. David. *Exploring Protestant Traditions: An Invitation to Theological Hospitality*. Downers Grove, IL: InterVarsity, 2006.

Chandler, Paul-Gordon. *God's Global Mosaic: What We Can Learn from Christians around the World*. Downers Grove, IL: InterVarsity, 2000.

Kärkkäinen, Veli-Matti. *An Introduction to Ecclesiology: Ecumenical, Historical and Global Perspectives*. Downers Grove, IL: InterVarsity, 2002.

Notes

Introduction

1. Paul Copan, *"True for You, but Not for Me"* (Minneapolis: Bethany, 1998); *"That's Just Your Interpretation"* (Grand Rapids: Baker, 2001); *"How Do You Know You're Not Wrong?"* (Grand Rapids: Baker, 2005); *Loving Wisdom: Christian Philosophy of Religion* (St. Louis: Chalice, 2007).

2. For a healthy discussion on, among other things, dependence on the transforming power of God, see J. P. Moreland, *Kingdom Triangle* (Grand Rapids: Zondervan, 2007).

Chapter 1 Why Not Just Look Out for Yourself?

1. Ayn Rand, *The Virtue of Selfishness* (New York: New American Library, 1961).

2. *Ice Age*, directed by Chris Wedge and Carlos Saldanha (20th Century Fox, 2002). Story (and screenplay) by Michael J. Wilson—with screenwriters Michael Berg and Peter Ackerman.

3. See chapter 11 in John Stott, *The Cross of Christ* (Downers Grove, IL: InterVarsity, 1985).

4. Gordon Graham, *Eight Theories of Ethics* (London: Routledge, 2004), 23–24.

5. Ibid., 21–22.

6. C. S. Lewis, "The Weight of Glory," in *The Weight of Glory and Other Addresses* (New York: Macmillan, 1965), 4–5.

7. See Scot McKnight's accessible elaboration on this theme: *The Jesus Creed: Loving God, Loving Others* (Brewster, MA: Paraclete, 2004).

Notes

Chapter 2 Do What You Want—Just as Long as You Don't Hurt Anyone

1. Jack Kevorkian, National Press Club, July 29, 1996, http://www.kevork.org/npc.htm (accessed January 30, 2005).
2. John Stuart Mill, *On Liberty*, ed. Alburey Castell (n.p.: Meredith Corporation, 1947), 104.
3. "Always to Care, Never to Kill: A Declaration on Euthanasia," The Ramsey Colloquium, *First Things*, February 1992, 45–47.
4. Stanley Hauerwas, *Suffering Presence: Theological Reflections on Medicine, the Mentally Handicapped, and the Church* (Notre Dame: University of Notre Dame Press, 1986), 14.

Chapter 3 Is It Okay to Lie to Nazis?

1. See Immanuel Kant, *Critique of Practical Reason*, trans. Lewis White Beck (New York: Bobbs-Merrill, 1956).
2. The movie *Sophie Scholl: The Last Days* (Zeitgeist Films, 2005) stars Julia Jentsch and is directed by Marc Rothemund.
3. Michael Shermer, *The Science of Good and Evil: Why People Cheat, Gossip, Care, Share, and Follow the Golden Rule* (New York: Henry Holt, 2004), chap. 6.
4. Joseph Fletcher, *Situation Ethics: The New Morality* (Philadelphia: Westminster, 1966), 164–65.
5. Lewis B. Smedes, *Mere Morality: What God Expects from Ordinary People* (Grand Rapids: Eerdmans, 1983), 236–37.
6. In this chapter I include a number of insights from chapter 18 ("Truth-Telling") in Glen H. Stassen and David P. Gushee, *Kingdom Ethics: Following Jesus in Contemporary Context* (Downers Grove, IL: InterVarsity, 2003).
7. See "Best Norman Rockwell Art," http://www.best-norman-rockwell-art.com/norman-rockwell-saturday-evening-post-article-1943-03-13-freedom-from-fear.html (accessed May 12, 2007).
8. Taken from Dietrich Bonhoeffer, *Ethics*, trans. Neville Horton Smith (New York: Macmillan, 1965), 367–68. For a Christian position taking an opposing (no-deception) view, see Paul J. Griffiths, *Lying: An Augustinian Theology of Duplicity* (Grand Rapids: Brazos, 2004).
9. Bonhoeffer, *Ethics*, 370.
10. Ibid., 369.
11. Stassen and Gushee, *Kingdom Ethics*, 386.
12. Regarding traveling from Galilee to Jerusalem for the Feast of Booths, Jesus tells his unbelieving brothers, "Go up to the feast yourselves; I do not go up to this feast because My time has not yet fully come" (John 7:8). Yet Jesus comes later during the feast. Was Jesus being deceptive here? No, *Jesus declares that the Father had not moved him to go to the feast*. So for the moment, he was planning on staying behind. The only reason he went to Jerusalem partway through the feast was because his Father had revealed that he should. See D. A. Carson, *The Gospel according to John* (Grand Rapids: Eerdmans, 1991), 308–9.

13. I. Howard Marshall, *The Gospel of Luke*, New International Greek Testament Commentary (Grand Rapids: Eerdmans, 1978), 897.

14. Stassen and Gushee, *Kingdom Ethics*, 388.

Chapter 4 Why Is God So Arrogant and Egotistical?

1. Bede Rundle, *Why Is There Something Rather Than Nothing?* (Oxford: Clarendon, 2004), 18. The citation from David Hume is from N. Kemp Smith's second edition of *Dialogue Concerning Natural Religion* (Edinburgh: Nelson, 1947), 226. Thanks to Charles Taliaferro for pointing out this quotation and for his other helpful suggestions in this chapter.

2. Some insights in this essay are taken from Charles Taliaferro, "The Vanity of God," *Faith and Philosophy* 6 (April 1989): 140–54, which has been reprinted elsewhere.

3. Lewis B. Smedes, *Love within Limits* (Grand Rapids: Eerdmans, 1978), 31.

4. C. S. Lewis has some wise insights on pride and humility in book 3, chapter 8 ("The Great Sin") of *Mere Christianity* (New York: Macmillan, 1952).

5. D. C. Searle, s.v. "Humility," in *The New Dictionary of Biblical Theology*, ed. T. Desmond Alexander et al. (Downers Grove, IL.: InterVarsity, 2000), 568.

6. Michael Martin, *The Case against Christianity* (Philadelphia: Temple University Press, 1991), 171.

7. Actually, the "treasure room/storeroom" (*tameion*).

8. From A. B. Bruce, cited in John R. W. Stott, *Christian Counter-Culture: The Message of the Sermon on the Mount* (Downers Grove, IL: InterVarsity, 1978), 127.

9. Dallas Willard, *The Spirit of the Disciplines* (New York: Harper & Row, 1988), 173.

10. Arthur O. Lovejoy, *The Great Chain of Being: The Study of the History of an Idea* (1936; repr., Cambridge: Harvard University Press, 1971). This "principle of plenitude" contains rich ideas for fruitful theological thought, but it can also be taken in unbiblical and philosophically problematic directions (e.g., pantheistic or Neoplatonic).

11. N. T. Wright, *For All God's Worth: True Worship and the Calling of the Church* (Grand Rapids: Eerdmans, 1997), 7.

12. Some of these thoughts are taken from chapter 1 of J. I. Packer, *Knowing God* (London: Hodder & Stoughton, 1973).

13. Richard Bauckham, *Bible and Mission: Christian Witness in a Postmodern World* (Grand Rapids/Carlisle, UK: Baker/Paternoster, 2004), 37.

14. For example, see Exod. 20:5; 34:14; Deut. 4:24; 6:15; 29:20; 32:16, 21; Josh. 24:19; 1 Kings 14:22; Ezek. 8:3 (a graven "idol of jealousy"); 16:38, 42–43; 39:25; Joel 2:18; Nahum 1:2; Zeph. 1:18; 3:8; Zech. 1:14; 8:2; 1 Cor. 10:22.

15. Thanks to Charles Taliaferro on this point.

16. Some people may object to this point by bringing up passages such as Isa. 43:21 ("The people whom I formed for Myself will declare My praise") or Ps. 8:2; Matt. 21:16 (God's ordaining praise from the mouths of infants). See also Eph. 1:6, 12, 14. Such passages, however, can easily be reconciled with the point I have made.

17. C. S. Lewis, *Reflections on the Psalms* (New York: Harcourt Brace Jovanovich, 1958), 94–95.

18. Lewis, "Weight of Glory," 4–5.

19. *Larry King Weekend*, September 29, 2004, http://www.biblebb.com/files/MAC/mac-lkl.htm (accessed February 1, 2005).

20. See Martin Hengel's *Crucifixion in the Ancient World and the Folly of the Message of the Cross* (London: SCM Press, 1977).

21. Richard Bauckham, *God Crucified: Monotheism and Christology in the New Testament* (Grand Rapids: Eerdmans, 1998), 51.

22. For further discussion, see Bauckham, *God Crucified.*

23. Martin Hengel, *The Son of God: The Origin of Christology and the History of Jewish-Hellenistic Religion*, trans. John Bowden (Philadelphia: Fortress, 1976), 1.

24. Colin E. Gunton, *The Christian Faith: An Introduction to Christian Doctrine* (Oxford: Blackwell, 2002), 181.

Chapter 5 Miracles Are Unscientific

1. Cited in Jaroslav Pelikan, *Jesus through the Centuries* (New York: Harper & Row, 1985), 190. Chapters 5 and 6 are adapted from material in Paul Copan, *Loving Wisdom*, ch. 11.

2. I myself have experienced and have known trustworthy people who have witnessed specific indicators of divine involvement in their lives and remarkably precise answers to prayer. For a sampling, note the personal experiences recounted in J. P. Moreland and Klaus Issler, *The Lost Virtue of Happiness* (Colorado Springs: NavPress, 2006), 113–14, 172–75; J. P. Moreland, *Kingdom Triangle* (Grand Rapids: Zondervan, 2007), which is full of such stories; Helen Roseveare's story about a dying baby, a hot water bottle, and a doll in *Living Faith* (Minneapolis: Bethany, 1987); Tom Morris's story of the beach ball in *Philosophy for Dummies* (New York: IDG Books, 1999), 233–36; A. T. Pierson, *George Müller of Bristol* (repr., Grand Rapids: Kregel, 1999)—or George Mueller's autobiography; the story of Sadhu Sundar Singh's dramatic conversion in Charles E. Moore, *Sadhu Sundar Singh: Essential Writings* (Maryknoll, NY: Orbis, 2005), 11–15; Pauline Selby, *Persian Springs: Four Iranians See Jesus* (London: Elam Ministries, 2001); David H. Greenlee, *From the Straight Path to the Narrow Way: Journeys of Faith* (Waynesboro, GA: Authentic Media, 2005); Craig S. Keener, *Gift and Giver* (Grand Rapids: Baker, 2001), esp. 175–76. While some may explain many of these testimonies and answers to prayer as coincidental or otherwise ambiguous, I think the activity and concern of God offer a more plausible context to explain them.

3. Technically, supernatural acts alone don't establish any religious claim but must be understood by the broader religious and theological backdrop (Deut. 13:1–5; 2 Thess. 2:9–10; Rev. 13:13; 16:14).

4. I've coedited three books on this topic: *Will the Real Jesus Please Stand Up?* (Grand Rapids: Baker, 1998); *Jesus' Resurrection: Fact or Figment* (Downers Grove, IL: InterVarsity Press, 2000); *Who Was Jesus? A Jewish-Christian Dialogue* (Louisville, KY: Westminster John Knox Press, 2001). Also, scholars such as William Craig, N. T. Wright, Stephen Davis, and Gary Habermas have done much good work on Jesus' resurrection.

5. Frank Kirkpatrick, *A Moral Ontology for a Theistic Ethic* (Burlington, VT: Ashgate, 2003), 55.

6. Rudolf Bultmann, *Kerygma and Myth* (New York: Harper, 1961), 4–5.

7. C. S. Lewis, *Miracles* (New York: Macmillan, 1960), 3.

8. John Earman, *Hume's Abject Failure* (New York: Oxford University Press, 2000).

9. See Gary R. Habermas, "Resurrection Research from 1975 to the Present: What Are Critical Scholars Saying?" *Journal for the Study of the Historical Jesus* 3, no. 2 (2005): 135–53.

10. Efforts to find parallels between Christianity and these mystery religions "have failed, as virtually all Pauline scholars now recognize," and to do so "is an attempt to turn the clock back in a way now forbidden by the most massive and learned studies on the subject." N. T. Wright, *What Saint Paul Really Said* (Grand Rapids: Eerdmans, 1997), 172, 173. Historian Michael Grant notes that Judaism was a milieu to which doctrines of deaths and rebirths of mythical gods seem so entirely foreign that the emergence of such a fabrication from its midst is very hard to credit. In addition, no dying-and-rising-god cults existed in first-century Palestine. *Jesus: An Historian's Review of the Gospels* (New York: Scribner, 1992), 199.

11. N. T. Wright, *The Resurrection of the Son of God* (Minneapolis: Fortress, 2003), 710.

12. James D. G. Dunn, *Jesus Remembered* (Grand Rapids: Eerdmans, 2003), 855.

Chapter 6 Only Gullible People Believe in Miracles

1. See Charles Taliaferro and Anders Hendrickson, "Hume's Racism and His Case against the Miraculous," *Philosophia Christi* n.s., 4 (2002): 427–41.

2. Earman, *Hume's Abject Failure*, 43.

3. Rundle, *Why Is There Something Rather Than Nothing?* 28.

4. Even Harvard scholar Helmut Koester notes that it is never claimed that Osiris rose from the dead. *Introduction to the New Testament (I): History, Culture, and Religion of the Hellenistic Age* (Philadelphia: Fortress, 1982), 190.

5. Gary Habermas, "Resurrection Claims in Non-Christian Religions," *Religious Studies* 25 (1989): 167–77.

6. See David K. Clark's excellent essay, "Miracles in the World Religions," in *In Defense of Miracles*, ed. R. Douglas Geivett and Gary R. Habermas (Downers Grove, IL: InterVarsity, 1997), 199–213.

7. Available from the Smithsonian's Department of Anthropology in Washington, DC.

8. On the historicity of Jesus' miracles, see Graham H. Twelftree, *Jesus the Miracle Worker* (Downers Grove, IL: InterVarsity Press, 1999).

Chapter 7 Don't People from All Religions Experience God?

1. Cf. George Appleton, ed., *The Oxford Book of Prayer* (Oxford: Oxford University Press, 1985). Some of this material is adapted from a section on religious

experience in Paul Copan, *Loving Wisdom: Christian Philosophy of Religion* (St. Louis: Chalice, 2007).

2. Cf. G. W. Hansen, "The Preaching and Defence of Paul," in *Witness to the Gospel: The Theology of Acts*, ed. I. H. Marshall and David Peterson (Grand Rapids: Eerdmans, 1998).

3. Rudolf Otto, *The Idea of the Holy* (New York: Oxford University Press, 1958). We won't deal here with sensory or visionary experiences, given their greatly varied nature.

4. For some qualifying remarks on Otto, see Winfried Corduan, *The Tapestry of Faiths* (Downers Grove, IL: InterVarsity, 2002), 204–5.

5. Richard Swinburne, *The Existence of God* (Oxford: Clarendon, 1979), 254. William Alston shows that "mystical perception" is parallel to sense perception in *Perceiving God: The Epistemology of Religious Experience* (Ithaca, NY: Cornell University Press, 1991). While not equivalent, they're *somewhat* alike, and the principle of credulity can aptly be applied to both.

6. See R. Douglas Geivett, "The Evidential Value of Religious Experience," in *The Rationality of Theism*, ed. Paul Copan and Paul K. Moser (London: Routledge, 2003); Keith Yandell, *The Epistemology of Religious Experience* (Cambridge: Cambridge University Press, 1993).

7. Also William Wainwright, *Philosophy of Religion*, 2nd ed. (Belmont, CA: Wadsworth, 1999), 120–38. Cf. J. P. Moreland's nice summary in *Scaling the Secular City* (Grand Rapids: Baker, 1987). Some people object to religious-experience arguments because they can't be "cross-checked"—presumably by sense experience or "scientific" criteria. But since religious experience provides us with our primary access to divine reality, and since God reveals himself when and as he pleases, we shouldn't expect that there necessarily has to be independent justification for religious experience (Wainwright, *Philosophy of Religion*, 132).

8. Andrew Newberg, Eugene D'Aquili, and Vince Rause, *Why God Won't Go Away: Brain Science and the Biology of Belief* (New York: Ballantine, 2001), 7.

9. Ibid., 8–10.

10. See my *"How Do You Know You're Not Wrong?"* which has three chapters on the body-soul relationship (Grand Rapids: Baker, 2005).

11. Justin L. Barrett, *Why Would Anyone Believe in God?* (Walnut Creek, CA: AltaMira Press, 2004).

12. Christian Smith, *Moral, Believing Animals: Human Personhood and Culture* (New York: Oxford University Press, 2003), 110, 122.

13. From chapter 8 in Barrett, *Why Would Anyone Believe in God?*

14. From Geivett, "Evidential Value of Religious Experience."

Chapter 8 Does the Bible Condemn Loving, Committed Homosexual Relationships?

1. Sy Rogers, "One of the Boys," http://www.syrogers.com/products/messages.php (accessed July 2, 2007).

2. Jack Rogers, *Jesus, the Bible, and Homosexuality* (Louisville: Westminster John Knox, 2006). In this chapter, I take some comments from Robert A. J. Gagnon, "Jack

Rogers's Flawed Use of Analogical Reasoning in *Jesus, the Bible, and Homosexuality*," http://www.robgagnon.net (accessed December 15, 2006).

3. Richard A. Burridge, *Imitating Jesus: An Inclusive Approach to New Testament Ethics* (Grand Rapids: Eerdmans, 2007), 127-8.

4. See J. Robertson McQuilkin, *An Introduction to Biblical Ethics* (Wheaton: Tyndale, 1989), 101.

5. Compare Stanley J. Grenz's book, *Welcoming but Not Affirming* (Louisville: Westminster John Knox, 1998).

6. Bruce Winter, "1 Corinthians," in *The New Bible Dictionary*, ed. D. A. Carson et al. (Downers Grove, IL: InterVarsity, 1994), 1169.

7. Ben Witherington III, *Conflict and Community in Corinth: A Socio-Rhetorical Commentary on 1 and 2 Corinthians* (Grand Rapids: Eerdmans, 1995), 166.

8. On the question of original sin and our sinful orientation, see chapters 14 and 15 in Copan, *"How Do You Know You're Not Wrong?"*

9. John Boswell, *Christianity, Social Tolerance, and Homosexuality* (Chicago: University of Chicago Press, 1980); see also John Shelby Spong and Daniel Helminiak, *What the Bible Really Says about Homosexuality* (San Francisco: Alamo Square, 1994).

10. On this point, see David F. Wright, "Homosexuals or Prostitutes? The Meaning of [*ARSENOKOTAI*] (1 Cor. 6:9; 1 Tim. 1:10)," *Vigiliae Christianae* 38 (1984): 148–49.

11. See Richard B. Hays, "Relations Natural and Unnatural: A Response to John Boswell's Exegesis of Romans 1," *Journal of Religious Ethics* 14 (1986): 184–215.

12. See Donald J. Wold, *Out of Order: Homosexuality in the Bible and the Ancient Near East* (Grand Rapids: Baker, 1998).

13. Richard B. Hays, *The Moral Vision of the New Testament* (San Francisco: HarperSanFrancisco, 1996), 395.

14. Paul Johnson, *Art: A New History* (New York: HarperCollins, 2003), 33.

15. R. T. France, "From Romans to the Real World," in *Romans and the People of God*, ed. Sven K. Soderlund and N. T. Wright (Grand Rapids: Eerdmans, 1999), 245.

16. Gagnon, "Jack Rogers's Flawed Use."

17. William J. Webb, *Slaves, Women, and Homosexuals: Exploring the Hermeneutics of Cultural Analysis* (Downers Grove, IL: InterVarsity, 2001), 88–90.

18. Derrick S. Bailey, *Homosexuality and the Western Christian Tradition* (London: Longmans Green, 1955).

19. Other Jewish literature makes the strong connection between Sodom and sexual sin: the Sodomites were "sexually promiscuous" (*Testament of Benjamin* 9:1); Sodom "departed from the order of nature" (*Testament of Naphtali* 3:4); the Sodomites were "polluting themselves and fornicating in their flesh" (*Jubilees* 16:5; cf. 20:5–6). Cited in Thomas E. Schmidt, *Straight and Narrow? Compassion and Clarity in the Homosexuality Debate* (Downers Grove, IL: InterVarsity, 1995), 88–89.

20. See John Stott, *Involvement II: Social and Sexual Ethics* (Old Tappan, NJ: Revell, 1986), 221.

21. See Wold, *Out of Order*, 86–87.

22. Joseph Gudel, "'That Which Is Unnatural': Homosexuality in Society, the Church, and Scripture," *Christian Research Journal* (Winter 1993): 13; Michael Ukleja, "Homosexuality in the Old Testament," *Bibliotheca Sacra* 140 (July–September 1983): 263, 264.

23. On understanding the odd- and harsh-sounding Levitical laws, see chapters 12 and 13 in Copan, *"How Do You Know You're Not Wrong?"*

24. Hays, *Moral Vision*, 381.

25. Ibid., 389.

26. David F. Wright, "Homosexuality," in *Dictionary of Paul and His Letters*, ed. Ralph Martin et al. (Downers Grove, IL; InterVarsity, 1993), 413; see also Wright's essay, "Homosexuality: The Relevance of the Bible," *Evangelical Quarterly* 61 (1989): 291–300.

27. Schmidt, *Straight and Narrow?* 33.

28. Tim Stafford, "Coming Out," *Christianity Today*, August 18, 1989, 28.

29. Schmidt, *Straight and Narrow?* 82–83.

30. This is precisely the point made (though not advocated as good) by Randy Thornhill and Craig Palmer, *The Natural History of Rape: Biological Bases of Sexual Coercion* (Cambridge, MA: MIT Press, 2000). When human males can't find a mate, they force themselves upon a female because they have a (subconscious) biological drive to survive and reproduce.

31. John J. McNeil, "Homosexuality: Challenging the Church to Grow," in *Homosexuality in the Church*, ed. Jeffrey S. Siker (Louisville: Westminster John Knox, 1994), 53.

32. Schmidt, *Straight and Narrow?* 65–66.

33. Paul elsewhere asserted that he and Peter were Jews "by nature [*physis*]" (Gal. 2:15)—that is, "by birth." For further commentary on this Romans 1 passage, see Schmidt, *Straight and Narrow?* 68–85.

34. Bruce W. Winter, *After Paul Left Corinth: The Influence of Secular Ethics and Social Change* (Grand Rapids: Eerdmans, 1995), 133.

35. Hays, *Moral Vision*, 381.

36. Some comments on this passage are taken from Winter, *After Paul Left Corinth*, 110–20.

37. Wright, "Homosexuals or Prostitutes?" 125–53.

38. Hays, *Moral Vision*, 381.

39. Boswell, *Christianity*, 107. Despite Boswell's sweeping claim, he offers absolutely no evidence for it, and he neglects to note Paul's clear use of Lev. 18 and 20 (LXX) for his terminology.

40. Winter, *After Paul Left Corinth*, 119.

41. Gudel, "Unnatural," 13.

42. Stanley Hauerwas, personal correspondence (January 28, 1992).

43. Schmidt, *Straight and Narrow?* 62–63 (his emphasis); cf. also 58.

Chapter 9 Aren't People Born Gay?

1. William A. Henry III, "Born Gay?" July 26, 1993. Available at http://www.time.com/time/magazine/article/0,9171,978923,00.html (accessed February 25, 2008); Larry Thompson/Bethesda, "Search for a Gay Gene," June 12, 1995. Available

at http://www.time.com/time/magazine/article/0,9171,983027,00.html (accessed February 25, 2008); Traci Watson et al., "Is There a 'Gay Gene'?" *US News & World Report*, November 13, 1995, 93.

2. Alfred C. Kinsey,Wardell B. Pomeroy, and Clyde E. Martin (Philadelphia: Saunders, 1948).

3. A well-researched and wisely-written book that I use in this chapter is Stanton L. Jones and Mark A. Yarhouse, *Homosexuality: The Use of Scientific Research in the Church's Moral Debate* (Downers Grove, IL: InterVarsity, 2000).

4. See Elizabeth Moberly, "Homosexuality and the Truth," *First Things* 71 (March 1997): 30–31.

5. Peter Kreeft, *How to Win the Culture War* (Downers Grove, IL: InterVarsity, 2002).

6. Schmidt, *Straight and Narrow?* 133.

7. See Judith Reisman and Edward Eichel, *Kinsey, Sex, and Fraud* (Lafayette, LA: Huntington, 1990).

8. Abraham Maslow and James M. Sakoda, "Volunteer Error in the Kinsey Study," *Journal of Abnormal and Social Psychology* 47 (April 1952): 259–62.

9. Reisman and Eichol, *Kinsey, Sex, and Fraud*, 23.

10. Richard Grenier, "The Homosexual Millennium," *National Review*, June 7, 1993, 52; Gordon Muir, "Homosexuals and the 10% Fallacy," *Wall Street Journal*, March 31, 1993; and Reisman and Eichel, *Kinsey, Sex, and Fraud*, 194–95. For further information regarding percentages of homosexuals, see Schmidt, *Straight and Narrow?* 101–5. One Harris poll indicated that 4.4 percent of males and 3.6 percent of females surveyed claimed to have had homosexual sex with someone within five years of the interview. Felicity Barringer, "Measuring Sexuality through Polls Can Be Shaky," *New York Times*, April 25, 1993, A1.

11. Jones and Yarhouse, *Homosexuality*, 73.

12. Michael King and Elizabeth McDonald, "Homosexuals Who Are Twins: A Study of 46 Probands," *British Journal of Psychiatry* 160 (March 1992): 407–9.

13. Simon LeVay, "A Difference in Hypothalamic Structure between Heterosexual and Homosexual Men," *Science* 253 (1991): 1034–37.

14. Joe Dallas, "Born Gay?" *Christianity Today*, June 22, 1992, 20–23.

15. Cited in Mark Hartwig, "Is Homosexuality Destiny or Choice?" *Citizen*, November 16, 1992, 13.

16. See N. E. Whitehead, "Born That Way? Puberty Studies Show Not So," http://www.mygenes.co.nz/Puberty.htm (accessed July 7, 2007).

17. For example, Dean H. Hamer, S. Hu, V.L. Magnuson, N. Hu and A.M.L. Pattatucci, "A linkage between DNA markers on the X chromosome and male sexual orientation," *Science* 261 (1993): 320-26; S. LeVay and Dean H. Hamer, "Evidence for a biological influence in male homosexuality," *Scientific American* 270 (1994): 20-25. See Jones and Yarhouse, *Homosexuality*, chap. 3.

18. Some of this information is taken from the research of Joseph Nicolosi, *Reparative Therapy of Male Homosexuality* (Northvale, NJ: Aaronson, 1991).

19. Chad W. Thompson, *Loving Homosexuals as Jesus Would* (Grand Rapids: Brazos, 2004), 113–15, 119–21.

20. Referenced in an essay by behavioral scientist George Rekers, "The Development of a Homosexual Orientation," in *Homosexuality and American Public Life*, ed. Christopher Wolfe (Dallas: Spence, 1999), 66.

21. Moberly, "Homosexuality and the Truth," 32.

22. Elizabeth R. Moberly, *Homosexuality: A New Christian Ethic* (Cambridge: Clark, 2001), 2.

23. This "interactionist" model is used by Jones and Yarhouse, *Homosexuality*, chap. 3.

24. Jones and Yarhouse, *Homosexuality*, 33 (their emphasis).

25. Slightly modified from Schmidt, *Straight and Narrow?* 152.

26. Jeffrey Satinover, *Homosexuality and the Politics of Truth* (Grand Rapids: Baker, 1996), 130–45.

27. Ibid., 135–36 (author's emphasis).

28. For more details on Hooker's biased study, see Jones and Yarmouth, *Homosexuality*, chap. 4.

29. David M. Fergusson, L. John Horwood, and Annette L. Beautrais, "Is Sexual Orientation Related to Mental Health Problems and Suicidality in Young People?" *Archives of General Psychiatry* 56, no. 10 (October 1999): 876–80. This study revealed that gay teens were "over 6 times as likely to have attempted suicide, 4 times as likely as their peers to suffer major depression, almost three times as likely to suffer generalized anxiety disorder, nearly 4 times as likely to experience conduct disorder, 5 times as likely to have nicotine dependence, 6 times as likely to suffer multiple disorders." Even researcher J. Michael Bailey (co-researcher with Pillard) admits, "These studies contain arguably the best published data on the association between homosexuality and psychopathology, and both converge on the same unhappy conclusion: homosexual people are at substantially higher risk for some forms of emotional problems, including suicidality, major depression, and anxiety disorder." http://www.narth.com/docs/archives.html (accessed October 18, 2006).

30. Jones and Yarhouse, *Homosexuality*, 103.

31. Ibid., 114–15.

32. Some of my comments below are taken from Moberly, *Homosexuality*, chap. 4.

33. Thompson, *Loving Homosexuals*, 23.

34. Ibid., 26.

35. These insights are taken from Joe Dallas's talk on homosexuality at Palm Beach Atlantic University (West Palm Beach, FL), January 24, 2008.

36. Taken from Joe Dallas, "How Should We Respond?" http://www.bridges-across.org/ba/dallas_lwo_respond.htm#repent (accessed July 2, 2007).

37. I am grateful to Dr. Julie Hamilton (a licensed marriage and family therapist) of Palm Beach Atlantic University for her comments on these chapters on homosexuality. Thanks too to my friend Justin Green, a former homosexual, for his comments as well, and to Joe Dallas for his encouragement.

Chapter 10 What's Wrong with Gay Marriage?

1. Moberly, "Homosexuality and the Truth," 33.

2. Jeffrey Satinover, *Homosexuality and the Politics of Truth* (Grand Rapids: Baker, 1996), 62.

3. Noted and documented in Thomas Schmidt, *Straight and Narrow?* 114.

4. Chad W. Thompson, "Treat Gays with Respect, but Don't Add Bias to Curricula," *Des Moines Register*, April 27, 2004, 9A.

5. Thompson, *Loving Homosexuals*, 58–61, 63.

6. Hadley Arkes, "The Family and the Laws," http://www.fww.org/articles/wfpforum/harkes.htm (accessed October 18, 2006).

7. But didn't the Bible permit polygamy? Did Jacob, David, Solomon, and others have more than one wife? In response, the spirit of Scripture seems to be that God *tolerates* such arrangements because of human hard-heartedness. However, we are regularly pointed back to God's original design: "from the beginning it was not so," Jesus says (Matt. 19:8). Some of the points here are taken from Francis Beckwith, "Street Theatre in the Bay Area," *National Review Online*, February 26, 2004, www.nationalreview.com.

8. From David Orgon Coolidge, "The Question of Marriage," in *Homosexuality and American Public Life*, ed. Christopher Wolfe, 200–238.

9. Robert P. George, *The Clash of Orthodoxies: Law, Religion, and Morality in Crisis* (Wilmington, DE.: ISI Books, 2001), 75.

10. David Popenoe, *Life without Father* (New York: Free Press, 1996), 145. See especially chap. 5, "What Do Fathers Do?"

11. Maggie Gallagher, *The Case for Marriage: Why Married People Are Happier, Healthier, and Better Off Financially* (New York: Doubleday, 2000).

12. Study cited in Stanley Kurtz, "Unhealthy Half Truths: Scandinavia Marriage *Is* Dying," *National Review Online*, May 25, 2004, http://www.nationalreview.com/kurtz/kurtz200405250927.asp.

13. Ibid. See also Stanley Kurtz, "The End of Marriage in Scandinavia: The 'Conservative Case' for Same-Sex Marriage Collapses," *Weekly Standard* 9, no. 20 (February 2, 2004), http://www.weeklystandard.com/Content/Public/Articles/000/000/003/660zypwj.asp.

14. Stanley Kurtz, "Unhealthy Half Truths."

15. NAMBLA's "Welcome Page," http://216.220.97.17/welcome.htm (accessed October 16, 2006).

16. Edward Brongersma, "Boy-Lovers and Their Influence on Boys: Distorted Research and Anecdotal Observations," *Journal of Homosexuality* 20 (1990): 160.

17. Referenced in NARTH, "The Problem with Pedophilia" (1998), http://www.narth.com/docs/pedophNEW.html (accessed October 18, 2006).

18. Cited in Jeffrey Satinover, "The 'Trojan Couch': How the Mental Health Associations Misrepresent Science," *NARTH*. Available at http://www.narth.com/docs/TheTrojanCouchSatinover.pdf (accessed February 28, 2008).

19. See Gregory Rogers, "'Suffer the Children': What's Wrong with Gay Adoption," *Christian Research Journal* 28, no. 2 (2005), http://www.equip.org/free/JAH050.htm (accessed October 17, 2006). The failure of heterosexual couples to parent adequately isn't itself an argument for the superiority of homosexual adoption. Studies advocating the positive results of gay parenting tend to be biased,

limited, anecdotal, and inadequate. Exceptions shouldn't be the basis for shaping public policy.

20. Greg Koukl, "Same-Sex Marriages: Challenges and Responses," (May 2004), http://www.str.org/site/News2?page=NewsArticle&id=6553 (accessed October 17, 2006).

21. Os Guinness and John Seel, *No God but God: Breaking with the Idols of Our Age* (Chicago: Moody, 1992).

22. Tacitus, *Annals* 3.27 (or "laws were most numerous when the Republic was most corrupt").

Chapter 11 How Can the Psalmists Say Such Vindictive, Hateful Things?

1. Psalms 35, 69, and 109 are almost entirely imprecatory. Interestingly, apart from (predominantly messianic) Psalms 1, 22, 110, and 118, these three imprecatory psalms are the most frequently quoted psalms in the New Testament. Walter Kaiser, *Toward Old Testament Ethics* (Grand Rapids: Zondervan, 1983), 293.

2. Eugene H. Peterson, *Answering God* (San Francisco: HarperOne, 1989), 98.

3. Lewis, *Reflections on the Psalms*, 20–33.

4. Some of these observations are taken from Elizabeth Achtemeier, *Preaching Hard Texts of the Old Testament* (Peabody, MA: Hendrickson, 1998), 105–10.

5. Peterson, *Answering God*, 100.

6. Ibid., 99.

7. Lewis, *Reflections on the Psalms*, 30.

8. Ibid., 30–31.

9. Some material here taken from William J. Webb, "Bashing Babies against the Rocks: A Redemptive-Movement Approach to the Imprecatory Psalms." Paper presented at the Evangelical Theological Society, Atlanta (November 2003).

10. D. J. Wiseman, *The Vassal-Treaties of Esarhaddon* (London: British School of Archeology in Iraq, 1958), 60–78.

11. We could also add that pagan curse prayers or incantations were manipulative, attempting to control the gods. This is a far cry from Israelite prayers, which viewed God as just and beyond manipulation. While the all-powerful God was responsive and willing to relent, he was not to be controlled.

12. D. A. Carson, *How Long, O Lord?* (Grand Rapids: Baker, 1991), 97–98.

13. Derek Kidner, *Psalms 73–150* (Downers Grove, IL: InterVarsity, 1975), 460–61.

14. John H. Sailhamer, *The NIV Compact Bible Commentary* (Grand Rapids: Zondervan, 1994), 346.

15. Peterson, *Answering God*, 98.

16. Derek Kidner, *Psalms 1–72* (Downers Grove, IL: InterVarsity, 1973), 28–29.

17. J. Clinton McCann Jr., "Psalms, Book of," in *Dictionary for Theological Interpretation of the Bible*, ed. Kevin J. Vanhoozer et al. (Grand Rapids: Baker, 2005), 648–49.

18. John Stott, *Favorite Psalms* (Chicago: Moody, 1988), 121.

19. Ibid.

20. Kidner, *Psalms 1–72*, 31.

21. Taken from Webb, "Bashing Babies."

22. Ibid.

23. Leslie C. Allen, *Psalms 101–150*, Word Bible Commentary 21 (Waco, TX: Word, 1983), 242–43.

24. See Copan, *"That's Just Your Interpretation."*

25. Tremper Longman III, *Making Sense of the Old Testament: Three Crucial Questions* (Grand Rapids: Baker, 1998), 78–86.

26. See Tremper Longman III, *How to Read the Psalms* (Downers Grove, IL: InterVarsity, 1988), 139–40.

Chapter 12 Aren't the Bible's "Holy Wars" Just Like Islamic Jihad? (I)

1. Shermer, *The Science of Good and Evil*, 39–40.

2. See Norman Geisler and Abdul Saleeb, *Answering Islam* (Grand Rapids: Baker, 1999). See also the "Answering Islam" website, http://www.answering-islam. org, which offers comprehensive discussion of such matters.

3. Copan, *"That's Just Your Interpretation."*

4. For example, see Paul Copan, "The Moral Argument," in *The Routledge Companion for Philosophy of Religion*, ed. Chad Meister and Paul Copan (London: Routledge, 2007); Paul Copan, "The Moral Argument," in *The Rationality of Theism*, ed. Paul Copan and Paul K. Moser (London: Routledge, 2003).

5. Alvin J. Schmidt, *How Christianity Changed the World* (Grand Rapids: Zondervan, 2004); Jonathan Hill, *What Has Christianity Ever Done for Us? How It Shaped the Modern World* (Downers Grove, IL: InterVarsity, 2005); Rodney Stark, *The Victory of Reason* (New York: Random House, 2006); Dinesh D'Souza, *What's So Great About Christianity?* (Washington, DC: Regnery, 2006).

6. John Goldingay, *Old Testament Theology: Israel's Gospel*, vol. 1 (Downers Grove, IL: InterVarsity, 2003), 475.

7. Christopher J.H. Wright, *Old Testament Ethics for the People of God* (Downers Grove, IL: InterVarsity, 2004), 478.

8. Compare the account of Joshua's death and burial in Josh. 24:28–31 and Judg. 2:6–9. Notice also the literary connection in Joshua, Judges, and 1 Samuel with the use of "the hill country of Ephraim": Josh. 17:15; 19:50; 20:7; 24:30; 24:33; Judg. 2:9; 3:27; 4:5; 7:24; 10:1; 17:1; 17:8; 18:2, 13; 19:1, 16, 18; 1 Sam. 1:1; 9:4 (cf. also 2 Sam. 20:21; 1 Kings 4:8; 12:25; 2 Kings 5:22). (Note: in the Hebrew Old Testament, these "books" are consecutive; in the Hebrew canon, Ruth comes after Proverbs. So the early part of the Hebrew Bible is "Ruth-less"!)

9. Wright, *Old Testament Ethics for the People of God*, 474–75; see also Iain Provan, V. Philips Long, Tremper Longman III, *A Biblical History of Israel* (Louisville: Westminster John Knox Press, 2003), 149. Similarly, the ages of those living before the flood may be symbolical—in keeping with the ancient Near Eastern use of numbers. See R. K. Harrison, "From Adam to Noah: A Reconsideration of the Antediluvian Patriarchs' Ages," *Journal of the Evangelical Theological Society* 37, no. 2 (1994): 161–68; Carol A. Hill, "Making Sense of the Numbers of Genesis," *Perspectives on Science and the Christian Faith* 55, no. 4 (December 2003): 239–51.

10. Gordon J. Wenham, *Exploring the Old Testament: A Guide to the Pentateuch* (Downers Grove, IL: InterVarsity, 2003), 137.

11. For example, Walter Brueggemann, *An Introduction to the Old Testament: The Canon and Christian Imagination* (Louisville: Westminster John Knox, 2003), 109–13. John Goldingay notes a combination of four categories: *military campaign, migration, social revolution,* and *cultural differentiation.* Goldingay, *Old Testament Theology: Israel's Gospel,* 488.

Chapter 13 Aren't the Bible's "Holy Wars" Just Like Islamic Jihad? (II)

1. I am very grateful for the generous help and research of Joshua Lingel of Biola University ("Jihad Project" paper). Thanks, too, to my colleague Gerald Wright for his discussion on this topic.

2. For a good discussion of jihad, see David Cook, *Understanding Jihad* (Berkeley: University of California Press, 2005); also *The Oxford Encyclopedia of the Modern Islamic World,* s.v. "Jihād," ed. John L. Esposito (Oxford: Oxford University Press, 2001), 2:369–73. Some of my comments in this introduction are taken from Cook and Esposito.

3. *The Qur'an: An Encyclopedia,* s.v. "Jihad/Jahada," ed. Oliver Leaman (London: Routledge, 2006), 331.

4. *Encyclopedia of Islam,* s.v. "Djihad," ed. Jane Dammen McAuliffe (Leiden: Brill, 1960–2003).

5. Cook, *Understanding Jihad,* chap. 3.

6. *Tabari* 9:82; *Sahih Muslim* 19:4294.

7. *Bukhari* 4:63.

8. For thorough documentation on this and other phenomena related to Muslim rule over Christians and Jews, see Bat Ye'or's excellent book *The Decline of Eastern Christianity Under Islam: From Jihad to Dhimmitude* (Teaneck, N.J.: Farleigh Dickinson University Press, 1997).

9. From Michael Cromartie's interview with Ye'or, "The Myth of Islamic Tolerance," in *Books and Culture* 4, no. 5 (September–October 1998): 38, http://www.christianitytoday.com/bc/8b5/8b5038.html.

10. Bat Ye'or, "Persecution of Jews and Christians: Testimony vs. Silence." Lecture given at the Ethics and Public Policy Center, Washington, DC (April 2, 1998), http://www.dhimmi.org (accessed August 27, 2007).

11. Ye'or, "Myth of Islamic Tolerance."

12. Ibid.

13. Taken from Joshua Lingel, "Jihad Project."

14. Bernard Lewis, *The Crisis of Islam: Holy War and Unholy Terror* (New York: Modern Library, 2003), 37–38.

Chapter 14 Aren't the Bible's "Holy Wars" Just Like Islamic Jihad? (III)

1. A few remarks in this chapter are taken from the Answering Islam website, www.answering-islam.org.

2. Norman Anderson, "Islam," in *The World's Religions,* 4th ed. (Downers Grove, IL: InterVarsity, 1975), 128.

3. Ibid., 129.

4. During King David's reign, he exerted political power over a wider region and exacted payment from peoples under him. This kingdom would soon divide after his son Solomon's rule.

5. Wenham, *Exploring the Old Testament*, 137.

6. J. A. Thompson, *Deuteronomy*, Tyndale Series (Downers Grove, IL: Inter-Varsity, 1974), 223.

7. Some of this material is taken from William Lane Craig's unpublished essay, "Jesus of the New Testament or the Qur'an?"

8. This and other points are taken from various articles at www.answering-islam.org (accessed December 29, 2006).

9. This section slightly adapts from ch. 3 in John Goldingay, *Theological Diversity and the Authority of the Old Testament* (Grand Rapids: Eerdmans, 1987).

10. Goldingay, *Theological Diversity*, 85. Goldingay goes on to talk about the next stage of the judges and monarchy: "being an institutional state means that God starts with his people where they are; if they cannot cope with his highest way, he carves out a lower one. When they do not respond to the spirit of Yahweh or when all sorts of spirits lead them into anarchy, he provides them with the institutional safeguard of earthly rulers" (86).

11. Ibid., ch. 5. See also Paul Copan, "Is Yahweh a Moral Monster? The New Atheists and Old Testament Ethics," *Philosophia Christi* n.s. 10/1 (Summer 2008).

12. Goldingay, *Old Testament Theology*, 1:480.

13. Ibid., 481.

14. Kenneth Woodward, "In the Beginning There Were the Holy Books" *Newsweek*, February 11, 2002, http://www.msnbc.com/news/698874.asp#BODY. Accessed June 15, 2002.

15. See http://www.ee.bilkent.edu.tr/~history/topkapi.html.

16. The next verse confusingly adds, "But if the enemy inclines toward peace, do thou also incline toward peace, and trust in God" (8:61).

17. Nabeel T. Jabbour, *The Crescent Through the Eyes of the Cross* (Colorado Springs: NavPress, 2006), 111; see Jabbour's discussion of warfare and tolerance in ch. 7.

18. Freedom House, www.freedomhouse.org (accessed January 8, 2007).

Chapter 15 Was Jesus Mistaken about an Early Second Coming? (I)

1. Bertrand Russell, *"Why I Am Not a Christian" and Other Essays on Religion and Related Topics* (New York: Simon and Schuster, 1957), 20–21.

2. Another alleged "delay of the parousia" passage is John 21:21–24, where Peter inquires about the apostle John's death: "yet Jesus did not say to him that [John] would not die."

3. See Richard Bauckham, *Jude, 2 Peter*, Word Biblical Commentary 50 (Waco, TX: Word, 1983), 290–95.

4. Luke 21:10–36 (which we won't be examining) makes reference to the destruction of Jerusalem as the first part of Matthew 24 does.

5. From Richard Bauckham, "The Delay of the Parousia," *Tyndale Bulletin* 31 (1980): 3–36.

6. Bauckham, *Jude, 2 Peter*, 308–9.

7. See Bauckham, "Delay."

8. See also *2 Baruch* 21:25 ("Do not delay!") and *2 Baruch* 21:19 ("How long?").

9. R. T. France. *The Gospel of Mark*, New International Greek Textual Commentary (Grand Rapids: Eerdmans, 2002), 539. Some critics argue that Jesus wasn't really *predicting* an event, but that the gospel writers were writing of this only after the event (*ex eventu*). However, consider the following: Why didn't Jesus mention that the temple would first be *destroyed by fire* (Josephus called it "one mass of flame")? And why would Jesus encourage the disciples to pray that the flight may not be in *winter* when Jerusalem was actually captured in the *summer*? Craig A. Evans, *Mark 8:27–16:20*, Word Biblical Commentary 34B (Nashville: Nelson, 2001), 295–98, 317.

10. Brant Pitre, *Jesus, the Tribulation, and the End of the Exile* (Grand Rapids/Tübingen: Baker Academic/Mohr Siebeck, 2005), 248.

11. See Anthony Thiselton, "Realized Eschatology at Corinth," *New Testament Studies* 24 (July 1978): 510–26.

12. Pitre, *Jesus, the Tribulation, and the End of the Exile*, 248.

13. E.g., Ralph P. Martin, *James*, Word Biblical Commentary (Waco, TX: Word, 1988), 190–92; Douglas J. Moo, *James*, Tyndale Series (Downers Grove, IL/Grand Rapids: InterVarsity/Eerdmans, 1985), 167–70.

14. Evans, *Mark 8:27–16:20*, 299.

15. See France, *Gospel of Mark*; R. T. France, *Matthew*, Tyndale Commentary, rev. ed. (Downers Grove, IL: InterVarsity, 1985); R. T. France, *The Gospel of Matthew*, New International Commentary on the New Testament (Grand Rapids: Eerdmans, 2007); R. G. V. Tasker, *Matthew*, Tyndale Commentary—an earlier edition prior to R. T. France's *Matthew* (Grand Rapids: Eerdmans, 1961); G. B. Caird, *The Language and Imagery of the Bible* (Philadelphia: Westminster, 1980). Also, see N. T. Wright, *Jesus and the People of God* (Minneapolis: Fortress, 1996), 339–68 (though Wright sees the events in Matthew 24 and Mark 13 as referring *solely* to the events surrounding the destruction of Jerusalem in AD 70, which I take to be only *partly* right); Pitre, *Jesus, the Tribulation, and the End of the Exile* (though I disagree with him at certain key points).

16. France, *Gospel of Matthew*, 899.

17. As Mark 13 and Luke 21 emphasize almost solely the destruction of Jerusalem, the word *parousia* does not occur in them. France, *Gospel of Matthew*, 895n.

18. The word *parousia* ("presence")—as opposed to *apousia* ("absence")—suggests that Jesus' final return, as G. K. Beale notes, will be a sudden appearing from a formerly invisible realm or dimension—not necessarily a descent from the sky to the earth. In 1 Thess. 4:15–16, the suggestion is that Christ's presence is dramatically manifested upon his arrival. (See 2 Thess. 2:8—"the appearance [*epiphaneia*] of his presence [*tēs parousias*].") G. K. Beale, *1 and 2 Thessalonians* (Downers Grove, IL: InterVarsity, 2003), 138n. This would be comparable to 2 Kings 6:17, where Elisha's servant is suddenly shown, like a veil being torn away, the formerly

invisible heavenly dimension and God's protecting armies. Josephus comments on Elijah praying for God's "power and presence [*parousia*] [to be manifested] to his servant (*Ant.* 9.55; see also 3 Macc. 3:17; *Ant.* 1.296; 3.203; 18.284 for further uses of *parousia* as "presence"). *Parousia* as "presence" is found in the New Testament as well: 2 Cor. 10:10; Phil. 2:12 (ibid., 138–39n).

19. Luke 19:43–44 speaks of how the Romans—in AD 70—will "level you [Jerusalem] to the ground and your children within you, and they will not leave within you one stone upon another, because you did not recognize the time of your visitation."

20. France, *Jesus and the Old Testament* (Downers Grove, IL: InterVarsity, 1977), 141.

21. France, *Gospel of Mark*, 534n.

22. Ibid., 342.

23. Ibid., 613.

24. R. T. France, review of D. A. Carson, "Matthew," in vol. 8 of the *Expositor's Bible Commentary*, *Trinity Journal* 6, no. 1 (Spring 1985): 112.

25. France, *Jesus and the Old Testament*, 235.

26. France, *Gospel of Mark*, 534.

Chapter 16 Was Jesus Mistaken about an Early Second Coming? (II)

1. Against such end-times popularizing, see Stephen Sizer, *Christian Zionism: Road Map to Armageddon?* (Downers Grove, IL: InterVarsity, 2005) and *Zion's Christian Soldiers* (Downers Grove, IL: InterVarsity, 2007).

2. Much detail of these events below is given by Evans, *Mark 8:27–16:20*, 304–14.

3. France, *Gospel of Mark*, 511.

4. Against Pitre's claim that there weren't any leaders of Jewish movements in the first century who claimed to be the Messiah/Christ (*Jesus, the Tribulation and the End of the Exile*, 240–42). However, 1 and 2 John speak of "antichrists." So Jesus' language isn't surprising.

5. France, *Gospel of Mark*, 510.

6. Ibid., 511.

7. France, *Gospel of Matthew*, 910.

8. Ibid., 904.

9. For further details, see Evans, *Mark 8:27–16:20*, 309–13.

10. France, *Gospel of Matthew*, 904–5.

11. France, *Gospel of Mark*, 517.

12. Ibid.

13. N. T. Wright, *Jesus and the Victory of God* (Minneapolis: Augsburg Fortress, 1997), 349; France, *Gospel of Mark*, 523.

14. France, *Gospel of Mark*, 523.

15. D. A. Carson, "Matthew" in *Expositor's Bible Commentary*, vol. 8, ed. Frank Gaebelein (Grand Rapids: Zondervan, 1984), 501.

16. France, *Gospel of Matthew*, 913.

17. Ibid., 911.

18. Carson, "Matthew," 501.

19. France, *Gospel of Mark*, 527.

20. Carson, "Matthew," 504–5.

21. E.g., Carson, "Matthew," 504–5; Craig L. Blomberg, *Matthew*, New American Commentary 22 (Nashville: Broadman and Holman, 1992), 361–62. As Scot McKnight writes, "Indeed, it is difficult to interpret 24:29 ('immediately') and 24:34 in any other way than as a primary (if not total) reference to the destruction of Jerusalem in A.D. 70." "Matthew, Gospel of," in *Dictionary of Jesus and the Gospels*, ed. Joel B. Green et al. (Downers Grove, IL: InterVarsity, 1992), 532.

22. France, *Gospel of Matthew*, 919.

23. Wright, *Jesus and the Victory of God*, 362, also 354–55.

24. France, *Gospel of Mark*, 530, 533.

25. Ibid., 534.

26. France, *Gospel of Matthew*, 923.

27. This Zechariah 12:10 passage is cited along with Daniel 7:13 in Revelation 1:7, but here they are applied more broadly (globally), as the context is different than Matthew 24/Mark 13.

28. France, *Jesus and the Old Testament*, 237; France, *Gospel of Mark*, 534–35.

29. France, *Gospel of Mark*, 535.

30. France, *Gospel of Mark*, 536.

31. France, *Gospel of Matthew*, 927–28.

32. See prophetic references to fig trees and their fruit to symbolize God's obedient people: Jer. 8:13; 24:1–10; Hos. 9:10, 16–17; Micah 7:1; cf. a similar parallel in Luke 13:6–9.

33. See chap. 13 in N. T. Wright, *The Climax of the Covenant* (Minneapolis: Fortress, 1993).

34. On "this generation," see also Matt. 16:4; 17:17; Luke 9:41; cf. Acts 2:40.

35. Again, this goes against what N. T. Wright says in his *Jesus and the Victory of God*.

36. France, *Gospel of Mark*, 542.

37. Ibid., 543.

Chapter 17 Why Are Christians So Divided? Why So Many Denominations?

1. I've slightly modified this (anonymous) joke. http://www.bible.org/illus.asp?topic_id=1380 (accessed March 31, 2005). Thanks to Nick Byrd for some helpful comments in a paper he wrote on this topic of denominations.

2. C. S. Lewis, *Mere Christianity* (San Francisco: HarperSanFrancisco, 2001).

3. John Stott, *Basic Christianity*, rev. ed. (Grand Rapids: Eerdmans, 1981.

4. N. T. Wright, *Simply Christian: Why Christianity Makes Sense* (San Francisco: HarperSanFrancisco, 2006).

5. Mendelius was an irenic Lutheran theologian and pastor living in Augsburg during the early seventeenth century. His given name was Peter Meiderlin. He spoke out during the fierce dogmatic controversies and the horrors of the Thirty Years' War (1618–48). The citation is from *Paraenesis votiva pro Pace Ecclesiae ad Theologos Augustanae Confessionis, Auctore Ruperto Meldenio Theologo*: *"In necessariis unitas, In dubiis libertas, In omnibus autem caritas."*

6. Cited in Jaroslav Pelikan, *The Christian Tradition: A History of the Development of Doctrine*, vol. 1 (Chicago: University of Chicago Press, 1971), 133.

7. Donald Bloesch, *The Church: Sacraments, Worship, Ministry, Mission* (Downers Grove, IL: InterVarsity, 2005), 90.

8. Veli-Matti Kärkkäinen, *An Introduction to Ecclesiology: Ecumenical, Historical and Global Perspectives* (Downers Grove, IL: InterVarsity, 2002), 85.

9. Bloesch, *The Church*, 43.

10. C. S. Lewis, *God in the Dock: Essays on Theology and Ethics*, ed. Walter Hooper (Grand Rapids: Eerdmans, 1970), 61.

11. Pelikan, *Christian Tradition*, 1:9.

12. Interview with Jaroslav Pelikan, "Why We Need Creeds," *Speaking of Faith* (National Public Radio), May 18, 2006, http://speakingoffaith.publicradio.org/programs/pelikan/index.shtml.

13. Ernst Käsemann, *Perspectives on Paul* (London: SCM, 1971), 60.

14. In this section, I borrow from W. David Buschart, *Exploring Protestant Traditions: An Invitation to Theological Hospitality* (Downers Grove, IL: InterVarsity, 2006).

15. Ibid., 263.

16. Bloesch, *The Church*, 45.

17. In this section, I borrow heavily from Kevin J. Vanhoozer, *The Drama of Doctrine: A Canonical Linguistic Approach to Christian Theology* (Louisville: Westminster John Knox, 2005), 231–37.

18. *Catechism of the Catholic Church*, par. 82. Both tradition and Scripture flow from the "same divine well-spring" (par. 80).

19. John Calvin, *Institutes of the Christian Religion*, trans. Henry Beveridge (Grand Rapids: Eerdmans, 1979), 4.9.8; 4.9.13.

20. Vanhoozer, *The Drama of Doctrine*, 237.

Paul Copan (PhD, Marquette University) is the Pledger Family Chair of Philosophy and Ethics at Palm Beach Atlantic University. He has lectured on many university campuses in the United States and internationally. He is the author or editor of various books, including *That's Just Your Interpretation, True for You, but Not for Me, Will the Real Jesus Please Stand Up?* and *How Do You Know You're Not Wrong?*